beautiful chaos
the psychedelic furs

dave thompson

First Edition
Published in 2004 by Helter Skelter Publishing
South Bank House, Black Prince Road, London SE1 9SJ
www.helterskelterpublishing.com

A CIP record for this book is available from the British Library.
Cover and contents design by Anna Dorfman, with additional prepress
work by Caroline Walker.
Printed in Great Britain by CPI, Bath.
ISBN 1-900924-47-1

CONTENTS

ACKNOWLEDGEMENTS

IT JUST DAWNED ON ME THAT this book took 17 years to write. No, make that 17 years to get written. I first started thinking about a Psychedelic Furs book back in 1986, at the same time as their remake of 'Pretty In Pink' was finally breaking them into the Big Time, and even then the group and I went way back – although just how far back I only realised, if this makes sense, while writing this volume. Memory plays weird tricks upon you, and I long ago established in my mind that the first time I saw the Psychedelic Furs play, it was an icy night in early 1979, probably at the Pegasus in Stoke Newington, but conceivably at any one of the 20-plus different venues they visited around London during the first half of the year.

They were, of course, phenomenal – a quarter of a century on, the 'original' Psychedelic Furs remain one of the five most exciting bands I've ever witnessed live (the others, not that you care, are the Adverts, Eddie and the Hot Rods, Mott The Hoople and the Doctors Of Madness.) But what really leaped out at that first show was the fact that six musicians played seven instruments. Two guitars, one voice, bass and drums, a saxophone and a vacuum cleaner. And it was the vacuum cleaner that blew me away. Haha.

They only used it that once, which means I was extremely lucky to have witnessed it. But I never forgot it, and hoped they wouldn't either. Every time a new record came out, I would dutifully play it twice, once full blast while I listened intently, once even louder while I vacuumed the rug. So far as I remember, it fit perfectly every time.

But where was that momentous gig? Was it the Pegasus in early '79? Talking with different band members over the years, and encouraging other writers to make the same enquiry when they interviewed the group, that always seemed in doubt. Maybe the Nashville, then, or the Rock Garden? No. It was the Roxy, halcyon hall of Punk dreams supreme. And, though I was right about it being cold and wintry, it was a full year earlier, in 1978. Meaning: by the time I first approached publishers with the Psychedelic Furs story, they had already equalled the Beatles' lifespan and, if I was feeling especially hyperbolic about it, were easily just as important.

Nobody was interested in publishing such a book. So, when gathering together all my thank-yous to the people who helped make sensible order from *Beautiful Chaos*, the first one goes to Sean Body at Helter Skelter, for finally making it happen. I was working on a pair of articles for a US magazine at the time, one documenting the Psychedelic Furs' turbulent origins, the other celebrating the success of their reformation. It was Sean who wanted to know what happened in between-times.

Next, the Psychedelic Furs themselves, that is: Richard Butler, Tim Butler, John Ashton and, from way back when, Roger Morris. Except where noted, all the quotes in this story are drawn either from my own interviews with the band members, conducted for various magazines and articles over the past decade, or were kindly donated by journalist Jo-Ann Greene, whose history in the American *Goldmine* magazine in 1997 provided the most coherent chronological framework of any I encountered. Many thanks, then, to Jo-Ann as well.

Additionally, in the autumn of 2003, Richard Butler, Tim Butler, John Ashton, Duncan Kilburn, Vince Ely and Les Mills, read the first draft of the manuscript and offered additional input by email, phone or, in the case of Vince and Les, in person. Les Mills in particular gave especially generously of his time and came up with the lion's share of the photographs in this book. Howard Thompson, Bruce Dickinson and Oedipus all offered valuable insights into the world behind the band; Howard Kayman and Mark Volman, the legendary Flo and Eddie, shared their recollections of their own time with the Psychedelic Furs; and Amy Hanson sat down with the near-finished manuscript and helped knock it into shape. I'm grateful.

Anna Dorfman, of the awesome Psychedelic Furs website Burneddowndays.com, was pivotal in helping track down Vince and Duncan, she also helped way beyond the call of duty in a variety of ways – from reviewing the manuscript, helping track down photographers and other personnel, providing pictures, and also in helping with the cover and contents layout and design. She also put me in touch with Furs expert André Huckvale, who helped with facts and discographical information as well as providing record sleeves and memorabilia.

And that just leaves everybody else who brought the beast to life: Dave Makin, Gaye and Tim, the Schecklers and Samantha, Anchorite Man, the Bat family and Crab, Blind Pew, Barb East, Ella and Sprocket, Gef the Talking Mongoose, the Gremlins who live in the furnace, my jellyfish finger-puppet, K-Mart (not the store), Geoff Monmouth, Mrs Rat, Nutkin, Snarleyyowl the Cat Fiend, Sonny, Mrs Nips, a lot of Thompsons, Neville Viking and the Walrus Ball. Thank you, and may your vacuum cleaners never need new bags.

INTRODUCTION

THIS BOOK IS INTENDED AS AN HISTORICAL documentary, the story of a band, but not necessarily a biography of its members. It details the group's development from without, as opposed to attempting to interpret its evolution from within – and it's important to make that distinction right away. Biography, even within the realms of its loosest definition, implies that it tells the story of a life, with all the minor details and petty irritations of which a life is comprised. It is the study of the individual tree within a dense forest, the inspection of a single stone within a quarry of boulders. It is the painstaking unravelling of the multitudinous strands that make a person the person they are.

This book does none of those things, and often it does quite the opposite. There's the tree, let's look at the forest. There's the stone, let's look at the quarry. These are the musicians, let's look at the band.

Popular music – let's call it rock'n'roll, although any one of a hundred definitions fit as well – is unique in the annals of modern art in that is completely interactive. Once a movie has been made, a TV series screened, an opera staged or a play presented, its parameters are set in stone. It can be revised – a scene cut here, a laugh track added there, an extra line of dialogue if it fills a special need – but, essentially, what's done is done and the film, the show, the whatever, will live and die by that simple law.

Rock'n'roll is different. It is not bound by those same limitations. Unless a machine is so well-greased and oiled that its owners couldn't tweak it even if they tried, every concert is a different experience, every song is a different event, and every day is a blank canvas. It's the musicians' job to colour each one in. But… there's a reason why landscape painting is not a team event, and portraiture is not a spectator sport. Rock'n'roll demands the highest standards of its participants, and rewards them with the lowest working conditions. Check out the cheap racks at your local used record shop, the place where they keep all the bands that no-one's heard of. Then, contemplate what they were up against, every day of their ill-starred existence. Suddenly, the marvel is not that so many dreams are doomed to fall by the wayside, unfulfilled and unfulfillable. The wonder is that so many others came true.

The Psychedelic Furs dared to dream and they made it all seem so simple. This is the story of what happened while all that was happening.

So, are you sitting comfortably?

Too bad.

PREFACE

THE COACH HOUSE CONCERT HALL in San Juan Capistrano isn't the kind of place where history gets made on a regular basis. A long, low, single-storey building, directly behind the San Juan Tire Center, its white façade partially shrouded by a clutch of well-tended climbing bushes, it squats on the Camino Capistrano, three turns off the I-5 freeway as it runs from Los Angeles down to San Diego.

The Coach House doesn't leap out at you. A lot of Orange County looks like this, and most visitors are more interested in the ruins of the old mission church which helped give the city its name and which, every March, around St Joseph's Day, becomes home to the thousands of swallows that stop off here as part of their annual migration, building mud nests within walls which took nine years to build, but stood for just six, before an earthquake toppled them in 1812.

It doesn't figure on too many live itineraries either, although it's hardly starved for attractions. Berlin played there in March 2002, and so did Neil Finn, while Tony Levin dropped by in April. And the Coach House's 480-capacity crowd is often there for the food as much as the entertainment – book dinner with your tickets and the best seats in the house are yours, closer to the stage, and more central, too. The earlier you book, the better your seats.

The food's good. Swordfish is a specialty, and the jalapeno peppers are out of this world. And who can resist a chocolate wipe-out to hold it all down? It's a great place, a friendly crowd, with a decent sound system and reasonable prices. But, again, it isn't the kind of place where history gets made on a regular basis. Unless you were there on 10th December 2001, to see the Psychedelic Furs return, closer to their "classic" line-up than they have been in twenty years. History wasn't simply made that night. For three songs, it was reborn.

That "classic" line-up needs no introduction. Three of them are even still on board – brothers Richard and Tim Butler, who formed the Psychedelic Furs in 1976 and have led it ever since; and guitarist John Ashton, the baby of the band, though he's been a member since 1978.

The others, however, have scattered to the farthest corners of the world.

Once the most raucous saxophonist on the entire London circuit, Duncan Kilburn was fired in 1981 and is now a businessman in Phnom Penh, Cambodia, a partner in the Globe Café and Restaurant. Sharing (with Air France) a restored French colonial building next door to the Royal Palace, the Globe is the first port of call for most European and Australian ex-pats and visitors, and the weekend's entertainment usually includes a set by Kilburn's latest combo, the jazz and bluesy house-band, the Lost Boys.

The powerhouse heart of the Psychedelic Furs' rhythm section, Vince Ely now lives in Spain. His energy and sense of timing drove the band relentlessly. Vince hadn't been apart from the band for as long as Duncan. He played drums for the band's 1990 tours of the US (including five nights at CBGBs), UK and Europe. Since then he'd been working as Van Morrison's personal assistant. It was good to be back behind the drum kit!

And finally, there was Roger Morris, the group's original lead guitarist, and a partial architect of the entire wall of sound that was the Psychedelic Furs' calling card when they first started attracting attention. Never one for flashy leads and Billy Big Banana posturing, he always seemed happiest with his amp at full blast, lashing out a symphony which made jet engines sound hoarse.

Half feedback, half bolero, but always completely controlled, Morris put the beauty into the group's Beautiful Chaos and, more than 20 years after he left, his work remains as painstakingly intricate. Today, he lives and works in Los Angeles where, in partnership with his wife, he is regarded among America's leading Chinoiserie artists, applying centuries-old Chinese painting and gold and silver-leafing techniques to reproduction antique furniture.

He'd not played a guitar in anger in something like 15 years, but – seemingly alone of the wayward trio – Morris never lost touch with his old band mates. He usually met up with them when they passed through town, to catch the show and hang out for a while, and that was what he was expecting on 6th December 2001, when the Psychedelic Furs headlined Hollywood's House Of Blues. But his erstwhile band mates had other plans.

It was after the show that the band dropped the bombshell, when Ashton asked if he fancied joining them onstage two nights later, when they returned to the House Of Blues. Morris immediately agreed. In the event, it didn't work out. Because the band had already done one show at the club, they were not given a soundcheck for the second and, with no chance to rehearse, Morris stood down. Twenty years and two weeks had passed since he last took the stage with the Psychedelic Furs and, while Los Angeles has always been loyal to the band, you can take spontaneity too far. But 48 hours later, the group was playing again, just down the road in San Juan Capistrano. And this time there was no going back.

Morris arrived at the club exactly as the band's own bus pulled in. They hung around, soundchecked, then retired to the bus to watch DVDs. And that was when it hit him: the old familiarity of being back with the band, a feeling of rising anticipation, set against the knowledge that there was absolutely nothing to do right now. Nervous and bored – is it any wonder so many musicians find other ways of killing so much time?

The capacity audience had no advance warning of what was in store. As far as they were concerned, simply seeing the Psychedelic Furs was enough – no matter that this was the band's third spin through California in under 18 months, for eight years before that, the group had been non-existent. There was a lot of reacquainting to be done.

Without a word about the treat in store, the current incarnation of the group – the Butlers, Ashton, keyboard player Gordon Raphael and drummer Frank Ferrer – opened their set as usual, pounding through the crowd-winning overture of 'Love My Way,' 'Only You And I,' 'Run And Run.' And then, a stir to the side of the stage, a seventh member moving to the stage, plugging in, looking around…

Morris: 'I'm not due up there until half-way through the set. Now I'm really getting edgy. Sitting at the side of the stage, counting down the songs until I'm on. A roadie tells me when there's one song to go. I'm either going to run out of this place screaming, never to be heard of for another 20 years, or get up there and have a blast. Finally, it's time, I walk on, and Richard introduces me. I can't remember if the audience cheered or booed, I'm so wound up. Probably "Who's that then?"'

They piled into 'Imitation Of Christ' and it wasn't really quite like the old days. Where the sax once yowled, the keys now washed; where the band once thrashed, they now merely (merely?) glowered. But it was just like the old days as well, Ashton and Morris going hell for leather, their guitars weaving weirdness across the Coach House walls, each spinning its own magic web, but blending and blurring together regardless, an edifice of sound which sounds so natural, it's as though not a day has gone by since the last time they merged.

'I settle into the music, trying not to rush it, and I'm having the time of my life.' He'd forgotten how much he enjoyed playing, and how much he'd missed it. He'd had a couple of bands after he departed the Psychedelic Furs, but none had lasted, none had accomplished much. 'This is great, highly recommend it.'

The song was over in no time and Morris left the stage, eagerly awaiting his next cue, watching as the band continued with their programmed set. A gaggle of new songs to remind onlookers that, just because the group had reformed, it didn't have to be a revival as well; a delicious 'Virginia Plain', to spite Roxy Music who neglected the song on their own reunion; and a delirious 'Heartbreak Beat', because you have to get round to the hit singles sometime. And then, another signal from the roadie, and Morris was on his feet again.

'Sister Europe' closed the set as dramatically as, once, it had opened it. Morris continues: 'Go back out there, manage not to mess it up, leave with the band, and then back for the encore, "Pretty in Pink". After the show I'm surrounded by a fan who wants an autograph, God bless him. And that's about it. The lads are packed in to the bus for a lovely drive to Phoenix, I drive home to my bed.' He'd had a blast – but the audience just looked blasted.

Some of them probably weren't even born when Beautiful Chaos first came to their country, and most of the others would have been too young to attend. But if they'd ever dreamed of what it must have been like, ever played the two albums which bookended the Psychedelic Furs' first American tour, and marvelled at the legend that tells them that vinyl can barely paint half of the picture, what they saw tonight would have helped wipe out at least a little of the guesswork. They had just witnessed a piece of history. At the Coach House Concert Hall in San Juan Capistrano. Who ever would have expected it?

YOU DON'T HAVE TO BE GOOD TO GET INTO IT

THERE'S AN OLD EASTERN PROVERB about a man who went out to build a house on the top of a mountain. Before he set off on his quest, he made sure he had everything he needed for the task ahead of him – provisions, supplies, wood, bricks and mortar. And, though it took many years and even more setbacks, though he lost friends on the way and got lost more than once, finally the summit was in sight. At which point he stopped climbing, dropped everything he had carried so far, then turned around and marched straight back down again.

He returned home. The villagers who'd been following his progress flocked around him to ask what had happened. Did he lose hope? No, he knew he could do it. Did he lose heart? No, he'd never felt better. Did he lose his head? No, he was as rational as ever. So, they demanded, why did you stop? Why did you not take those last final steps?

The mountaineer took a deep breath, then explained. All the time he was climbing, he said, the only direction he looked was straight up... the next ledge, the next outcrop, the next place he could rest. Not until he reached that very last stop, at the very last minute, was he actually able to look all around him. 'And quite simply, I didn't like the view.'

The story of the Psychedelic Furs is a lot like that proverb. They, too, set out for the top of the world; they, too, came so close they could reach out and touch it. It seems strange even to contemplate the fact today, but there was a moment – a fairly long one as well, nudging two years from beginning to end – when the Psychedelic Furs were on their way to becoming one of the biggest bands on the planet. One more tour, one more album, one more final push and they'd be there. But they never took that final step because, not only did they not like the view, they didn't like the reflections which that view mirrored back at them. So they turned their backs on all they had worked for, and made their way back down to earth again, back to where they began.

Of course, another ancient proverb tells us that we can never go back to a place we have left, no matter how much we want to and how right it feels. And so it proved. Times had changed, people had changed, the Psychedelic Furs themselves had changed. After four years of increasingly fractious company, forever looking over their shoulders at what they'd forsaken, the band members parted in 1992. Another eight years would elapse before they joined forces again and the only reason they were able to do so was that they knew they would never go scaling that mountain again.

There are no mountains in East Horsley. In fact, there's not really much of any-thing in East Horsley. Look for it on a map of southern England and you'll find it in that odd dog's leg of highways and railways that lurks just a few miles to the south of London. Guildford and Leatherhead are the nearest big towns, and Waterloo Station's less than 40 minutes away.

But the iron horse didn't even start grazing East Horsley until the early 1930s, by which time the village had already adopted a lot of its character – quiet, unruffled and just a little eccentric, the legacy of a 19th century nobleman, the First Earl of Lovelace, who chose the village as the site for a vast French-style chateau, then built it with such a dogged strength of purpose that the rest of the village couldn't help but take on the character of the edifice it hosted.

East Horsley Towers is not the most attractive stately pile in the land. Lovelace, of course, was Lord Byron's son-in-law and he inherited his kinsman's taste for drama and intrigue. JJ Norwich's *The Architecture of Southern England* describes East Horsley Towers as 'a grotesque Victorian Disneyland which has to be seen to be believed – and may not be, even then.' But growing up in its shadow wasn't that big a deal – the kind of things that most strike outsiders very rarely are. Life went on around the turrets and towers, in the Duke of Wellington pub and the cricket club down the road and, though the outside world drew closer every year, East Horsley didn't seem to mind that much. It took what it needed and didn't heed the rest.

Nice normal towns breed nice normal people, and the Butler brothers fit that bill. They were young, of course, but they'd soon grow out of that – by 1976, Richard, the eldest – he'd just turned 23 on 5th June (though later he would under-state his age by up to three years) – was doing well at Epsom Art School. Simon, the middle one, was on the edge of university, where he would study engineering. And Tim, the youngest, had promise as well. Lovely boys. It was just that… well, it was just that they could be a little noisy sometimes, especially when they invited their friends to the house, and started playing their Punk Rock. There was a lot of that going on in 1976.

A quarter of a century on from Year Zero, the spectre of Punk continues to haunt British rock. Maybe it's because it was the last musical movement to evolve from the street, not the studio; from the heart, not the head; from the gutters, not the press. Latter-day historians can trumpet all they like about situationist art installations and the algebraic calculations which a few well-placed minds spray-painted across the consciousness of a generation and it's true. There was an ele-ment in Punk which was absolutely calculated.

But there were a lot more that weren't which erupted despite – and, maybe, *to* spite – the mathematical manipulations of the scene's so-called godfathers. Punk was an explosion simply waiting to happen, because it couldn't have done anything else. Look at the facts. For anyone actually growing up in the mid-1970s, the rock music scene as they knew it was dead. Bands that flourished with such promise and brilliance earlier in the decade had sickened and died, but refused to lie down, and even the most woolly-hat-headed prog-rocking hobbit was tiring of the convoluted excuses for art which its idols were now distributing. You could love Yes as much as anyone, but *Tales From Topographic Oceans* was twaddle, and *Relayer* really was no better. Peter Gabriel left Genesis with a half-cocked concept double, and now they were back with their drummer singing lead. Barclay James Harvest, Emerson, Lake & Palmer, heavy metal, jazz rock… oh, need the condemnations continue?

But where did you go when you saw through those disguises? Glam Rock, the last positive force that actually seemed to speak to its audience from outside of the industry – for what record company insider would ever have incited a gay pop insurgence in those drab early '70s? –, had swallowed its last mouthful and wiped off its lips with the pay cheque. David Bowie was off in Los Angeles, making soul music and looking like death. Roxy Music were disbanding in order to fulfil Bryan Ferry's solo ambitions. Steve Harley, whose Cockney Rebel once promised the earth, was hurtling the wrong way down a musical *cul de sac*. Sparks had sunk, T Rex were forgotten and Slade were crooning ballads.

If that was life at the top of the gene pool, it only grew worse at the bottom. Check the gig guide, go down the pub. It was the golden age of live entertainment, and every brewer worth his hops had a stage and a booker on call to keep it jumping. But the most exciting R&B bands were time-locked in another age and, for every band which did make you smile – Ducks Deluxe, Dr Feelgood, Eddie and his red hot Hot Rods –, there were another three dreaming that the Eagles might discover them, and whisk them away to the motel California to sip on tequilas and watch another sunrise. Country Rock from the Kentish greenbelt. Right on.

And then, a lot of things happened, all at once, and suddenly everything changed. A few of them did involve the people who said that they started it all: Malcolm MacLaren *did* discover the Sex Pistols, Bernie Rhodes *did* ferment the Clash and, if they looked on their creations as an exclusive club, for a short time around spring 1976, they had the whole place to themselves. By summer, however, the dance floor was packed. And by late September, when the 100 Club hosted Britain's first ever fully-fledged Punk Rock Festival, the queue crocodiled halfway down Oxford Street, and its shadow was cast across the whole country.

A few miles down the road from East Horsley, in the commuter 'burb of Woking, the juvenile Jam were just stepping out with their spiked-Ribena reruns of classic Motown and Who. A little further afield, in Chiddington, the Guildford Stranglers were making a foul-smelling cocktail from smouldering Doors riffs and nubiles and rats. In Guildford itself, the first stirrings of Crisis were making themselves heard. And in Hersham, Jimmy Pursey was studying toilet wall graffiti in search of a suitable band name. 'Sham' was a contraction of the town's name. 69

referred to the local non-league football team's last year of triumph. Of course it did.

Not one of them had anything to do with what was transpiring in the capital, but all were drawn inexorably to its nexus regardless – drawn there and drawn in, until the sound of the suburbs was screaming as loudly as the ugly urban sprawl. For the sake of argument, we might agree that Punk was (or became) a deliberate invention. But Punk Rock was a happenstance that no-one could control.

For anybody living on the outskirts of London – and that means Surrey, Essex, Kent, wherever – there never was a local scene as such. Other cities took flash-points and made them their own. In the northern conurbations in particular, a single event might resonate for weeks within the confines of a group of like-minded friends, to be twisted, in turn, around their own unique view of what they thought they saw happening. In Manchester, an early Sex Pistols gig was the catalyst for creation between what seems to have been half the audience. In Liverpool, the Clash had the same dramatic effect.

Further south, however, where the cities sprawled wider and the suburbs soaked up the overflow, such bonding is less inclined to take place. In Liverpool, there was really only one place to go and see bands, so that's where everyone went, to Eric's on Matthews Street, just down from the site of the Beatles' old Cavern. In London and its surrounding satellites, there were dozens of places – and the focus blurred accordingly.

What did not change, however, was the sense of awareness that permeated every mind, the knowledge that something was going on all around and the belief that everybody was invited to take part. In late 1976, the East Horsley Butlers decided to form a band.

Richard had been wanting a group of his own for a while now; for as long, in fact, as he'd been writing poems and lyrics, and all the more since he realized, with all the knowing arrogance that is the divine right of literate teens, that he was actually rather good at it. Besides, he was convinced that it beat his current calling, the solitary life of a rather good artist, particularly at a time when his nose was stuck in books about Andy Warhol, and his brush was tracing the outlines. 'I loved Warhol, I loved the Factory, [and] there I was, doing oil paintings stuck in the studio.' What, he was now wondering, if he could turn painting into sound, pictures into music?

Could he sing? That didn't matter. Butler had long ago realized that it wasn't the quality of a voice that mattered, it was what that voice was capable of portraying – Bob Dylan proved that, and you only had to look at the pile of Dylan albums that Butler had amassed to know that that proof wasn't lost on him. But, if it was more contemporary evidence you were after, there was the Sex Pistols.

The first time he saw that band, Butler realised, 'God, it's not about singing, it's about being a "vocalist." [Johnny Rotten] made sense to me, he made sense to a lot of people. It wasn't about being a great musician; it was about finding the minimum framework in which you could put your ideas across, and making those ideas intelligible.' Interviewed for *Ink 19* 25 years later, Butler still felt that way. 'I don't really like "singers",' he observed. 'Whitney Houston is a "singer." Bob Dylan is a "vocalist." I like "vocalists".'

Did he know any musicians, then? No, but that didn't matter, either. Yes were musicians, Pink Floyd were musicians, Gentle Giant were musicians. Look where listening to them had got us. Now it was time the non-musicians had a go, and the Sex Pistols were a role model there, too. Or, at least, they seemed to be. It is only with hindsight that Tim Butler acknowledges that the non-musicians were always on a hiding to nothing.

'It's everybody's dream to be in a well-known rock band, especially back then, with the "anybody can do it" attitude. The whole Punk thing was that anyone could get up and play a song, but it wasn't true! You listen to the Pistols' album, and they're all good players. Joe Strummer had played for five years in a pub band. It was a pretty stupid ethic, really, that "anybody can do it".'

But that didn't stop people trying, and it certainly didn't stop the Butlers. They were going to form a group.

The exact date doesn't matter, and hasn't been recorded if it did. It was shortly before Tim's 18th birthday on 7th December and a few weeks after the three brothers took the train up to London to catch the Sex Pistols, the Clash and the hastily formed Siouxsie and the Banshees among the attractions at the 100 Club Punk Festival, a gathering of the clans which cemented once and for all the fact that there was more to the movement than the Sex Pistols' tailor.

The two brothers were playing records and talking, when Richard asked whether Tim wanted to form a band.

'I can't play anything,' Tim responded.

'What do you want to play?' Richard countered.

'Bass.'

'Well, buy one. Learn to play it, then you can be in the band.'

Ah, the impetuosity of youth. 'He said bass because he figured it was easier to learn, as it only had four strings, and he was probably right,' Richard muses. And, over the next few months, he did learn to play it, after a fashion, of course. Commandeering Richard's copy of the first Stooges album, Tim started at the beginning – the anthemic '1969' – then simply worked his way through the record: 'I Wanna Be Your Dog,' 'We Will Fall' (okay, maybe *not* 'We Will Fall')… By the time he reached the last song, 'Little Doll,' he was at least as proficient as much of the competition, and probably more so than most of it. Judging from the number of other bands who took to mutilating their favourite Pop songs, most bassists never got past 'No Fun'.

Elder brother Simon was roped into the conspiracy because he could already play guitar a little and, early in the new year, two of his friends, aspiring saxophonist Duncan Kilburn and fellow guitarist Roger Morris – 'Dog' to his friends – were brought in to broaden the sound even further. Both lived in Epsom, about half an hour away, but could usually be found at the Butlers' place anyway.

Morris recalls, 'Their house was the local meeting place, having the most tolerant parents of any of us. We'd listen to music – Dylan, the Stooges, the Velvet Underground – and pass around Simon's guitar, taking turns to abuse it.'

Like Simon, both of the newcomers were graduates of Therfield School in Leatherhead; Simon and Duncan Kilburn also attended City University together until the latter dropped out in 1974 – 'we shared digs in various slums in London for a year,' Kilburn explained. But the pair brought both enthusiasm and expertise to the band. Indeed, Kilburn, with a career working with Stock and Commodity markets for Reuters already in his palm, had just returned from a posting to New York City, 'where I spent 1976 living on 53rd and 3rd. In my spare time I was studying the theory of music, and saxophone with a great teacher who'd played in the Broadway pits on most of the 50s shows.'

Roger Morris, a British Rail track maintenance worker by day, was himself a proficient player, while Simon Butler, says Kilburn, was an 'excellent' guitarist, not to mention 'something of an electronics genius. It's important to understand Simon's contribution to the Furs in order to understand how it all came together.'

In later years, Kilburn continues, 'Richard often referred to our lack of musicianship, which was a very Warhol thing to come up with, and very inaccurate. Like the Velvet Underground, Richard liked to think that he brought a bunch of willing accomplices around him and gave them instruments and told them to play. This may have been true with Tim, but not with myself, (I was trained from a young age on piano, have always read music and played alto and tenor sax as well as guitar, trombone etc etc) and Roger was, and I gather still is, an awesome guitarist, as was Simon. But it fitted the bill and I could never be bothered to correct him in full flight.'

Richard insists that he never wanted to imply that his cohorts were clueless musically, he just wanted to distance the group from self-indulgent virtuosity. 'We knew chords and how to play, but we were beginners as musicians. I said we couldn't play, but I'd say it to be abrasive. I was saying it as a blow against Yes and ELO. Were we comsummate musicians? No!'

Maybe the initial Furs line-up was, as Tim Butler puts it, 'just friends getting together, bashing around, learning to play their instruments.' But it also possessed a very strong musical core from the outset.

One of Richard's art school friends, Nick Sealy, was installed on a rudimentary drum kit, and a few reasonably coherent rehearsals convinced the sextet that they were ready for the world. 'Before Punk Rock there was a big blur between being a fan and being a person who could actually do it,' Richard reiterated years later. 'Then, after the Pistols came along, it was like, you learn three chords and it's more about attitude than musicianship. You realise you don't have to be that good at it to get into it.'

He never intended for the group to be simply a Punk band, however. In later years, Butler would coin the description 'glam-Punk rock with good lyrics' and, while it was some time before anybody outside of the band could hear it, from the outset that was the mood they were aiming for. 'It's not like I sat back and said I wanted the lyrics to sound like Dylan and the saxophones like Roxy Music, but I wanted that kind of aesthetic. I wanted that sneer. There was something about it that was a lot crueler and a lot more snide than Punk. Johnny Lydon was great for his time, but next to Bob Dylan he sounded like a child throwing a tantrum.'[1]

Kilburn agrees. 'We were not really into the punk thing for a number of reasons. We were very middle class and clearly in comparison pretty well off. The nucleus of the band are very well educated. We were totally un-political. We hated being spat at. (Very often we'd just walk off when they started gobbing). And we considered ourselves to be in some ways artists, or at least I did. So what we were doing was creative, with no political bent, with some funding and some sort of a plan. Not punk.'

At Richard's suggestion, the band was christened RKO, in tribute to the flamboyant logo of the old film studio, and early into the long, hot summer of 1977, as the local teenaged garden party season got underway, the band landed their first-ever gig, in the front room of a friend's house in Leatherhead.

It wasn't a success. Indeed, far from drawing the party-goers in from the garden, RKO actually succeeded in driving the handful of onlookers outside with everyone else. 'Nobody was really interested,' Tim recalls with touching understatement. A clutch of tentative originals, all-but freeform renditions of the very formative 'Radio' and 'Blacks' among them, were met with blank stares and, by the time RKO launched into their version of Jonathan Richman's 'Roadrunner' – an interminable, rambling, and really not-very-good 'Roadrunner' – 'people walked out and shut the door on us. There were only about two people left. That wasn't a very auspicious start!'

Neither did RKO's immediate future dawn any less merciless. A few days later, Morris was in a coffee bar in town when he overheard someone discussing RKO – or 'some bloody awful Punk band they had seen that weekend. I kept a low profile.'

The RKO identity was abandoned after that first show, and most of the replacements that were suggested are now forgotten. A name would sound great for a while, but its allure would fade with the following morning's hangovers. For a time, the group vaguely considered rechristening themselves the Radiators, then switched to the Refrigerators. But they shut that door once they realised the ammunition they'd be handing their critics on a plate – they'd had enough 'frosty receptions,' 'icy glares' and 'cold shoulders' already.

What they needed was something eye-catching. With the exception of a handful of monosyllabic drudges, this was the age of the extravagant band name: Ed Banger and the Nosebleeds, Johnny and the Self Abusers, Siouxsie and the Banshees… The group played one show as Matt Vinyl and The Undercoats, but that lasted about as long as it would have taken to dry and they were back to square one.

Still intrigued by household items, they played another party as Radio. It didn't last. Though it was retained for a future song title, Radio was simply too dull for words, and words were important to Richard Butler: the way they sounded, the moods they embodied, the images they created. 'For instance,' he once reflected of his earliest attempts at songwriting, 'the song "Sister Europe." At the time I wrote that, I was going out with a girl… and she went off to Italy. But instead of saying "my bird's gone to Italy and I miss her", I tried to put over the feeling of being sad and low with images.'[2]

Images. If there was one image associated with the Punk movement, born of its appearance, sired in its songs and immortalized in the names of the musicians who performed it, it was violence: Sid Vicious, Menace, Penetration, 999. Conflict was the order of the day, mashed bloodily into a brutality which established the music's intentions from the outset.

What, however, if a name rejected those connotations? If it conveyed warmth instead of anger, cuddles instead of kicks? If it wrapped itself in a cocoon of adorable fuzzy fluffiness and waited until the crowd was safely inside the room, their hearts and souls begging to be bathed in beauty, before stepping out to deliver the *coup de* dis-*grace*?

'There were so many confrontational-sounding names,' Richard Butler recalls. 'And it eventually became the safe option. You'd look through the back of *Melody Maker* and that's all you'd see, so I was thinking, "what name would make me go 'what? What are they doing?'"' He was well aware that people were already wondering that, once they heard the band play. What he wanted was to start them guessing before they even left the house.

COUNTLESS MINUTES OF CHAOS

BRAINSTORMING IN THE PUB one night, the conversation turned to Iggy Pop and the Stooges, how they started life in 1967 as the Psychedelic Stooges, convinced that audiences immersed in the prevalent warmth of love and flowers would be sucked right into their clutches. And then the music would batter them into unconsciousness. It was the ultimate mindfuck for the fucked-up hippy minds and, ten years on, the trick was well worth playing again.

For a time, the band was uncertain precisely what Psychedelics they wanted to be – the Psychedelic Shirts and the Psychedelic Shoes were among the contenders. And then Richard came up with the Psychedelic Furs, 'and that's the one that stuck.'

In truth, the Psychedelic tag really wasn't too far off the mark, wrapping itself around the band's sound a lot more comfortably than a more fashionable tag would have. 'Psychedelia', after all, is one of those terms which has become hideously devalued over time, absorbed by the hippy *chic* notions of wasted pot-heads with too many guitars, noodling into a chemical eternity and burning their draft cards because war isn't cool. Man. Either that, or the Grateful Dead.

But what if Psychedelia hadn't been co-opted by the media the moment it surfaced; what if flowers and tie-dye and bubble-lamps had *not* become the standard bearers of the movement? Under those conditions, Psychedelia becomes something deeper and darker altogether – so deep, so dark, that the culture-crushing catastrophes which modern history holds high as the corollary of the entire shebang – Charles Manson, Altamont, Vietnam – are completely inverted, to become its logical consequence.

In that climate, Psychedelia indeed becomes the absolute freedom of thought, word and deed which is the true legacy of an expanded consciousness. There, it represents the total annihilation of such limited concepts as good and evil, right and wrong, love and hate; there, Man becomes one, not with God, but with himself. And Francois Rabelais' oft-appropriated mandate, 'Do What You Like,' ['Fait ce que vouldras'] becomes the only commandment that could ever mean anything.

In those hands, Psychedelia changes and its soundtrack is irrevocably altered as well. No more white rabbits or black cats, sugar lumps or donkey rides, no more songs or structure or verse-chorus-verse. Free your mind and your ass will follow. Freak out in a moonage daydream. Let it *all* hang out. The Psychedelic Furs played a formless, tuneless, endless, nameless racket. And *that*, in every alternate universe but our own, is what Psychedelia was all about.

The Psychedelic Furs' earliest influences could be read off a cue-card, of course. The icicle sheen of vintage Roxy Music was in there, but so was the minimalist twist of Suicide – if Andrew Loog Oldham had jumped in as their producer. The arrogant swagger of Lou Reed, the beautiful pummelling of Iggy and the Stooges.... Richard Butler coolly latched onto the singing styles he most fervently admired, and tried to combine them in his own: the laconic sneer of the Pistols' Johnny Rotten, the nasal intuition of the young Bob Dylan, the affected inhumanity of David Bowie.

As a songwriter, Butler's favourite Bowie record was (and remains) 1971's *Hunky Dory*, the word-hungry, tune-laden masterpiece that was cut when fame and fortune were still a love affair away. 'Queen Bitch' with her own blatant nod to the Velvet Underground sashay and tat; the labyrinthine mysteries of the 'Bewlay Brothers'; the doom-in-sheep's-clothing of 'Oh You Pretty Things'; the stark idolatory of 'Andy Warhol': all were moods that Butler himself intended to pursue.

As an acolyte, however, it was the popsicle-cold tones of *Station To Station* and *Low* which he most purposefully echoed. There, Bowie's words were merely the messenger; the actual message was in the tone. Many of Butler's earliest lyrics are little more than vignettes. It is the impact of the band that transformed them into epics.

It was what they did with these influences that mattered. Most bands mentioned the Velvets, then lurched into an awful cover of 'White Light, White Heat' – to file alongside the 'No Fun' they'd desecrated earlier. The Psychedelic Furs weren't interested in the songs, though. It was the attitude that they wanted to re-create, the shocked words and observations that flood from the Velvets' early press mentions as straight minds attempted to come to terms with the ultimate twisted fantasy.

In 1966, New York journalist Richard Goldstein wrote of one Velvets' performance: 'the sound is a savage series of atonal thrusts and electronic feedback. The lyrics combine sado-masochistic frenzy with free association imagery. The whole sound seems to be the product of a secret marriage between Bob Dylan and the Marquis De Sade.' In 1977, the Psychedelic Furs set out to discover if someone might write the same thing about them.

Simon Butler was first to drop out of the band. According to Tim, 'he didn't want to get into the band proper, because he thought it would be like the Bee Gees [Richard compared the sibling grouping to the Osmonds] or something. So he went off to university, and the rest of us carried on.' Simon eventually relocated to the US, settling in San Rafael, California; he is now Principal Engineer at an electronics 'start-up' company in nearby Palo Alto. By mid-1977, Sealy, too, had departed, to be replaced for a time by one Phil Snow. The drummer's seat never seemed to be occupied for very long, though, and the band soon grew accustomed to the revolving door of drummers. It helped keep things interesting.

Undeterred by the comings and (more frequently) goings, the Psychedelic Furs continued expanding their horizons, fitting music – or, at least, droning rhythms – around Richard's lyrics, then tinkering with cover versions until they were unrecognisable chasms of noise, and new lyrics could be slipped over them as well.

Later immortalised as 'We Love You', but originally known as 'Cars', a chanted litany of all the things one could fall in love with, from the Supremes to the twist to the BBC, the Furs' first song was built upon a rhythmic foundation whose origins in 'Waiting For The Man' are still apparent – but only if it had first been appropriated by the Stooges, *circa Fun House*.

If it was a cacophony when you stood in the same room as the band, it was even worse when heard through the unsoundproofed walls of a suburban home. The Butler household's neighbours were as unsupportive as the most disdainful party-goer and, by late summer, 1977, the Psychedelic Furs had been expelled from their living room roost by the growing complaints of the rest of the street. It was time to leave East Horsley behind.

The group relocated its headquarters to London: Morris and Kilburn were already halfway there, with a flat in Kingston; now, the Butlers leapfrogged them to the heart of north London, and a shared flat on Grasmere Road, close by Muswell Hill Broadway. It was an area steeped in rock'n'roll history – the Kinks once lived there, Alvin Stardust was born there, Rod Stewart was schooled there, Fairport Convention formed there – and later, they'd discover, mass murderer Dennis Nilsen hung out there, frequenting the same local pubs as the Butlers, in search of fresh bodies to cut up and boil.

Duncan Kilburn recalls those early days as little more than 'a jumble of memories of filthy North London rehearsal space, scrabbling for gigs, and replacing drummers (nine I believe in the first couple of years). I had some pretty cool bosses at the time who turned a blind eye to late morning appearances and my appearance in general, which was becoming decidedly Cramps at that time.

'There were some great gags at the time. I remember Tim and Richard walking down Muswell Hill Broadway both actually hungry. Richard says "Stop complaining Tim, when The Clash first started they had to eat wallpaper paste" (apparently it expands in the stomach and stops hunger pains – don't try it kids its got some nasty stuff in it these days). To which Tim replies "Lucky bastards". I think the same night they actually ended up fighting and Tim threw Richard through a shoe shop window. Tim recalled waking up surrounded by left shoes!' The group had one additional advantage over countless others in their position – Kilburn's BMW, and sufficient disposable cash (Kilburn again) to pay for rehearsal space and demos.

The rehearsals continued. Democratically, the group rented a studio smack in between the members' homes, in a converted warehouse on Lotts Road, Chelsea, in the shadow of the old power station. There, they honed the set into a presentable shape, then began calling round in search of a gig.

The first outside venue to offer the unknown, untried Psychedelic Furs a break was the Duke of Lancaster pub in Wealdstone, a few stops up the Northern Line from the Butlers' home base. It was an unprepossessing place with undiscerning punters, a low stage and a tiny PA. It was also completely unprepared for the sheer cacophony with which the Psychedelic Furs intended entertaining the tiny, curious crowd. Backs turned, doors slammed, the room emptied – and not only were the Psychedelic Furs banned from ever again darkening the Ducal doorstep again, but word quickly spread that other venues might want to think very seriously, and feel very desperate, before booking the group for themselves.

The group was dismayed, but scarcely discouraged. They acknowledged, however, that some serious strategy was called for. 'If [venues] wanted to hear a demo,' Richard reveals, 'we'd play them something we'd taped off a record that they didn't know, something very hip, so they didn't have a clue. Then we'd play, and they'd say, "We'll never have you back again." So, we'd go the next week with a tape of...I don't know...the Velvet Underground's third album, and say it was us. We'd say we'd gone acoustic, and they'd book us back. Then we'd turn up and do exactly the same thing as before.' In fact, the band did consider going acoustic for real, but a handful of rehearsals (and a change of name, to the Europeans) swiftly showed them the error of their ways. It was back to business as usual.

Tim Butler, too, still relishes the subterfuge that the band would indulge in, in the search for shows. 'We'd play certain gigs, and they'd say you can't come back, because you're too loud. We'd go back with a different name, and say, "Hey, we're different now, we're not as loud." Then we'd set up and play just as fucking loud! So we didn't get very popular with quite a few pub and club owners.'

To compound the band's sense of hardship and sacrifice, they were also bedevilled by a chronic lack of transport. Roger Morris remembers: 'One feature of playing those gigs... was having to walk back to Muswell Hill afterwards, usually lugging a Marshall 100 watt amp. Freezing cold, flat broke (spent cab fare in pub), and a hangover just starting to take hold.'

They cut a sorry sight on those occasions – so sorry that, one night, a police van stopped as it cruised past them and, having ascertained the musicians actually owned the equipment they were struggling with, stopped and gave them a ride home.

As autumn 1977, turned towards winter, gigs began to come faster and, as the band's experience mounted, so did their ability to actually start communicating with the audience – not verbally, perhaps not even musically, but certainly on a deeper level, one which acknowledged that at least the Psychedelic Furs were trying something different, something that strived, within the rent-a-riff cauldron that now passed for Punk Rock, to offer more than another three chords to pogo to.

'We were definitely different from what was around at the moment, those sort of conveyer-belt Punk acts,' Tim Butler reflects. 'We were pretty much writing songs onstage, everybody in the band just jamming because nobody really knew how song structures worked. In the end, everybody wanted to be in the limelight, so we tended to have a wall of melody. Then, we'd come to a screeching halt, and I'd be detuning the bass while I was playing songs.'

Draped in as much darkness as they could find in the shadows of the stage, with Richard the garishly painted ghost of a ghastly vaudeville tart, croaking and crooning until he ran out of words, it was a disconcerting experience, to say the least.

'We'd play each song for about 15 or 20 minutes, until we got bored with it, and we'd just stop, walk around talking to each other, then start something else.' Sometimes, circumstances did wreak a respite. Broken strings were rarely an impediment to the band – if Morris lost one, he still had five more, and it wasn't as if he needed use them all, anyway. But band meetings took place in the full view of the audience, and shouted orders to the bar were as likely to punctuate a song as its lyrics.

'I think the reason the songs went on forever is that we didn't have very many of them,' Richard reasons. 'They told us we had to play for half an hour, so we'd just fill it out with different noises, carry on ranting, breaking things, just really filling out three songs to fit half an hour. It was a good idea in a way, we liked the idea of having the songs all segue into each other, and we were probably afraid to stop in case people didn't clap. We wanted to get done and get off.'

He later recalled 'playing whole shows with my back to the audience. I used to feel very self-conscious about being onstage because I wasn't sure I was any good, or whether what we were doing was any good.'[3] Other shows, he would simply lie on the floor and let the band – themselves no more certain of their validity than he was, but able, at least, to hide behind their instruments and volume – wash over him.

The ensuing timeless improvisations were not wholly indulgent, however. Within a year or so, many of these same ingredients had been stirred into the sonic tureen which band and critics alike dubbed 'beautiful chaos.' For now, however, beauty had little to do with it. Roger Morris explains, 'We used to play "Blacks", then segue into "Radio", and that transition became known as "Chaos". And it was a real bloody racket sometimes. But it was also where we jammed, and worked on ideas for new songs. So, if "beautiful chaos" had a literal meaning, it was referring to one of the methods we used to write. And it sounded cool, a bit self-contradictory, a bit of Warhol, a bit of anarchy, a bit of psychedelia.'

Many of the songs that comprised the Psychedelic Furs' first album were devised during these marathon excursions, whether onstage with an audience or during equally intense rehearsal jams. Here a bass line that Tim had inadvertently stumbled upon, that Richard hurried over and told him to remember; there a sax break or guitar riff that scythed unexpectedly through the mayhem of the mix and embedded itself upon someone's awareness. No good ideas were wasted, although plenty were probably lost as the moment passed before anyone noticed, and it'd be blind luck alone if it ever returned again.

Richard was as improvisational as his band mates. He was constantly writing lyrics in readiness for the day when a song might coalesce round them, but he was equally adept at simply letting rip unscripted, spitting out whichever words came into his head. Indeed, the band's primary source of on-stage direction came directly from the frontman and whatever he was ad-libbing at the time. And that, in itself, was a wonder to behold. Even after the Psychedelic Furs' repertoire cemented itself around a distinct set of songs, the lyrics rarely remained the same. Sometimes, Richard would simply change a few key words – other times, he'd come out with entire new verses. And occasionally, he'd pick up a book or a newspaper and start reading aloud from that.

Not until the Psychedelic Furs had a record out, and audiences began demanding something they might recognize, did the singer fall out of the habit of simply shooting off at manic tangents midway through a familiar riff and, as time passed, he got out of the habit altogether. Still, the intriguing spoken-word close to 'Pretty In Pink' bears permanent witness to his ability to let go – and, even more intriguingly, he admits that he's never been able to remember every word.

From the other side of the stage, where the audience shifted uncertainly, the chaos was no less illuminating. Occasionally, through the roar, a phrase would strike out which might resolve itself, later, into an actual song title: 'Fall In Love', 'Sex', 'Cars' (an early version of 'We Love You' but also, for a time, titled 'So In Love'), 'Shoes.' Sometimes, one might even sense (but rarely hear) an abrupt tempo change from one player or another, the cue or a clue that one song had ended and a new one begun.

The group did not seem to understand the concept of volume controls, and they certainly hadn't thought of co-ordinating their settings. If you were ever caught alongside the PA while they played, your balance could be shot for days. It was, in short, an absolute din.

But there was something compelling about it regardless: the notion that, if you could only break through the pain threshold that the Psychedelic Furs erected around their songs, you might discover something waiting on the other side that was very precious indeed.

Kilburn quit for a time, but returned soon after, filling the group with renewed vigour. A new drummer, Paul Wilson, seemed to offer further stability and, in early November, the newly reconstituted group landed what seemed certain to be their big break. They'd been booked to play the Covent Garden Roxy.

The Roxy had fallen on hard times since the halcyon days of early 1977, a mere nine months previous but several musical lifetimes before. Back then, it was the rapidly beating heart of Punk London, the host of 100 nights of… So many modern rock history books recall those shows as undiluted ecstasy, as the Adverts, the Damned, Generation X, Chelsea, Wire, the Buzzcocks, X-Ray Spex, the very icing of the Punk Rock cake, turned out to shake the very foundations of modern society with unmitigated primeval brilliance.

In fact, the place was a dump, with probably half the bands that filed through its doors barely worthy of the name, and a bunch more still a few months-worth of rehearsals short from mastering their first actual song. But hey, it was Punk Rock and that's what it was all about. Besides, no matter how rose-tinted your spectacles are when you look back on the first days of the Roxy Club, once a change of ownership snatched away the aura of exclusivity which let it get away with murder, you need solid crimson lenses.

Except for the night when the Psychedelic Furs played.

Actually, their first appearance was little short of a disaster. Billed only as the Furs – somebody, either the promoter or the band themselves, felt that the "Psychedelic" tag might be pushing things a bit too far – they'd been recruited to open one of the club's regular audition nights, on 14th November 1977.

They wouldn't be paid for appearing, of course, because that wasn't what auditions were about. They would be rewarded, if they merited it, with a return booking, and that was incentive enough. A few names of some future renown had already emerged from such evenings – the very first public audition, at the end of June, threw Bernie Torme and Rikki Sylvain into a spotlight of sorts. Another unearthed the Killjoys, so soon to be reborn amid Dexy's Midnight Runners.

But history records those shows as a lurid exception to the rule. On a bill 'topped' by the immortally named Jesus Savage, who'd already played the Roxy a few weeks before, the Psychedelic Furs would be duking it out with the similarly unknown, equally obscure The Pitiful. If the audience response of boos and jeers was any barometer of their performance, it really was a dreadful show, the Duke of Lancaster to the power of ten. But the Roxy management was made of sterner stuff – or, at least, was more forgiving. The Furs were promptly offered a second gig, on January 20th 1978.

It was a night that will never be forgotten.

BEAUTIFUL CHAOS IS IN
THE EYE OF THE BEHOLDER

ASK THE PSYCHEDELIC FURS today about the night that they added a hoover to their arsenal, and their memories tend not to be too rosy.

'A hoover, you say,' replies Roger Morris. 'That does ring a bell, must have been from our "household-appliances-as-art" phase. You didn't catch the sink plunger show?'

'It was horrible,' continues Richard Butler. 'It didn't work at all.' Or, most damning of all, from brother Tim, 'It sounded like a gorilla fart.'

At the time, however, it was a magnificent idea, a roar within a roar that would increase the group's already unsettling powers of dislocation to hitherto untapped heights. One needed only remember the hysterical reaction to Lou Reed's *Metal Machine Music* three short years before; how even people who had long and lovingly championed Reed's talent for the experimentally unexpected had run screaming from earshot as four sides of vinyl ground out one long concerto of anguished electronic wailing. Lou had never returned to those pastures, and anyone else who ventured near them – Throbbing Gristle, for example, or Cabaret Voltaire – did so safe beneath the bushel of art, with a very large capital A.

The Psychedelic Furs, however, had no such pretensions. 'We'd heard that Iggy Pop used some appliances on stage, so we thought why not use a vacuum cleaner?' Tim explains. Noise, as David Bowie once said, was what the world was all about. And noise was what the Psychedelic Furs excelled at.

The evening began inauspiciously. Arriving at the Roxy for load-in, the band found the back doors of their rental van were stuck. 'We couldn't get the gear out,' remembers Richard, 'so this wide-boy character who ran the place came up, and told us, "Oh, I'll get it open". Then, he bent the door handle back and forced the door open. The van was useless after that, but at least we got the gear out.'

Again billed as the Furs, they were the first band on. Above them on the bill, the Plague, the Purge and Guildford's own Crisis stood around the venue, each anxious only for those below them to play and clear off. The audience, many of whom had only turned up because they couldn't get into Elvis Costello's freebie at the Roundhouse, was even more impatient. The sight of the Furs setting up as the club opened, all Velvets shades and nervous shuffling, wasn't even greeted with a half-hearted murmur, while the sight of the sax even drew a few groans: the discordant honking of X-Ray Spex notwithstanding, there wasn't a band in the land which had rehabilitated that instrument from the days of the dreaded jazz-rock insurgents. The practice squawks that punctuated the tune-up only deepened the sense of gloomy trepidation.

Then the band started playing – and then they switched on the hoover.

It's hard to say if it was the sound of the hoover, or the sight of it, that made the greatest impression. Probably, it was neither. The small knot of drifters shifting list-lessly around the dance floor instinctively recoiled when the noise first erupted, and the band themselves looked a little taken aback.

But, to a handful of people watching from the back – and being drawn ever closer by the mystifying barrage – there was something compelling about it, regard-less. Bands didn't do things like that at the Roxy. They didn't even do it at the ICA. They just went onstage with their guitars and their attitudes, then strummed and thrashed and shouted a lot, hey diddle diddle, that's our song. And now, here were these unknown Furs, plugging it in and switching it on... And it was wonder-ful: a dense, infernal bellow which was louder than anything else on the stage, unyielding in its sonic obesity, but obscenely undulating as well, until it sounded like somebody really was playing it, and the other instruments were deliberately weaving around. Either that, or they were trying to escape.

'Oh no...the hoover!' Tim Butler recoils. 'We thought it would be really cool, but, of course, all it did was sound like the bass was feeding back.'

They never repeated the experiment.

Time passed. Spring 1978 found the Psychedelic Furs making their first tenta-tive trips out of London, westwards to Reading and Aylesbury, – where they were witnessed by a young Peter Murphy, a year or so away from launching Bauhaus; north into East Anglia. Tim Butler: 'We played the Boogie House in Norwich, which was a bit eye-opening. We never played again in Norwich in our lives! It was in this place that was a don't-blink-or-you'll-miss-it town. I don't think the guy that got us in there knew what he was getting into.'

Paul Wilson departed, and the drum stool was filled by Tommy, a friend of a wrestling promoter who was professing an interest in managing the group at that time. Tommy's surname has long since been forgotten, but his unswerving sense of band loyalty lives on in Psychedelic Furs mythology to this day.

The band had landed another London gig, opening for the Zaine Griff Band at the Rock Garden in Covent Garden. A New Zealander and former student at Lindsay Kemp's dance school (where he worked alongside the young Kate Bush), Griff was one of those peculiar souls who emerged just as the firestorms of Punk first abated, positing one of several possible directions in which the Next Big Thing might lurch – in this case, a pre-Gary Numan drift towards the painted artiness of a New Wave David Bowie.

Griff's show, both with the band and, later, when he struck out as a solo artist, was actually a lot more fun than the disdainful sneering of received rock history lets on. Unfortunately, you would not have known that, if you spent that night at the Rock Garden.

According to Richard, 'we were in the dressing room after the show, and Tommy came in, looking very pleased with himself. He'd managed to wrench this big plug that carried all the wires off the back of the deck, so that Zaine Griff couldn't actually play his set. He said, "People will leave here remembering us, this is a great thing!" And I remember, we were all pissed off and thought it was very unfair. Plus, we thought we were going to get lynched. But nobody ever realized.' And nobody remembered it either.

Tommy left, to be replaced by another character whose surname has been lost to time, a visiting Frenchman who may have been named Jean Paul, but was certainly known as Denis by his band mates – Roger Morris recalls the group clubbing together to buy him a copy of the latest Blondie single for his birthday (it was also called 'Denis'). His guitar-playing roommate Dominic came as part of the package and, briefly, the Psychedelic Furs imagined themselves pioneering a revolutionary brand of New European chic. It was a short-lived dream. The duo played one show with the band, then returned to France.

Such turmoil could not disguise the fact that the Psychedelic Furs were coming on by leaps and bounds. Nigel Gray, just starting out on the production career which, within a couple of years, would lead him to triumph with the Police, the Passions and Siouxsie & the Banshees, caught a show and was sufficiently enthused to offer his help recording some demos. Regretfully, the band turned him down – they couldn't afford the studio time.

But an audience was certainly beginning to gather around their increasingly frequent (if still under-attended) shows and, after you'd seen the band a couple of times, the relentless wall of noise really did seem to resolve itself into moments you recognised from an earlier gig. It was still utter confusion, wholly indecisive, a chaotic construction that managed to stay upright as much by luck as judgement. But it worked. 'It was just weird stuff,' Tim Butler admitted. 'But I guess people liked it.'

Few people who saw – or, should that be, survived – a Psychedelic Furs show could ever resist returning for another. And that included the band's own members. Since quitting the group earlier in the year, Paul Wilson had been drumming with the Unwanted. Now that they were splitting up, he wanted back into the Psychedelic Furs – and they, having just been rendered drummer-less again, were quick to welcome him home.

The Unwanted were one of the great also-rans of Punk – great because, at their best, in the seething dungeon of the original Roxy, they left witnesses utterly boggled by how bad they were, a comedy turn which laughed at its own shortcomings, then laughed at the audience for being so shocked by them. They cut the first Punk cover of 'These Boots Are Made For Walking,' and it stomped all over every other version you've ever heard. But critical disdain, commercial neglect, and increasingly miserable returns for their seldom-less-than-wonderful live show took their toll.

The group's membership, too, was in constant tumult. Since the band formed in March 1977, on the very eve of their recorded debut, onstage for the *Live At The Roxy* Punk sampler, every place in the line-up had been occupied by at least two different musicians and some by more than that. By mid-1978 then, vocalist Ollie Wisdom and bassist Dave Postman were hanging onto the band by the skin of their teeth and, though hopes were high for the future, that future was itself on its last legs. Unwanted by name, unwanted by nature. The only positive aspect of the entire affair was that Ollie had decided not to stick with his original choice for a band name. Heaven knows what would have happened to Smak.

Wilson had been one of two new recruits as the Unwanted wound down: also joining Wisdom and Postman was guitarist John Ashton, a London-born, Leicestershire lad who migrated back to the city in 1977, specifically to seek his Punk Rock fortune. There was, after all, little in that line to keep him at home – home being Lutterworth, a village best known for its annual air show, and as the last resting place of the Avro Vulcan jet bomber.

Ashton hit the city with his best friend, Dave Martin, and it was Martin who was first to fall on his feet. In October 1977, he landed the vacant rhythm guitar slot in Chelsea, then riding high on the strength of the ultra-anthemic 'Right To Work'. Ashton took a little longer to touch down. When he did land a gig, wanted by the Unwanted, he was just in time to see the whole thing to go unpleasantly pear-shaped.

The end came suddenly, in October 1978. A recording session was booked, but Wilson never showed up. Gamely, the band tried to press on without him, but even Ashton, whose first studio visit this was, admitted, 'it was a pretty disastrous session. We made a recording, but it wasn't very good, and that was the end of that.'

A couple of weeks later, however, Ashton answered his door to find the errant Wilson standing there. 'He said, "Oh yeah, I couldn't make it, I had something to do, but anyway there's this band, the Psychedelic Furs, and they're looking for another guitarist. I'm going to go rehearse with them in two weeks' time, here's a tape, check it out." So I did, and I really liked it.'

The rehearsal fell on Ashton's 21st birthday, 30th November 1978, but any propitious omens he could deduce from that coincidence were more than quashed by nervousness. By the time he was ready to leave for the meeting, he'd all but decided to go somewhere else entirely. Only the exertions of his girlfriend, Tracey Collier, finally persuaded him to go along.

The Psychedelic Furs themselves were not expecting to audition a guitarist that night but, as Tim Butler put it, 'Hey, we were loose and ready for anything at that time.' Recalling that the first song he ever heard the band play was 'Cars', Ashton continues, 'I met them all, listened to them rehearse a bit, went out and got some beer, watched them rehearse a bit more, got some more beer, and then I think I couldn't get any more beer, so they asked me to get up and play, and I did. Then, later that night, Richard came back to Tracey's and my flat, and asked her to manage the band.' A former club promoter with a diary full of contacts and the knowledge to make them work, she agreed.

The following Saturday, 9th December 1978, Ashton and Collier attended their first Psychedelic Furs concert, at the Green Man pub in Islington. It was, even by the group's usual standards, a memorable performance, one that culminated with Richard, holding a chair on the top of his head, careening around the dance floor until he smashed into the cigarette machine.

Ashton remembers, 'Much drinking followed, and I started rehearsing with them the next week.' A few days later, the guitarist sought out Dave Martin and his Chelsea bandmate James Stevenson, at the Marquee, to pass on his news. They burst out laughing. What sort of band was called the Psychedelic Furs?

It was Ashton's arrival, with a manager in tow, which added the finishing touch to the band's dynamic: a coruscating edge to what was already a fiercely opinionated community and a brand new power bloc to be negotiated whenever they fought. Which was a lot, as Kilburn made clear the following year: 'You've got six people who are thrown together, there's no way they can be naturally compatible, there's bound to be clashes. If there weren't clashes, then it wouldn't be constructive.' 'There's been a conflict,' Ashton agreed. 'The make-up of the band has been taut. There've been personality clashes.' But he, too, was adamant. 'The point is, we've got to learn to live with each other.'[4]

'We used to start out a rehearsal date at the pub drinking,' Tim Butler explains. 'Then we'd go to the rehearsal studio and have a few more beers, which would loosen us up. Then we could start jamming.' But it was a temporary respite. 'We'd hook onto an idea, and then start arguing about it. Of course, maybe that's where the aggression of those songs came from – gritting our teeth and staring angrily at each other – and then we'd play more aggressively still.'

'The thing about the band,' Ashton elaborates today, 'was you had to have an argument to have anything accomplished. That was what the chemistry was all about. It wasn't like a leader telling the troops to do this, that or the other, or like a team. Everybody was in there putting their two cents in, and making little alliances with one another. And the alliances were always changing.'

With Collier assuming much of the workload Richard had hitherto shouldered, some of that tautness relaxed a little. Ashton recalls, 'She got us gigs, she knew people at record companies, she knew promoters and everybody else.' Ashton, too, proved to be happily well-connected – numbered among his own musical friends was Les Mills, Siouxsie and the Banshees' road manager, who proved more than willing to loan that band's equipment to Ashton when they didn't need it themselves.

'I had lived for a time with John and Tracey in Wightman Road,' recalls Les.

'John had played me a tape of "The Psychedelic Furs" in November 1978, which I remember as being pretty awful. I advised him not to join them! Fortunately he ignored my advice.'

Before the Psychedelic Furs could go out and the equipment that Les was providing, however, Collier wanted to be sure of one thing. If she was going to manage the band, she wanted to know that they were actually worth managing. They had potential, they had power, they were brimming with possibilities. But that was no longer enough. Now they had to deliver, and that didn't mean turning in a good gig every so often. From now on, every gig had to be a good one. And, if they could stick to that side of the bargain, she'd be able to stick to hers.

She pulled the band off the road, booking them instead into six weeks of solid rehearsal time at a little studio in Turnpike Lane: 'It was run by the Arthur Daley of rock'n'roll,' Morris remembers. 'Always trying to flog us effects pedals. "Just got a new shipment in. No, sorry, I can't give you a receipt. What warranty?"' It was also close enough to the flat she shared with Ashton that she could drop by any time she wanted, to make sure the pub hadn't deflected the band from its duties. She wanted new material, tighter arrangements, a stronger stage presence.

Collier, meanwhile, was planning her campaign, a series of gigs which opened at the Rock Garden, supporting Random Hold on 30th January 1979, and then thrust the Psychedelic Furs into each and every venue she could land – which turned out to be virtually every significant club, pub and dive in the Greater London area. Richard and his girlfriend pulled extra hours screen-printing posters for the band, announcing their imminent arrival.

Finally, everything was in place. On February 5th, the Psychedelic Furs headlined the Pegasus in Stoke Newington, the pub in whose car park Johnny Rotten was razored during the Punk-thumping summer of 1977. Five days after that, they were at the Windsor Castle, on the Harrow Road; on February 13th, they debuted at the Moonlight Club in West Hampstead, the old Klook's Kleek of Swinging Sixties legend, but now a key site in a brand new rock underground swirling around the capital rock scene. Camden Town's Brecknock pub was next, then it was back to the Windsor Castle on the 23rd, where the group so impressed the pub's management that they were promptly offered a six-week residency, every Wednesday until the end of March.

'Residencies were very important,' affirms Duncan Kilburn, 'because gigs were always hard to find and so if there was a following they generally didn't know where to see you next. So if you could promote one gig on the back of another it was a big plus. The promoter could also monitor progress in the numbers coming through the door, and move you up the bill. In other words they would offer you the opening slot and if you could pull in a couple of hundred people they would move you up to second on the bill. After four weeks we were headlining and the place was sold out with queues. It was truly amazing.'

'The first Wednesday, there weren't many people there,' Richard agrees. 'But, by the end of the month, the place was getting pretty crowded.' Another member of Bauhaus, bassist David Jay, meanwhile, caught the group when they returned to the Rock Garden. 'They were the coolest thing on earth at the time, they were amazing. It was wild, very exciting, really interesting.' Joy Division frontman Ian Curtis was another early convert: 'He used to come down and see us a lot,' recalls Tim Butler.

By March 1979, there was clearly a buzz building around the band; more than that, there was a palpable sense that something was about to happen. The Psychedelic Furs were destined to be in the thick of it, as Duncan Kilburn explains: 'One of the great things about this time was hanging out in rehearsal studios with other bands in a similar position to us. Some didn't make it, but others, like Adam and the Ants, went on to great stardom. None of us knew at the time who would make it, and so it gave us a great spin on fame.' And a wider range of experiences to draw from.

Without ever considering themselves eligible for any of the pacts or packages which then comprised the British rock scene – and there was certainly enough of them around in 1979-80 – the Psychedelic Furs suddenly found themselves embroiled in one regardless, a neo-psychedelic ferment which drew its essential energies from the powers unleashed by Punk, but took its inspiration from the succession of musical pioneers whose own example had, in some way, fired Punk's earliest strivings.

The Velvet Underground and the Stooges were in there, inevitably, those self-appointed exterminators of the cultural and sonic taboos which permeated the first decade of rock'n'roll, and which were still clinging on into the third. But so were the poetry of politics and the wrath of Bob Dylan; so was the Glam Rock of Bowie, Roxy, Sparks and T Rex; and so was the leftfield eclecticism that they so flamboyantly disguised as pop.

The melding of these disparate ingredients was not, of course, new. In the mid-1970s, the Doctors of Madness dispensed a similar cocktail, and the likes of Rikki and the Last Days of Earth, the formative Japan and the early (pre-Midge Ure) Ultravox drank deep from their glass. But it was an idiom in desperate search of identity, and it took Punk to cast the last of the shadows that would finally coalesce into a tangible form, by tearing up the formbook that had excluded it in the first place.

Punk created community from what had hitherto been even less than a cult: the outsiders, the misfits, the miserable buggers that every schoolroom closeted in deepest isolation, to be labelled 'weird' by the captain of the football team, and 'creepy' by the girls who taped the Bay City Rollers to the lid of their desks.

From Liverpool, The Teardrop Explodes and Echo and the Bunnymen; from Manchester, Ian Curtis' Joy Division and Howard Devoto's Magazine; from

Northampton, Bauhaus; from Sussex, neighbouring county to the Surrey hinterland of the Psychedelic Furs, Robert Smith and the Cure; and, from further afield, Scotland's edgy Simple Minds and the dangerous Doll By Doll; Wales' Gene Loves Jezebel; Ireland's Virgin Prunes and the nascent U2, then a very far cry from the blustering demagogues of future fusty renown.

All delved into musical regions that had been developed by Punk, but they looked deeper back and further forward, too. What was astonishing was that, in almost every case and certainly in every city, such communities emerged in utter isolation, only discovering common ground in other regions when it was finally pointed out by the music press, obsessed as always with finding and binding the Next Big Thing. Once it had been noted and formally christened – 'New Musick'! 'Positive Punk'! – there was no escaping its clutch.

Sensibly, few bands even tried to wriggle away, the Psychedelic Furs included. Ashton occasionally railed against the 'clever, arty groups' who haunted the fringes of the Psychedelic Furs' own territory – 'The Pop Group are crap,' he sniffed to *Zig Zag*. 'It's unbelievable, [the singer] sounds like Norman Wisdom.' But Morris recalls, 'We really didn't pay it much attention. It seemed to have more to do with other people's needs than our own. We never purposefully pursued any particular performance sound or style in order to perch in any specific pigeonhole. Christ, we could hardly agree on which pub to go to ...'

Only Tim Butler acknowledges that there was a case to be made for some kind of stylistic unity among bands 'who were considered at the forefront of the music that was coming out of Punk, kind of trippy and psychedelicy, but still with energy.' And it didn't hurt at all that his band was the trippiest, psychedelic-est and most energetic of them all.

4

THE GUITARISTS ARE TOTALLY
OUT OF THEIR TREES

ON 26TH FEBRUARY 1979, the Psychedelic Furs played their biggest gig yet, opening at the Music Machine for EMI power-pop hopefuls, The Flys (fronted by Neil O'Connor, brother of singer Hazel). It was an awkward pairing, but it was to be repeated more than once over the next few months and, according to Tim Butler, it did the Psychedelic Furs no harm whatsoever. 'I guess people liked us, because the dance floor in front of the stage would be full for us, and when the Flys came on, they'd walk away to the bars.'

That first night was a rough one, though. Morris and Ashton both broke strings in the first song, and neither had thought to pack any more. By the end of the set, they were getting by on one and three strings respectively but, backstage after the gig, there was no time for recriminations. Les Mills dropped by to say hello with Banshees Siouxsie and Severin beside him, ready to confer their seal of approval on the band.

Mills was back at the Music Machine a few weeks later to see the Psychedelic Furs open for the Boys – and this time, the band pulled out all the stops. The sound was astonishing, the act was amazing, and Richard – his face a spectral white against the darkness that still enveloped his band mates – was absolutely mesmerising. It was that night that Mills decided he had to become involved with the Psychedelic Furs. 'It was awesome,' he recalls. 'Sonically it sounded like a squadron of B52's going overhead.'

At first, Mills simply helped out at gigs – check the gear, man the board, keep the drinks flowing, the usual stuff. Increasingly, however, he found other tasks to do, and there, too, the Psychedelic Furs were in good hands.

One morning a year or so earlier, during the seemingly interminable period when the Banshees hung unsigned from the rafters, a city full of record companies arrived at work to find the words SIGN THE BANSHEES: DO IT NOW neatly stencilled across their office facades. 'That was Les,' says Siouxsie proudly, and Mills' gift for publicity was confirmed. As the music press began moving in on the Psychedelic Furs, Mills became one of their first points of call, and he never disappointed.

'The Psychedelic Furs are in the vanguard of what's going to happen in a few months' time,' was a favourite prophecy. 'It's the Mod era at the moment' – Britain was then awash with Lambretta-and Parka-toting revivalists, lined up like landmines at the feet of the Jam – 'and that'll last another six months. Then, as soon as everybody gets fed up with it, they'll look for something else. The Psychedelic Furs have got a headstart. They've got twelve years to go on.'[5] Shortly after, Mills would leave the Banshees altogether, to become Collier's partner in the Psychedelic Furs' management.

'My original role with Siouxsie and the Banshees had mutated from fan to roadie to friend and confidant (particularly with Kenny Morris and John McKay) and finally to assistant manager,' Mills explains. 'It was as a result of an ultimatum by Banshees manager Nils Stevenson that I became co-manager of The Psychedelic Furs. Throughout May and June of 1979 I had been dividing my time between the Banshees, who were ensconced in Air Studio's making 'Join Hands', and the Furs. One day in late June, whilst Nils and I were up at Air, I remember feeling particularly exhausted. Nils, who knew about my increasing involvement with the Furs, turned to me and said "You can't work full time with both bands it's got to be either us or them". So I chose them. Tracey and I officially became partners in a management company that I named Amanita Artists on July 4th 1979.'

The Clash were next to check out the group. On 9th March, Joe Strummer and Mick Jones headed down to the Africa Centre on King Street, Covent Garden, where the Psychedelic Furs were headlining a four-band bill. They delivered a scathing verdict. According to Tim, 'they went up to Richard afterwards and said, "Hey, you're good, the bass player's good, but get rid of the guitarists, they're totally out of their trees!"' What the two professionals didn't know, of course, was that Ashton and Morris had spent the entire pre-show drinking. By the time they took the stage, Tim continues, 'they were propping each other up.'

Back at the Moonlight on 23rd March, the Psychedelic Furs came under the scrutiny of the national music press for the first time, at what they claimed was only their 14th-ever gig. Nick Tester, representing the now-defunct *Sounds*, wrote, 'While psychedelia is an influence (especially leaning on the Velvet Underground), they don't simply return to the form, but return it with their own updated colours and character... fast, assertive and rumbling rhythms dart deep beneath the strains of Duncan's sobbing, weeping sax, and Richard's yearning vocals.' In other words, whatever you were expecting from the Psychedelic Furs, they probably weren't going to be delivering. They were too individual for that.

The *Sounds* review had an immediate effect. 'It was very different in London then,' Richard recalls. 'It was very exciting, lots of bands, everybody was going out to clubs, everybody went out then.' A good review in any of the music papers could have people queuing round the block the next week, and the Psychedelic Furs were perfectly placed to take advantage of such enthusiasm. They became a fixture at Billy's for a while, the Soho heartbeat of the then-looming New Romantic movement, in the days before it actually had a name. For a time, arch-entepreneur Jock MacDonald, the club's promoter, appeared keen to take his own active role in the band's career, and that heightened their renown even further. Mercifully, perhaps, his interest faded – the Psychedelic Furs were never cut out to be stable mates for the Bollock Brothers. In fact Les Mills insists this was never really considered. 'Jock McDonald was a Glaswegian wide-boy who tried to latch on to the band but there was never a hope in hell that we would get involved with him.'

Word of mouth and, even, words on leather jackets were also telegraphing the news. Richard Butler: 'There were a couple of girls, very early fans of ours, who had leather jackets with PSYCHEDELIC FURS written on them. One day they were walking down Oxford Street when David Bowie walked up to them and asked, "What's that? What's the Psychedelic Furs?"'

Bowie then encountered the group themselves, backstage at Siouxsie & the Banshees' 7th April MENCAP mental handicap charity benefit, and quickly fell deep into conversation with Richard. According to legend, he walked up and announced, 'Hi, I'm David.' And Butler just stood there thinking, 'Christ, I *know* who you are. I'm Richard Butler.'

Formalities over, the pair fell to debating the Age of Consciousness or some such lofty concept, but the conversation was never resolved. Midway through, legend has it Tim broke up the party with a booming cry of 'you can't fucking act, can you?' 'Bowie came to see us at the Pegasus the week after,' Richard reflected. 'But he didn't speak to us.'

By the end of April 1979, the Psychedelic Furs had performed at least once at 21 different venues, all of them within London. Most nights were memorable, a few were even magical. However you looked at it, the Psychedelic Furs' reputation was gathering pace and plaudits wherever they went. On 30th May, they headlined the Music Machine for the first time; the following evening, they trouped down to the Victoria Venue to play *Zig Zag* magazine's tenth anniversary party.

At least, five of the band did. Paul Wilson, however, didn't join them.

Relations between Wilson and the rest of the band had been growing increasingly frosty over

Howard Thompson collection

Richard and David

recent months. 'We didn't like [him] much,' Richard admits. 'He started getting those Octoband drums, those really ugly heavy metal drums, and we hated it.' Tonight, it seemed, he was getting his revenge.

'We waited, waited, and waited,' Ashton recalls, 'but as the time got closer, we knew he wasn't going to come. John Lydon was in the audience, and he was all pissed off because he'd come to see us. He was shouting, "Just get up there and play!" We said, "We can't, we don't have a drummer!" He yelled back, "Well, we did it".'

And he might have done, but the Psychedelic Furs weren't going to take the chance. Finally, they called Wilson's mother, to learn the tragic news. The drummer had been involved in a terrible road accident earlier in the day. He wouldn't be able to make the show.

In fact, he'd been involved in nothing of the sort. He was, in actuality, playing a gig with the Clampdown that same night, but the Psychedelic Furs weren't to know that. Instead they spent the evening disconsolately watching last-minute stand-ins Levi & the Rockats melt the wallflowers with their high-octane rockabilly, and avoiding the attentions of Godfrey, a monstrous stuffed giraffe that had arrived with Siouxsie, and seemed intent on bashing every head it could reach.

Wilson did briefly return to the Psychedelic Furs, but his stay was short-lived. In June, he blew out another show, this time at the Moonlight Club – the band got through the set with the ever-ready Mills filling in on drums and, when they contacted Wilson to tell him he was sacked, it was to discover that he'd already quit. His girlfriend had given him the ultimate ultimatum: he could stay with her and work a steady job with the local council, or he could go off and play with the Psychedelic Furs. He chose the council.

Zig Zag forgave the band their non-appearance at the party, running a four-page interview in its next issue and championing them with almost delirious passion. 'The music is wild, rampant, atmospheric, dynamic and full of startling power,' author Kris Needs raved. Free-associating from the band's name back to the psychedelic Sixties, he noted, 'It's the spirit of attack and abandon [which] they've got in common with the most outrageous of the acid-rock groups,

André Huckvale collection

Furs make the cover of *Zigzag*'s 100th issue

Howard Thompson on the band minibus, USA, 1980.

Les Mills

Les Mills and Jack Rovner (Columbia marketing director) backstage, US tour, 1983.

Les Mills

plus the drama and barrage of '66 Velvets. *Low*-time Bowie and *Idiot* Pop prong the sound with '80s sheen. But their main attributes are their own devising... and, once the latest problem is surmounted – getting a new drummer – they'll be off the turd-strewn bumpy road and onto the escalator.'

After a handful of auditions turned up no-one of note, Tracey Collier finally recommended they recruit Rod Johnson, of post-pub rockers Straight Eight. Johnson was also with 'Camera Club', a Trevor Horn incarnation that was also signed to CBS. He wasn't immediately compatible, swiftly alienating his new band-mates with a musical taste that leaned dangerously close to the New Wave of British Heavy Metal – Saxon, Angelwitch, Girlschool and co made awkward points of reference for the rest of the Psychedelic Furs. But there was no time to waste getting precious about it. On 25th June, they were scheduled to play the Nashville again, co-headlining with the rising Spizz Energi and hopefully impress-ing at least one special guest, CBS A&R man Howard Thompson.

Thompson, like so many other people, was first attracted to the band by their name – he saw it in the gig guide and was immediately intrigued. A few days later, both Muff Winwood's Personal Assistant, Ben Kay, and *Sounds* journalist Giovanni Dadomo informed him the band was as fascinating as their name sug-gested. (Ms Kay later became the first Mrs Duncan Kilburn.) Thompson went along and was not disappointed. Midway through The Furs' set, a fight broke out in the audience and the band jumped in to help. It was, of course, a supremely Sex Pistols-shaped moment – some of that band's earliest notoriety was earned after they, too, stopped playing on the Nashville stage, to take part in a battle going down on the floor. The difference was, their singer didn't look like a gothic Mime. The memory of the white-faced Butler piling into the melee was a vision that Thompson would not readily forget.

The fight brought the curtain down on that evening's show, but Thompson had already seen enough. Over the next few weeks, he caught the band at virtually every show they played: Goldsmiths College, the Music Machine, the Pegasus... Introducing himself to the group, he confirmed what he already suspected: that CBS was neither the first label to court the Psychedelic Furs, nor would it be the last. He prided himself in the knowledge, however, that it was one of the few who might stay, after all of the others had walked away. The group was not an easy beast to deal with.

The first hint Thompson was given of the band's obduracy was when he asked if they had a demo tape that he could play to his boss, Muff Winwood. You could have sliced the silence with a box-cutter. Aside from a handful of rough cassettes recorded for their own amusement, the Psychedelic Furs had never taped anything remotely resembling a 'demo'; had never shopped their music to the record industry. Why should they? If a label really wanted them, it would come to them. Only once had they ever even ventured into a studio, a small set-up out Wimbledon way, to try to capture a fraction of their onstage fission – Roger Morris remembers stabs at 'Blacks', 'Radio' and 'Sex' – but they abandoned the attempt with the tapes barely rolling.

Thompson improvised. According to Tim Butler, 'Howard Thompson… has the best collection of live Furs' cassettes, even more than I've got. Every show he went to, he was allowed to bring his tape machine into, so he'd put his tape machine on the mixing deck.' And the night Winwood accompanied him to a Psychedelic Furs show, at the Music Machine, Thompson's tape was rolling as well. 'He actually has a tape of Muff Winwood talking about signing us. He says, "Howard, go talk to Tracey, their manager and get her to come by the office tomorrow, and we'll talk about…".'

Les Mills recalls things slightly differently:

'Howard played me the tape from the Nashville. I do not recall Muff Winwood saying "Talk to Tracey". He said "Let's see if we can sign them". In fact Muff called me at the Banshees' office the day after the Nashville show, Nils answered the phone and was shocked when Muff said "Can I talk to Les Mills"?' Talk about… what? Sign in haste, repent at leisure was a maxim written loud and proud by the experiences of a thousand different bands and the Psychedelic Furs, young and innocent though they ostensibly were, didn't intend falling for the first handsome stranger who offered them a ride. Any label that they signed to had to guarantee they'd retain complete artistic control – and, unlike so many of the other acts who make a play for similar privileges, they knew precisely what they meant by that. The Psychedelic Furs would not tell their label how to sell records. The label, in turn, would not tell them how to make them.

The Psychedelic Furs' role model for this uncompromising attitude, of course, was Siouxsie and the Banshees. Even without Les Mills' input, the Banshees' example was a guiding light for every unsigned band looking to make an impact on the post-Punk landscape. For over a year, the Banshees had bided their time, turning down some labels, alienating others, purposefully pushing their own backs to the wall. Not until the Punkwagon was crashing into the scrapheap did they finally ink a pact with Polydor, and then the battling could really begin.

Nothing, not even success, could disturb the group's vision of its own artistic sanctity. When the Banshees' debut single, 'Hong Kong Garden,' flew into the Top 20, Polydor begged the band to include it on their forthcoming debut album. The group refused, not through the elitist Punk instinct of contrary snottiness, but because the song didn't fit. And Polydor accepted their decision. This was the power that the Psychedelic Furs set their sights on securing. And Thompson agreed they should have it.

In early July, Thompson arranged for the Psychedelic Furs to record a demo at Basing Street Studios in West London with producer Ed Hollis, manager of Eddie & the Hot Rods. Thompson, Hollis and, indeed, Winwood went way back – before they joined CBS, both Winwood and Thompson had worked A&R at Island

Records, where the Hot Rods were Thompson's very first signing. They knew how Hollis worked; he knew what they wanted to hear.

The Psychedelic Furs were booked in for a twelve-hour session, only for Rod Johnston to come close to scuppering the whole arrangement by arriving four hours late. Working a lot faster than they'd ever intended doing, the band completed four songs: a taut 'Sister Europe'; a chaotic 'Cars' – now retitled 'We Love You'; and the brutal 'Pulse', an iconoclastic apocalypse which at least some observers still insist was a savage assault on the Beatles in general ('four useless gods') and John Lennon ('war is over if you want') in particular. Best of all, though, was a viciously sneering take on the already seething 'Flowers' – an ugly song with a pretty title, loosely referencing one of Andy Warhol's last series of silkscreen images, but remarkable not only for its stark variation on musical themes which only Public Image Ltd were then extrapolating, but also for an intro section which would eventually be built into a new song in its own right, 'India'.

It is amazing in a way that the band made such fast progress. Says Les Mills: 'Recording with Ed Hollis was problematic as he had a heroin problem at the time and had to take long trips to the bathroom to service his habit. Then when he returned to the control room he could barely function.'

The tape was rough, but presentable, and was immediately pressed into service to help secure more work. John Peel at the BBC was one of the first recipients, and one of the first people to respond to it, too. The Psychedelic Furs were booked to record a session on 25th July – and, displaying an alarming tendency for repeating himself, Johnston was late for that as well. Nevertheless, patience and Peel alike were rewarded with a magnificent session, four songs ('Imitation Of Christ', 'Fall' – a song created at Johnson's first ever rehearsal with the band – and reprises for 'Sister Europe' and 'We Love You') which not only merited three repeat broadcasts, but also illustrated just how far the Psychedelic Furs had progressed in a matter of mere months.

'I think we developed very quickly between doing those live shows and the Peel session,' Richard confirms. 'We'd written some more songs, and started getting more serious. When we first went out, it was almost like… not an image we were presenting, but an attitude. Songs almost came later.' Now they were flooding out and with such precision that little of the band's repertoire was to be significantly altered in the run up to their first album. They would dispense with a Banshee-esque guitar break during 'Fall'. they would leaven Richard's penchant for Rotten-like sneering. But only 'Imitation Of Christ' received a major makeover, not only losing swathes of its broadcast melody, but also most of its lyric as well.

With the Butlers, Kilburn and Morris gathered at the five-bedroom squat on Turnpike Lane that served as home to Les, Tracey and John, as well as the band's management office, for an informal listening party, the Peel session was broadcast on 30th July, alongside a set by the only marginally better known Police, and an on-air request from Peel himself for aspiring drummers to contact the band post-haste. The situation with Johnson had finally broken down immediately after the session was recorded. Re-entering the room after saying goodbye, he caught one of the group – either Morris or Kilburn, their bandmates insist – bidding farewell with an offensive hand gesture. 'He didn't come back again,' Richard shrugs, but he wouldn't have been needed if he had.

Responding to Peel's SOS, Vince Ely got in touch almost immediately. Five other callers had already fallen by the wayside; Ely gelled at the first rehearsal – all the more so when Ashton discovered that he, too, was a former member of the Unwanted, during the group's summer 1977 heyday.

Vince Elite was his name back then, a fitting band mate for Tony Topic and Paul Grotesque, although (like them) he hadn't remained onboard for too long. By the end of the year, Elite was drumming for the Photons and moonlighting in the Moors Murderers, a provocatively named, and controversially opinionated cre-ation launched, by former Roxy Club proprietor Andy Czechowski, for the sole purpose of winding up the tabloids. What else?

Though everyone knew the source of the band's name – killers Ian Brady and Myra Hindley, whose tortured, slaughtered child victims were crudely buried on a desolate moor during an early 1960s reign of terror – these latest Moors Murderers meant nothing to most people. The Photons themselves were utterly unheard of; Chrissie Hynde was a former employee of Malcolm MacLaren who'd once had a few articles published in the *New Musical Express*; Steve Strange was a Welsh post-Punk scenester who was friends with the Rich Kids' drummer.

Photographs from the time, early 1978, preserve this obscurity. The Murderers' faces are hidden within bin-liners. It swiftly transpired that faceless outrage was all they had to offer. Adopting the Photons' own name for the occasion, the Moors Murderers played just one major show, albeit one with plenty of tabloid potential, opening for the Slits at an NSPCC (National Society for the Prevention of Cruelty to Children) benefit concert. Aired that evening, the group's tailor-made-for-con-troversy anthem 'Free Myra Hindley' managed to push almost every panic button in the national press, but the Murderers themselves proved less than a storm in the already well-agitated teacup of Punk.

Denounced as demons by the mainstream, the group was then dismissed as a bunch of sensation-seekers by Punk's own hardcore, and that was the kiss of death. While Hynde and Strange set sail for more conventional careers, Ely returned to life as a full-time Photon. The band never recovered from its recent associations, however. By the time Ely placed his call to the Psychedelic Furs, the Photons had already shattered.

Ely made his debut with the Psychedelic Furs at the Nashville on 26th August 1979, facing a completely sold-out room. Dispatched by *Sounds* for a second opin-ion on the band, writer Steve May first described the queue that was still wriggling

its way in when the support band took the stage: 'The fleshy moat around the
Nashville is a graphic indication of the Psychedelic Furs' rapidly growing audience,
a multi-hued crowd come to bear witness to perhaps the most uniquely exciting
band to emerge during this year.'

He was right; they were. In early September, Howard Thompson added them to
the roster of CBS's Epic Records subsidiary, proud label mates of ABBA, Dorothy
Moore and the Vibrators. It was one of Tracey Collier's final acts as the band's manager; within weeks she had assigned her rights in the band to Less Mills in return for a
significant financial settlement. Mills then became sole proprietor of Amanita Artists.

The CBS deal was signed on August 31st 1979 and record company execs
attended the band's show at the Nag's Head in High Wycombe in mid-September
for a signing photograph. Representing CBS were Managing Director David
Betteridge and A&R men Howard Thompson and Muff Winwood. The marriage
was consummated with full-length interviews running in all three major music
papers, *Melody Maker*, *New Musical Express* and *Sounds*. All three found the group
bristling with prickly confidence and becoming belligerence.

There'd been a suggestion, somewhere in the *NME* conversation, that signing
a record deal, making a record, would somehow dilute all of the band's bold intentions. But Richard – or Rep Butler/Butler Rep as he was now alternately styling
himself – was swift to disagree.

'We're trying to do something that we haven't heard before, and it requires…
work. It doesn't freeze. We're never gonna play it the same two nights running.
This band will never be like that and CBS might hate the fact. But I don't care.'

Upstairs at The Nags Head, High Wycombe, two days after signing to CBS:
L-R, Les, John, Vince, CBS MD David Betteridge, Muff Winwood, Duncan, Howard Thompson,
Richard, Tim, Roger, Tracey

5

NEEDLES ON THE BEACH AT GOA

THE FIRST MAJOR TEST of the Psychedelic Furs' ascendancy in this new rock hierarchy arrived just one week after the Nashville show, when they shared the bill at the London Lyceum with the Only Ones and Toyah Wilcox.

It was an intriguing billing, and not only for musical reasons. Shortly before he departed Island Records in 1978, Howard Thompson had passed on the opportunity to sign the Only Ones, leaving them free to flit to CBS instead. Now both Thompson and Muff Winwood, Island's head of A&R at the same time, had followed them. Vocalist Peter Perrett was left to rue, 'I felt that Howard Thompson didn't like us.' In fact, Thompson didn't like to see a band that packed so much obvious potential apparently frittering itself away through drugs and irresponsible behaviour. The Lyceum show was the Only Ones' opportunity to show him just how wrong he was. And they blew it.

Wilcox, the future Mrs Robert Fripp, was a more or less unnecessary irritant for the majority of onlookers – they were there for the battle between what was, undisputedly, the most intellectually astute band on the entire London circuit, the group

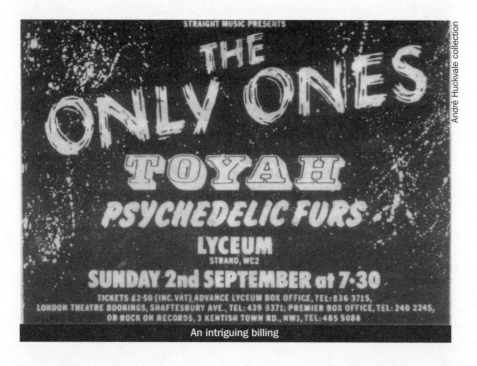

An intriguing billing

who gave us the masterful 'Another Girl, Another Planet', and the only convincing challengers they'd had since their reign began.

The challengers themselves sympathised with Perrett and co. Like them, the Only Ones had long laboured wearily beneath the burden of comparison with the Velvet Underground and, when *Zig Zag* raised that same spectre in relation to the Psychedelic Furs, John Ashton simply shrugged. 'That's cool, they've slagged off the Only Ones for years because of that.'

On the night and in the ring, however, the Psychedelic Furs were taking no prisoners. 'Our songwriter's better than yours,' they taunted when they met their rivals backstage, then they turned in a show which melted the stage, and sent the headliners home with their crown looking severely tarnished.

Scant weeks later, CBS released new singles by both bands, the Only Ones' fifth, the Psychedelic Furs' first. Barely promoted and cruelly under-sold, the Only Ones' 'Trouble In The World' disappeared without trace. Proud in its picture sleeve, and peacocked through the music press, 'We Love You' didn't bother the chart, but it made a lot of friends regardless. The changing of the guard was complete.

For all the fanfare that attended the Psychedelic Furs' arrival at CBS, there was a problem in trying to find the right producer for them.

Manager Les Mills had a producer in mind. He had been in attendance throughout the recording of The Banshees' *The Scream* and had got to know Steve Lillywhite quite well both as a producer and a friend.

'When I had become involved with the Furs I had convinced Steve to come down and see the band live', says Mills. 'Although he was reluctant to commit initially about production he gave me his blessing to use his name if it would help to secure a deal. In fact I had told Muff Winwood that we wanted Steve to produce us at my first meeting with him in July. When I originally approached Steve to work on the debut single he was busy in

We Love You single

Phonogram Studios, Marble Arch, London where he was working with Penetration. He said he would like to produce the album but as CBS were unwilling to wait to record, Steve suggested the names of a couple of engineers we might want to work with; Hugh Padgham was his first choice (he was unavailable) and the other was Ian Taylor, who was available, so we went with him. It is interesting to imagine what might have been had Hugh been available to record 'We Love You', 'Pulse' and 'Flowers' back then in the light of what he went on to achieve. It is also significant that it was Hugh that approached us to remix tracks on *World Outside* when he said that he had waited twelve years for an opportunity to work with The Psychedelic Furs. '

In the absence of the ideal producer, Howard Thompson had an idea – in the years before he moved into A&R, he'd worked in the disc-cutting/mastering suite at Trident Studios, exposed to a world of different production styles and learning sufficient tricks of the trade to more than hold his own in the recording booth. Since then, he'd co-produced a set of demos with Sham 69 (for Island Records) that featured what remains the definitive version of 'Borstal Breakout.' Now he suggested that he return to Basing Street Studios with the Psychedelic Furs to record a one-off single and use that as the lure for prospective producers. Steve Lillywhite's suggestion Ian Taylor was the engineer, and Les Mills insists that Taylor was the main force behind the sessions' production:

'I think Howard Thompson had his own agenda,' he says, 'as he wanted to break into production and, realising the band and Ian's inexperience, saw an opportunity to get himself a name check. His contribution to those sessions was negligible.'

First on the recording agenda were two versions of 'We Love You'. already ear-marked as the A-side: an unabridged take for commercial release, an expletive-deleted version to be sent out to radio: included in the song's constantly evolving litany of amours was a reference to reggae hitmakers Althea & Donna, and 'all that shit that goes uptown top ranking.' (Richard Butler would follow this line at early shows with the words, '...Stop wanking')

They also cut a furious 'Pulse', the single's eventual B-side, and had

André Huckvale collection

We Love You single

another stab at the seething 'Flowers', tighter than their last go, and reconciled to life without its original intro. And this was the band that the biggest names in the land all reckoned could not be recorded?

The choice of 'We Love You' as the band's maiden single was a contrary one – which, of course, was the whole point behind it. Richard Butler: 'We felt that three and a half minutes of withering sarcasm under the misleading title of "We Love You" was an ideal way to introduce the band.'[6] *That* and an enthused turbulence that spiralled through an almost dub-laden neo-gothic landscape of *noir*-esque perversity. A media that had wet its pants in anticipation of the Psychedelic Furs' first waxing greeted it with combination relief and gratitude.

Singer Tom Robinson, guest reviewer in the *NME* that week, called 'We Love You' one of 'the classic singles' of the year-so-far; Chris Bohn, in *Melody Maker*, opined, 'Richard Butler achieves more in three minutes than F Scott Fitzgerald could in 300 pages.' And so on. Reinforcing the term that was now on every observer's lips, the back of the record sleeve announced "the Psychedelic Furs are Beautiful Chaos."

Music press support for the record, however, was scarcely echoed by radio play. For all the strides that had been made in recent years – the slicing open first, of the BBC's broadcast monopoly; then of its once avowedly safety-first playlist – there was still a resistance to new bands, new music, new ideas. A market needed to prove itself before marketing would cater to it, which is why Gary Numan's 'Are Friends Electric?' sat unplayed for weeks before it got into the Top 30, but his follow-up 'Cars' went into rotation at once – and topped the chart as 'We Love You' was released.

There it did battle with the Police, Status Quo and Blondie, while the 2-Tone ska revival rode the retro metro out of the underground, and the Dooleys, Dollar and Dr Hook snagged all the places in between. Only John Peel aired 'We Love You' with any real enthusiasm, and he merely preached to the long-since converted. There *was* an audience out there for the Psychedelic Furs, and 'We Love You''s swift rise to #4 on the *Sounds* Alternative Chart – the all-encompassing predecessor of the later, specialist independent chart – proved it. But Wonderful Radio One was not about to help it climb any higher.

Neither were the group's first steps outside of the capital to prove especially blessed. The band members lived all over the city – Morris and Kilburn in Kingston, the Butlers in Muswell Hill, Ashton around Turnpike Lane, Ely in Chelsea. 'Starting a tour took half a day, as the bus had to cover most of London to collect everyone,' remembers Morris. Sometimes they wondered if it had been worth it. Night after night, the band arrived at venues to discover that the booking agency had never been bothered to confirm the show with the promoter – and some had not been arranged in the first place. The entire itinerary was submerged beneath a sea of cancellations, rescheduling and frantic cross-country dashes.

One gig, in late October 1979, placed them at the Manchester Factory on a night when it was closed; another, in November, had them appearing late night in Liverpool, then dashing down the length of the country to be in London the following evening. It's called 'paying your dues,' of course, and it's nothing that other bands have not had to endure since time immemorial. But if the Psychedelic Furs seemed a little less than psychedelic (and more fuzzy than furry) that night at the Electric Ballroom, that's why.

It didn't make much difference to the assembled throng that greeted them, though. 'At last,' enthused Jane Suck in the following week's *Sounds.* 'A band to write about.'

Work on the group's debut album would begin on December 5th, a task that was to keep them locked away until the very end of the year. As a farewell to action, then, and to reacquaint themselves with their roots before the studio turned their set to stone, they booked a pair of shows at the Nashville on the last two days of November.

They had, of course, far outgrown the pub and, indeed, that entire tier of clubs and bars. The opening night was still young when the frailty of the exercise hit home. Massively over-crowded within, bad-tempered latecomers clogging the North End Road outside, both shows were a total fiasco, marred by bad sound, scarred by zero security. The first night, flying glass from the audience struck Ely while he was playing; the second, the manager of the support band, the Soul Boys, laid his fists into Kilburn.

From now on, the band swore as they pulled away at the end, pubs were a place to go when you wanted a drink.

As much as Howard Thompson had struggled to find a producer willing to work with the group, the band members themselves had talked about any number of possible partners as they planned their first album. Having already proven themselves, Thompson, Taylor and Ed Hollis were all considered. But throughout, there was one name

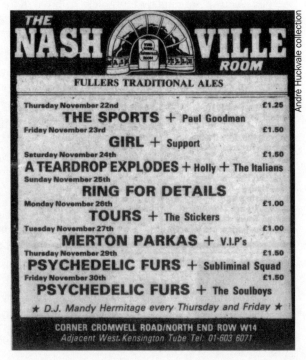

THE NASHVILLE ROOM

FULLERS TRADITIONAL ALES

Thursday November 22nd	**£1.25**
THE SPORTS + Paul Goodman	
Friday November 23rd	**£1.50**
GIRL + Support	
Saturday November 24th	**£1.50**
A TEARDROP EXPLODES + Holly + The Italians	
Sunday November 25th	
RING FOR DETAILS	
Monday November 26th	**£1.00**
TOURS + The Stickers	
Tuesday November 27th	**£1.00**
MERTON PARKAS + V.I.P's	
Thursday November 29th	**£1.50**
PSYCHEDELIC FURS + Subliminal Squad	
Friday November 30th	**£1.50**
PSYCHEDELIC FURS + The Soulboys	

★ *D.J. Mandy Hermitage every Thursday and Friday* ★

CORNER CROMWELL ROAD/NORTH END ROW W14
Adjacent West Kensington Tube Tel: 01-603 6071

that kept coming up: Steve Lillywhite.

One year Richard's senior, Lillywhite had long since graduated out of mentor Ed Hollis' shadow. His work with Ultravox, when they came in to Basing Street to cut their first demos, had prompted Island to sign both the band and the young producer, and Lillywhite co-produced (with Brian Eno) Ultravox's eponymous debut album.

Alongside Hollis, he scored his first chart hit with Eddie and the Hot Rods' *Life On The Line* and a cult smash with 'Terminal Stupid,' the first single by journalist Giovanni Dadomo's Snivelling Shits. He'd worked with Howard Thompson, on the Sham 69 demos; alone, he scored another success with the Leyton Buzzards' *Jellied Eels To Record Deals*. The Members, XTC, reggae band Steel Pulse and Johnny Thunders (the superlative *So Alone*) were all included in his resume. For the Psychedelic Furs, however, the clincher was Siouxsie & The Banshees' debut, *The Scream*.

The reviews for that album alone painted Lillywhite as a force to be reckoned with. After over a year of solid touring, the Banshees' basic repertoire was as familiar to fans as a pair of old shoes. It was Lillywhite who leavened an entire new landscape from those well-worn Wayfinders, prompting even seasoned observers to sit back and take stock of their stamina. Bare, spare, sparse and dark, *The Scream* hit the ears like a nor'easterly ice storm, with the spaces between the sounds as frigid as the pellets of music that punctuated them. It was discomforting, disassociating, dramatic. It was everything the Psychedelic Furs themselves dreamed of.

Les Mills, who knew the producer from those same sessions, made the introduction; Richard recalls their first meetings. Lillywhite had been keeping tabs on the band since catching them at the Windsor Castle during their Wednesday nights residency earlier in the year, and 'when we talked, he said he wanted to make a record that sounded like us playing a great live show, and that's what we went ahead and did.

'That's a great thing for a producer to do, especially when you're a young band in the studio. You don't quite know what producers do, how it all works and, if you get put into the wrong hands and get over-produced, you can come out sounding very slick. If you don't know how it all works, you could just think "this is how it always happens." Then, six months down the road, you realize that's not how it always happens. We were very lucky in a way, because we were very naive.'

It was Lillywhite who suggested they book the RAK Studios in St John's Wood, London, a converted Victorian schoolhouse opened by producer Mickie Most in 1976. He'd recorded the Banshees' *The Scream* at RAK's Studio 1, which was renowned for its drum sound – indeed the Furs were hoping to emulate the Banshee's drum sound from that album. Though the studio was an expensive proposition, it was also, Lillywhite assured the group, one that would pay for itself through the music.

In the event, the group spent 15,000 pounds in a little over two weeks, with Epic breathing down their necks the whole time, insisting the album be finished so they could get it into the stores. Lillywhite, too, wanted his charges somewhat under the gun: he came to the Psychedelic Furs straight from producing Peter Gabriel's third album, where he'd spent hours staring into space while Gabriel and keyboard player Larry Fast made noises at each other, trying to program the synthesizers. 'Sometimes,' Gabriel admitted later, 'Steve would get bored while we tried to get the right sound.' He didn't want to repeat that experience this time.

The crushing rush, Duncan Kilburn later condemned, certainly sloughed some of the intended edge off the record. 'We needed a producer like the ones at the BBC, who can put something out in eight hours,' he complained – BBC staff producer Trevor Dann and engineer Nick Gum handled the group's Peel session and *that*, he insisted, was 'the best thing we've recorded. It really had to be spontaneous and we were really concentrating hard, playing as well as we could, and it was mixed so quickly. Whereas Steve is very slow and spends a lot of time thinking and working things out.'[7]

It was, however, worth it – both sonically and as a learning experience. Richard explained, 'It was interesting working with Steve. Peter Gabriel hadn't been using any percussion [at his sessions], while Steve was famous for his drum sound at that time, he had a whole new drum sound that was very instantly recognizable. So, he decided he wanted to record all the drums on our album without using any cymbals or high hats.'

The band objected furiously when the idea was first mooted, but Lillywhite was adamant: 'If you really like them, then we'll put them in afterwards. But I just can't stand that riding on the high-hat business getting in the way of the drums.'

'So, that's what we did,' recalls Butler. 'Any high-hats we wanted, Vince got to ride them afterwards. Which was a good thing, because it was a good discipline. People are so used to hearing the whole kit; they're so used to the drummer keeping time on the high hat that it becomes part of the overall sound. And Lillywhite was, "I don't want that trashy chigga-chigga-chigga sound through everything." That was a great idea.'

Most of the songs were cut in one take; most of the vocals as well. Equally impressively, Butler refused to allow Lillywhite to add any effects to his voice, not even a hint of reverb. 'Because it was the first time,' Butler continues, 'I felt that the feeling is the important thing.' Only one track drew any special attention, 'Sister Europe'. After Butler's original vocal performance was rejected as too angry-sounding, Lillywhite told him to go down the pub. 'Have a couple of beers, and when you come back, I want you to sing like it's three in the morning, and you're talking on the telephone to someone.' Looking back, Butler acknowledges, 'it was a good way of putting it, and it was a good way of letting go of having to feel like you're angry with every song.'

Of course, the most important aspect of the entire affair was the opportunity, at last, to get at least a portion of their live set down on tape – even if it did arrive a little too late for a handful of existing audience favourites. When 'Useless' (swiftly retitled 'The Wedding Song') was written in the studio around a sax riff and a drum beat which appeared from who-knows-where, it immediately displaced something else – there was no time to record either 'Dumb Waiters' or 'Shoes'.

Elsewhere, 'Sister Europe' itself was displaced as the album's anticipated curtain-raiser by the newly composed 'India'; while the once-squealing 'Girl's Song' was tamed with a moodily moaning sax melody, duelling for supremacy with Richard's all-but spoken vocal (and Ashton's chanted 'girl song, girl song'). Even the live finale of the improvised 'Chaos' was compressed to barely a fraction of its traditional length, as a bridge in the medley of 'Blacks' and 'Radio', and Ashton still shudders as he recalls, 'I've forgotten (thankfully) how many takes it took to get that transition to sound like the Furs on a good night.'

Such disruptions were a necessary evil, though. The experiences of other bands, so many other bands, had long since proven that free-for-all free-fall seldom works within the confines of a gramophone record, no matter how exhilarating they may seem in a club and a crowd. The Psychedelic Furs were intent that they would not join that same sad rollcall. Their one unquestionable essay into experimentation, the twisted, spastic ambience of '****' (titled for a Warhol movie, but also casually referred to as 'Fuck'), a heartbeat pulse over which effects from elsewhere in the recording were spread and skewered, including parts of the intro to 'India' reversed, was reserved for a shortlived live intro tape and, later, as a UK B-side.

John Ashton: 'We obviously needed someone behind the boards who knew what they were doing. I think that the sound had [already] become refined between the first Peel session and when we went in to do the album. Elements of that wall of sound chaos thing were really quite small in retrospect. Songs like "India", "Pulse", "Blacks" and "Radio" were still an avalanche of sound, just a lot of energy really. But the tunes themselves, songs like "Sister Europe", would not have benefited from that kind of full-tilt approach. I always felt that the band had this incredible sort of power, but it also had this refined kind of almost laid-back feel at times.'

Tim Butler continues, 'Even though we were playing minimally back then, we were playing minimally in interesting ways, which made it sound more complicated than it was. Our songs were a wall of simple melodies, hummable melodies. Not that you can hum "India". I don't think I'll ever be at bus stop and hear someone whistling "India"!'

But you know what he means and it was the ability to isolate that knowledge and turn it into something more than a notion that Lillywhite brought to the sessions. And it was that, in turn, that encouraged the Psychedelic Furs' own confidence to flourish.

For each of the band members, Christmas 1979 was spent playing back a tape of the completed album, then reconvening to acknowledge that it didn't quite hit the spot. They could listen to 'Sister Europe', and know they had recreated the feel of the live experience. But they could pick holes in the versions of 'Fall' and 'Imitation Of Christ', and know that both needed to be completely remixed.

And there was more. Lillywhite's version of 'Flowers', all agreed, was certainly inferior to the one they'd taped with Taylor and Thompson during the sessions for their debut single; while 'Girl's Song' just didn't work at all. It would ultimately be dropped in favour of the 'We Love You'/'Pulse' 45 coupling, before elements were cannibalised for a completely new song, 'All Of This And Nothing'.

They could even admit, with an honesty that really wasn't shared by the fans who heard the same tape (bootleg cassettes were on the street market circuit some two months ahead of the actual album), that the medley of 'Blacks', 'Chaos' and 'Radio' wasn't all that it ought to be, either. 'They're a feeling more than anything else,' opines Ashton and the Lillywhite mix didn't quite nail it. On 7th January 1980, the Psychedelic Furs alone returned to the studio for three days to remix three tracks and reorganize the rest.

On the whole, however, it was impossible not to acknowledge that the band had done themselves, and their music, proud. John Ashton: 'The first album was about how it was great to be in a band, it was like: "This is what it's all about!" It was just such fun. That's all I ever wanted to do, play guitar in a band, and I spent a year or so being in London, just kind of being at loose ends, wondering what was going to happen. And then I met these guys and it just all started to avalanche, snowball.'

BLUE CARS, BIG BEAT

FOUR DAYS AFTER CHRISTMAS 1979, the Psychedelic Furs were scheduled to open for sub-Sixties warlords Hawkwind at the Electric Ballroom, Camden
Town. It would have been an uncompromising coupling – six or seven years previous, the Hawks had been in much the same position as the Psychedelic Furs, bub-
bling beneath the mainstream with a sound which was as densely packed as it was
oddly melodic, a heavyweight swamp out of which instruments hauled themselves,
heavy and oozing, to slash light through the bass-driven blackness around.

By the end of the 1970s, however, the Hawks' very existence strained the credi-
bility and it was the Psychedelic Furs who were grasping those same sonic accolades,
out-Hawking the Hawks with a set which bristled with musical confidence – not to
mention a light show which they had, in fact, rented from Hawkwind themselves.

The gig never happened. 'Somebody got sick,' Ashton sighs. 'I think it was
Duncan.' And when the venue rescheduled the Psychedelic Furs' appearance, this
time as headliners on 19th January 1980, Kilburn almost had to pull out of that one
as well. Visiting a night club over the New Year's holiday, he was attacked and left

André Huckvale collection

STRAIGHT MUSIC PRESENTS

HAWKWIND

PSYCHEDELIC FURS

ELECTRIC BALLROOM
184 CAMDEN HIGH ST. NW1 (NEAREST TUBE CAMDEN TOWN)
FRI/SAT 28th/29th DECEMBER at 7·30
TICKETS £3·00 (INC. VAT) ADVANCE ELECTRIC BALLROOM BOX OFFICE, TEL: 485 9006
LONDON THEATRE BOOKINGS, SHAFTESBURY AVE., TEL: 439 3371; PREMIER BOX OFFICE, TEL: 240 2245,
OR ROCK ON RECORDS, 3 KENTISH TOWN RD., NW1, TEL: 485 5088

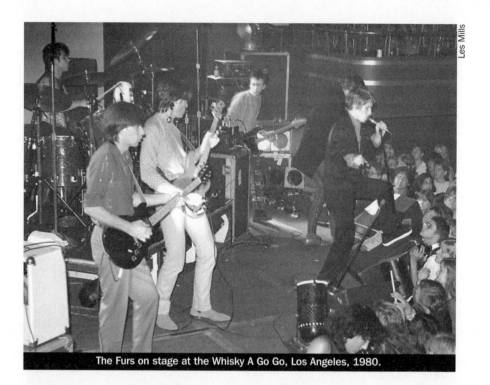

The Furs on stage at the Whisky A Go Go, Los Angeles, 1980.

Ricki Ostrov, Joanna 'Spock' Dean, and Les Mills at Columbia Records, LA, 1980.

with a broken jaw – not the sort of impediment that a saxophonist can readily over-look. Determined that the show must go on, though, Kilburn – who had already started draping some additional keyboards over the band's live sound – spent the next fortnight learning how to duplicate his sax parts on a newly procured synthe-sizer, and the gig went ahead as planned. It did sound bizarre, though.

Early February brought an equally unusual development, as the Psychedelic Furs transferred record labels, from Epic to the parent CBS. According to Tim Butler, 'it came to a point where the people at CBS were more into the band than at Epic. So, we went to the head of the company [Maurice Oberstein] and asked if we could transfer to CBS, and work with these guys who were more motivated. He said yes, so Howard [Thompson] then signed us to CBS.' (They remained with Epic in Japan, among others.)

The move was effected swiftly, but it was not without mishap. The Psychedelic Furs' next single, the epic 'Sister Europe' (backed by the out-take 'Fuck,' now politely retitled '****') was scheduled for release on February 14th, and the first copies had already come off the presses, bearing the expected Epic label. The issue was scrapped and destroyed long before any ever saw the shops, but around 25 copies did escape, to bedevil record collectors forever more. The record itself, meanwhile, was again received with mass media celebration – Single Of The Week in *Melody Maker*, it prompted *Sounds* to exclaim, 'there's more phasing in three minutes than I've heard in five years.'

Putting further weight behind the single's release, CBS freed up funds for the Psychedelic Furs to shoot their first video – still a novelty in rock musical terms, but one which was clearly going to impact very hard. Don Letts, the dub-loving DJ whose between-bands stints at the original Roxy did so much to forge the bonds which bound Punk and Reggae as outsider brethren, was directing; he had, after all, already shot one of the crucial celluloid documents of the Punk scene, 1977's *Punk Rock Movie*; in a medium which was still up for creative grabs, that qualified him as a virtual veteran in any onlooker's eyes.

Nor did he disappoint. With co-director Mick Calvert, Letts fashioned a shoot which was as intriguing as the band themselves, a Shepperton Studio lot draped in black, but punctuated by statues and the musicians bunched together, as claustro-phobic as the song, as dense as the rhythms. There is precious little visual footage of the early Psychedelic Furs in existence – the 'Sister Europe' video, seldom-seen though it is, stands as a dramatic indicator of their primeval passion. Which is incredible considering quite how drunk the band were when they made it.

'I turned up with John for the video shoot at around 11 am at Shepperton,' recalls Les Mills, 'to find half the band blind drunk. Don Letts had ordered in several bottles of vodka, as well as the usual beer the band would drink, so Richard and Tim were already out of control and Roger not far behind. Look closely at that perfor-mance and you can see the evidence.' Richard concedes they got drunk but maintains, 'It was actually a lot later than 11.00am – we were waiting around with nothing to do, so we just got drunk.' The post script was that I had the taxi driver who had taken them home turn up at my door that night demanding compensation as Richard and Tim had got into a drunken brawl and trashed his cab!'

Days later, on 2nd February 1980, the Psychedelic Furs were back on the road, this time opening for Iggy Pop. It was one of several tours they'd been offered in the run-up to the album's release – the Stranglers, the Ramones and CBS labelmates the Clash were all heading onto the road at that time, and all would have welcomed the added attraction of the year's hottest new band. The Psychedelic Furs, however, took one look at the elephantine schedules which each of those tours entailed, and turned all three of them down.

The Ig, on the other hand, was battering his way around the UK with just nine shows in 12 days; plus, he'd personally asked for the Psychedelic Furs to support him. As meaningful endorsements went, the man whose example had inspired the band's name took a lot of beating.

But, though the Psychedelic Furs accepted the need for such a showcase, that didn't necessarily mean they liked it. The group was anxious to make its own way round the country, with a massive headlining tour scheduled to begin the following month. Opening for Iggy might help introduce the group to a new audience, but that handful of extra bums on seats was scarcely compensation for the sacrifices that would have to be made in order to attract them. The sensation of being at the bottom of the food chain was distasteful in itself, but worse was the knowledge that, no matter how well they got on with the headlining artist, they were still 'the support act'.

At the Birmingham Odeon on 8th February, Iggy managed to miss his own soundcheck, so his band went on and did it alone. Then, just as the Psychedelic Furs were launching into their own, already-delayed check, in flounced the man of the moment and demanded the hall be cleared while he one-two'd. 'I hate supporting other bands,' Richard howled. 'It sucks.'

'Iggy was a real hero of the band,' insists Les Mills, 'but by the end of the tour they were pissed off with him. Iggy's crew would never mix the Furs' sound properly, so in the end I ended up mixing it. Vince would take the mickey out

André Huckvale collection

Promotional poster for the debut album

of Iggy's obsession with his physique by asking him, "Iggy, where's your bullworker?'"

The Iggy tour ended at the Hammersmith Palais, London, on St Valentine's Day, and with 'Sister Europe' sliding into the shops that same week, a return booking on the John Peel show offered the group a heaven-sent opportunity to plug the new single. They gleefully turned their backs on it, and chose to preview two new

songs instead. 'Susan's Strange' and 'Soap Commercial' were then capped with Kurt Weill and Bertolt Brecht's 'The Ballad Of Mac The Knife', the deliciously over-wrought saga of underworld hero-worship which the duo wrote in 1928 for their *Threepenny* adaptation of John Gay's *Beggar's Opera*, but which had been crying out for a rock reinvention ever since Bobby Darin painted it pop in the early '60s.

The Butlers had grown up with Weill recordings knocking around the house, and there was certainly a lingering ghost of Brecht's twisted lyricism in Richard's writing. Unlike some of the other people moving in on the German cabaret cata-logue at that time, it wasn't a matter of *if* he'd ever acknowledge the influence, so much as *when*. And, as the Psychedelic Furs discussed the upcoming Peel session, Richard and Duncan Kilburn determined to make it a performance to remember, working up an eight-minute-plus arrangement which not only offered each band member a chance to shine, it would also keep them on the air for as long as they wanted. In the end though, the elongated track was cut short.

'When we had listened back to the finished mix at the end of the session we had become uncomfortably aware that it had degenerated into a clichéd rock jam – which was anathema to the concept of the band – so we literally put a razor blade through the tape,' recalls Les Mills. 'I still clearly remember this sudden ending catching out John Peel when the session was originally broadcast.'

Enthused by the project nevertheless, the group earmarked the arrangement for further development and returned to RAK for their first ever attempt at self-pro-duction, working alongside Phil Thornally – assistant engineer on *The Scream* and

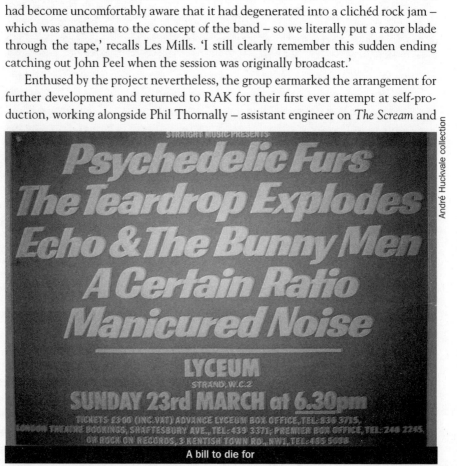

André Huckvale collection

A bill to die for

engineer on the Furs' debut album – to cut a new, four-minute version of the theatrical chest-beater, for use as a future B-side.

Then, with all of that out of the way, it was finally time for the album release.

The cover – briefly available in three day-glo shades – of *The Psychedelic Furs* gave away little that observers weren't expecting, its freckled two-tone mugshot frontage an indistinct clutter, its live shot backside (from the Nashville in November) nodding vaguely towards the reverse of the first Velvet Underground album. Inside, however, *The Psychedelic Furs* was laid out like a locomotive journey into the abyss, stygian concrete overlaid with a half-croaked sheen of majestic pop, a wall of noise and texture with, as Richard put it, 'everybody doing something different within the same number.'

Echoing the dynamic of the live show, the album built in intensity from the opening whisper. The deliberately buried intro to 'India' was a two-minute drift designed to make you turn your stereo up… up… up… to try and find out what's buried in the grooves. And then the band slammed in with zero remorse and all the ornaments fell off your mantelpiece.

Livid on its liquid bass, 'Sister Europe' and the revised 'Imitation Of Christ', its lyrics now firmly nailed to a title borrowed from medieval monk and theologian Thomas á Kempis, maintained the low-key pace. But 'Fall' – possibly the most distasteful expression of blissful love and romance ever written – upped the tempo to confirm the relentless drive that would wrap itself around the remainder of the record, and the harsh, churning ambience which the band summoned up from places the production didn't even touch.

'Pulse' and 'We Love You', revived from that earlier (but, since the band's shift between labels, damnably hard to find) single, led into the skirling 'Wedding Song', another of Richard's less-than-idealised visions of romance and, at a time when such comparisons could generally be received as a compliment, the song which most blatantly illustrated his debt to Johnny Rotten/Lydon. Public Image Ltd's mutant funk-dub *Metal Box* was still a recent development in chronological terms – the Psychedelic Furs' absorption of its lessons, condensed into one four-minute march, was as pioneering as the PiL disc itself.

By the time you arrived at 'Blacks'/'Radio' (and the concluding 'Flowers') then, you were accustomed to the carnage, just as the band were predicting. So, it was time to reach back into the bag and pull out something different, a taste of something you'd not heard before. There's a delicious moment about three minutes into the medley, which you have to play loud (with the bass even louder), where the drums start the heart attack, the sax and axe squeal and your stomach knows before your head that the planet has just shifted gear. It is quintessential Psychedelic Furs – it's what all the fuss had been about for the last year-and-a-bit. It was almost as good as the hoover.

'All we've ever wanted to do was create enjoyable music for people,' Richard Butler shrugged. 'If anyone tries to look too deeply into our music, they won't find any hidden meanings there at all.'

People tried, anyway. One reviewer sat down and painstakingly counted every time the word 'stupid' appeared in a song, as an illustration of Butler's presumed contempt for humanity. 'He came up with twenty-or-so "stupids" (and another dozen-odd "uselesses") and, even now when I'm making a record, I have to think about that. There's words that do get repeated over and over again.' Preparing the first *Love Spit Love* album for release in 1994, Butler reflected, 'this time it was the word "talk". I suddenly noticed it one day – "Jesus Christ, how many of these songs have the word 'talk' in them?" I went through and every single one did.' He ended up excising it from three of them. 'That seemed enough.'

In fact, he'd also slashed quite a few 'stupids' from the first album – 'Girl's Song,' the discarded live favourite which has never been heard since, was riddled with the things. But he dismissed any suggestion that the recurrence of the word had any significance – and, even if it did, so what? 'Rock music can't change what's going on,' he warned *Sounds*. At the very best, 'it can colour things' and it was that colouring that he wanted to pursue, as far as it could go.

'We're making our music and it's gradually gaining a lot of popularity. [But] I don't want hype or a lot of push, cause we're gonna gain popularity just by what we're doing. You get bands like the Clash who won't go on *Top Of The Pops*, [but] I want as many people as possible to hear this band, because we have something to say, and I think we have something very good to say. I don't mind going on *Top Of The Pops* and miming, as long as people who see us listen to what we say. I'd like to have something out on K-Tel.' In years to come, such a blatant hunger for the furthest reaches of fame and renown would come back to haunt him with a vengeance. For now, it was sufficient to know that those reaches were in reach.

Entering the chart within a fortnight of its 3rd March release date, *The Psychedelic Furs* barged ruthlessly into the Top 20, building sales as the band's latest tour got underway. Titled for the "Beautiful Chaos" appellation which remained the group's favoured self-description, it was a hectic outing, climaxing with a headlining show at the London Lyceum on March 23rd, supported by a veritable galaxy of talent: Echo and the Bunnymen, the Teardrop Explodes, A Certain Ratio and Manicured Noise were also on the bill, a post-Punk hydra-header which, today, seems implausibly magnificent. At the time, it was just another night out

Of course, the tour was not without its moments of fragility. Fuelled by alcohol and pills, the band spent much of its time running on nerves and adrenalin alone. Tim Butler recalls, only partially in jest, 'We'd do early soundchecks, then get drunk out of our minds. Then, [we'd take] some blues to wake us up, so we'd go on speeding our balls off, and who knows what happens? If you can remember those days, you weren't in the Psychedelic Furs!' Unfortunately, if you *were* in the Psychedelic Furs, you were also heading for the frontline of the latest war on drugs. And, on 14th March 1980, as they left the stage of Liverpool's Eric's, they stepped directly onto it.

The Liverpool constabulary had been glowering at the club almost since it opened. A late night hang-out for every misfit Punk in town, it only stood to reason in their bluebottle minds that it was also the hotbed for every manner of vice that the teenaged flesh was capable of devising. Liverpool had a graffiti problem: blame Eric's. It had a street crime problem: blame Eric's. And it had a drug problem: don't simply blame Eric's, bust it. 14th March 1980, was the date they set for the deed.

Roger Morris: 'Right after we finished our set, the local constabulary moved in and destroyed the place. They took the place apart, tearing light fittings off the walls, smashing the toilets – it looked like a bomb site by the time they'd finished. I remember they tried to arrest one guy, built like a brick shithouse – this guy put up so much resistance that the cops just gave up and picked on someone smaller. And then they had a good look at us...'

The group were seated in the dressing room when four guys barged in and announced they wanted to search everyone. 'We thought they were joking,' Richard recalls, 'so we carried on laughing. Then they said, "No, no, we're not joking, we're police officers," and they pulled out their badges.'

Unaware of the carnage being enacted outside, and knowing that, tonight at least, he had nothing to hide, Butler stood up and asked them to search him first, 'because I want to go to the bar and get a drink. Big mistake. They told me to empty my pockets, and I did. Then one of them said, "Okay, what's this then?"; put a matchbox in my hand, and said, "Let's have a look at this." He opened up, and it had some grass in it. I was actually planted with drugs by the police!'

Escorted out of the dressing room, while his bandmates watched in disbelief, Butler got his first glimpse of the remainder of Eric's. 'The bar was full of about 100 policemen. They'd turfed everybody out and were actually ripping the club to pieces. There were those round tables bolted to the floor, and they were pulling them up, pretending to look for drugs underneath. As if anyone would unbolt a table, hide some drugs under there, and bolt it back down!'

Handcuffed, Butler was thrown into the back of an already-crowded meat wagon, to spend the rest of the night in a cell.

The following day, Liverpool came to a near-standstill as a massive protest march wound its way through the city centre, demanding the re-opening of the club – to no avail. For Richard Butler, meanwhile, the last night of Eric's was to keep him occupied for much of the next six months. Released on bail the following morning, he found himself regularly summonsed back up to Liverpool as the wheels of justice commenced their slow, painful grind. Very slow, very painful. Time and again, he'd arrive to discover that the case had been adjourned once more before, finally, it was dropped altogether. 'The police didn't present their evidence,' Butler shrugged. 'I guess they felt sorry for me.' Or, maybe they'd already achieved their objective. Eric's had been padlocked, never to reopen.

It was in the midst of this entanglement, in early May 1980, that the Psychedelic Furs trouped out to meet producer Martin Hannett. 'He contacted CBS and said, "I want to work with these guys",' remembers Tim Butler, and the label celebrated because, of all the hip names on the scene at that time, Hannett really was an obvious choice for the band. Maybe even too obvious. Hannett's patented Spartan swirl was one of the essential components in the rise of Factory Records from ambitious local indy to the most fashionable label in Early '80s Land.

But he'd never stepped out beyond the local, northern scene – a shortlived, and mutually unsatisfactory dalliance with Island's recently acquired Irish hopefuls, U2 notwithstanding (he produced their label debut, '11 O'Clock Tick Tock'). Mention Hannett's name elsewhere, and the replies inevitably centred around one or other end of the Manchester Ship Canal.

OMD, Durutti Column, Magazine and, of course, Joy Division all filtered through Hannett's desk, to emerge infinitely more resonant and atmospheric for the experience; although, according to Richard, it was Hannett's handling of the acerbic poet John Cooper Clarke which most appealed to the Psychedelic Furs. 'We never cared for Joy Division.' Richard corrected journalists who suggested the two bands were a marriage made in some dark soulful heaven. 'We were just trying out producers, because Steve Lillywhite had said he never wanted to work with bands more than once.' At the back of their minds, the Psychedelic Furs themselves fancied a return to Ian Taylor, but as he had relocated to the United States, there was no guarantee that their schedules would gel.

Hannett, for his part, was completely enthralled by the band. 'I guess we had that dark sound that Martin liked,' Tim Butler continues. 'Although Joy Division were an even darker band – they made us sound like the Monkees. We did some good tracks with him, but when I think of Martin Hannett, I think of a cloud of pot smoke sitting behind the console!'

The Psychedelic Furs recorded four songs with the human smokestack: 'Susan's Strange', 'Soap Commercial', 'So Run Down' – a new song written about Richard Butler's experiences with the Liverpool law ('run round Lime Street...') – and an attempt at 'Dumb Waiters,' a song which had been in their live set for close to a year.

Not one of the four especially merited further attention, however, with the John Peel versions of the first two certainly edging the re-recordings in terms of atmosphere and passion. 'It's not that I want to slag him off,' Richard Butler mused, 'cos obviously he's right for a lot of the people he's produced. But it's always a "Martin Hannett sound." He's like John Wayne: no matter what the film was, John Wayne could only ever play himself and be John Wayne. It just wasn't our sound.'[8]

Indeed, only two of the four, 'Susan's Strange' and 'Soap Commercial', were ever considered for a British release, leaking out as B-sides over the next year or so. However, when CBS's American counterpart, Columbia, began preparing its own release for The Psychedelic Furs, those same two tracks looked very appealing indeed.

ALL DAY ON CHANNEL NINE

ALTHOUGH THEY HAD AN OPTION to do so, the US wing of Epic Records had decided not to release the Psychedelic Furs' debut album in America. Over the previous two or three years, the label had kept close tabs on the turbulence then passing as a UK music scene, and did indeed pick up a handful of the better-placed acts.

Reformed pub Punkers the Vibrators, the arty tangle of the Only Ones, Annie Lennox's Tourists and Stiff label mavericks Lene Lovich and Wreckless Eric were all recruited to the label, but only the Clash, the critics' own tip as the import-most-likely-to, had been able to break through the glass ceiling of prejudice and disdain with which the American media regarded that entire "New Wave" business. And even that hadn't been easy. Anyone who thought the Psychedelic Furs had even the remotest chance of breaking through where 'Another Girl, Another Planet', 'Blind Among The Flowers', 'Whole Wide World' and 'Clash City Rockers', had failed was clearly a few turkeys short of a Thanksgiving feast.

Nevertheless, when Bruce Dickinson arrived in New York as the latest recruit to sister label Columbia's product management department, the first thing he looked at

Les Mills

Richard with friend and Andy Warhol, backstage at The Ritz, 1983 was the schedule which listed forthcoming releases – and there, alongside the Psychedelic Furs' name, was one single damning word: PASSED. As in: REJECTED.

Dickinson was outraged. For the past nine months he'd been working in the mail room at Columbia's regional office in Boston, religiously tuning into WMBR, the college radio station attached to MIT (the Massachusetts Institute of Technology). With much of its programming adventurously geared towards Punk and the New Wave, the station had lost little time in throwing 'We Love You' onto the airwaves; had no hesitation in following through with 'Sister Europe'... By the time *The Psychedelic Furs* hit the import racks, Dickinson wasn't simply an acolyte. He was positively apostolic.

Dickinson: 'All the time I was working in the mail room, I remember sending the singles to Peter Philbin, who was the West Coast VP of A&R for Columbia, [with] letters saying why Columbia should sign the band.' Now, Dickinson was on the phone to Philbin, determined that Epic's loss should be Columbia's gain. 'I called him up, "Did you see this thing? Someone was going to put the Psychedelic Furs out on Epic, but they've passed on it – we've got to do that!" And Peter said, "Okay, let's do it." So, together with him and a couple more people on the West Coast, Ricki Ostrov and Joanna Dean (both assistants to various publicity and marketing people, Ostrov would relocate to London in 1981 to work for Les Mills) we put out the first Psychedelic Furs record.'

They would not, however, put it out in the form that it was originally issued. 'Blacks'/'Chaos'/'Radio' would be excised, to be replaced by two songs from 'the Martin Hannett session.

Partly, it was a marketing decision, based upon the historic belief that even Anglophile Americans needed to be courted with melody and song. For that reason alone, the medley was always on swampy ground when it came to Stateside sensibilities. But lyrically, too, there were issues to be addressed.

The Andy Warhol quotation which inspired 'Blacks' had always drawn a few disapproving grumbles from certain quarters, no matter how tongue-in-cheek both its source and delivery might have been. At the height of the Civil Rights movement in the 1960s, Warhol was asked what he thought about Black people. 'Oh, I love them,' he replied. 'If it wasn't for the Blacks in the south, my father's refrigerator factory would close down.' Having lifted the line *verbatim*, Richard assumed that the majority of his listeners were going to be smart enough to understand the joke, and so it transpired.

True, a handful of Portsmouth Polytechnic students got a little hot-and-bothered about it, convinced that they had unearthed a rat's nest of right-wing racism in the heart of these latest critical raves, and disrupting the Psychedelic Furs' campus gig with their placards and jeers. But they were apparently just as happy when they realized their mistake – even in the unforgiving climate of winter 1979, when the battle lines of racism were splitting open in every arena and the Anti-Nazi

League was rubbing a nation's face in the detritus, considered reaction was still winning out over hysterical knee-jerk responses.

In the US, however, irony not only had a nasty habit of mistranslating itself, it often snowballed completely out of proportion. Tim Butler: 'People were constantly asking, "What's this? Is this racist, or what?" And Richard would say, "No, Andy Warhol would say it as a way of poking fun at that whole thing".' But his defence rarely made the headlines that the original lyric was producing and, as Peter Philbin contemplated the forthcoming release, he knew the song was going to cause problems.

Besides that, excising the medley would open some space for a few more radio friendly, singable songs, as opposed to some dense cascading avalanche of melody. 'Susan's Strange' and 'Soap Commercial' were drafted in as Stateside substitutes, leavening a very different sonic vista across the disc; and paving the way, too, for a revision of that so-distinctive UK cover. Photographer Andrew Douglas had recently completed a session with the band, with one portrait in particular really standing out. Bruce Dickinson continues, 'We had this great photo, so we decided that, as it's now a different album, maybe we should do a different package.'

With the LP set for an autumn 1980 release, the Psychedelic Furs themselves headed for the US to play two nights at New York's Mudd Club, on 20th/21st June. 'We were flown over and put up for six days, which was great, as it was the first time we'd been to America,' Richard enthuses. 'It seemed like an incredible luxury to be flown over and put up in a hotel.'

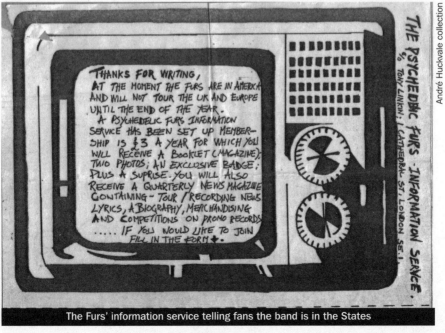

The Furs' information service telling fans the band is in the States

John Ashton in Texas, USA, 1981.

Roger Morris on the tour bus, USA, 1981.

It was scorching in the city when they arrived, the height of summer. But when they checked into the Gramercy Park Hotel, with the six band members, their manager and roadie crammed into two rooms, it was to discover that air conditioning was not on the menu. 'The janitor seem[ed] to be moving them around,' recalls Roger Morris. '200 rooms, 150 working air conditioners.' 'The temperature was over a 100° F,' says Les, 'and I had to call in a doctor as Duncan went down with strep throat. '

As much as they could, the band stayed away from the hotel, spending their free time in bars instead. But, if it was hot in their hotel rooms, the shows themselves would be hell.

Since opening in 1978, the Mudd Club had established itself as one of the New York underground's most exclusive niteries, its admission policy notoriously more dependent on celebrity and appearance than anything so mundane as actually wanting to see the band. It was not, of course, a million miles removed from the kind of door restrictions that London clubs like Billy's, Blitz and the Batcave were operating; there, too, a die-hard fan could be left on the street because his shirt was the wrong shape, but somehow the Mudd Club seemed even worse.

Richard Butler: 'They were terrible gigs. It was like Studio 51 – really snotty, with people wearing lurex tights and spaceboots. They were the only crowd being allowed in. If some poor bloke dressed up like us in jeans and a shirt, he'd get turned away. The promoter (who was paying all the Psychedelic Furs' expenses) lost so much money....'[9]

Outside, the crowd was beautiful. Inside, it turned ugly. The band arrived onstage to find a steel roll-up garage door-type contraption doing duty as a stage curtain – and also as a barricade. As they waited for the show to start, the band could hear bottles and glasses smashing against the metal. Roger Morris recalls, 'We look at each other the way people would in a plunging aircraft. Through the dry ice fog, lights and strobes, snapshot grainy faces of green, purple and red behind this iron curtain. The door begins to rise. We hear Vince count us in, "India" at 10 to the *nth* watt, and the sheer force of the music stops anything they throw at us from finding a target.'[10]

Welcome to America.

Still, though he confesses his memory may be addled due to an acid-trip celebration in honour of his impending birthday; Les Mills remembers some more positive aspects of the show:

'I do remember a huge sense of anticipation from the audience and people banging on the steel shutters shouting: "Furs, Furs, Furs". Lux Interior of The Cramps was at the very front going mental and the band being well received.'

Certainly the Mudd Club shows were lucrative. Club owner Steve Maas paid the band $10,000 plus all our expenses for the two nights.

'This was an unheard of sum for us at that time,' says Les Mills. 'A typical fee for

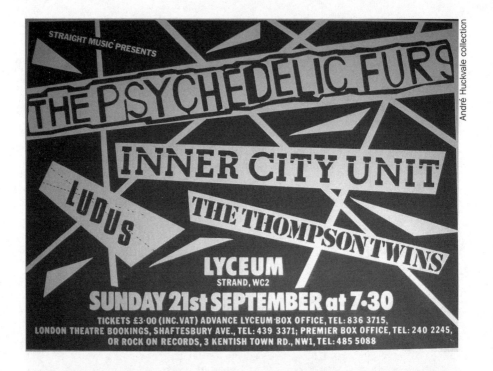

André Huckvale collection

Les Mills

Duncan Kilburn and Joanna 'Spock' Dean, Los Angeles, 1981.

a London Headline gig then would take £500.'

The Psychedelic Furs made their American TV debut that same week, appearing on a local cable music show, then returned home and moved straight into the pre-production phase of their next album, sessions which passed by with stunning, even unexpected ease, and emerged with joyful clarity. With Kilburn doubling on keyboards and sax, they completed well over a single LP's worth of new songs, great swathes of which were to be previewed at their next major performance, co-headlining the final night of the much-anticipated Futurama Festival, in Leeds on September 14th.

The group talked down the importance of the event – or, at least, their relevance to it. On the eve of the show, Richard told *Zig Zag* that the group was purposefully realigning its sound, shrugging off the doom and gloom mantel which the critics had wrapped around their sound. 'When we arrived… everyone was Punk and we tried to be different. Now everybody is playing depressing music and we want to change again. The whole country's in a very depressed state and it can't be very nice to be constantly reminded by depressing music.'[11]

Nevertheless, Futurama was tailor-made for the Psychedelic Furs, and for the wealth of other bands percolating within what the media was still terming 'New Musick'. Organized by local promoter and F Club owner John Keenan, it was the first national event to specifically acknowledge the widening schism in the Punk/New Wave consciousness, the fact that a vast aesthetic difference had developed within the musical culture, and a massive audience wanting to hear all it had to offer. Over the course of two days, 13th/14th September 1980, Leeds' Queens Hall would host 42 bands, harbingers of the new breed one and all.

Siouxsie & the Banshees, the Psychedelic Furs and the recently revitalized Gary Glitter were the headliners; behind them lined up Echo & The Bunnymen, Clock DVA, Athletico Spizz 80, Hazel O'Connor, the Soft Boys, the Young Marble Giants, Durutti Column, U2 and Classix Nouveaux… and that's only the names that most people remember. Wherefore, today, the Mirror Boys, VenaCava, the Acrobats of Desire, Eaten Alive By Insects, Boots For Dancing, Or Was He Pushed…?

The entire event was recorded and filmed (by Virgin), and it was certainly successful enough to merit repeat performances in each of the following two years. But, once the reviews had been written and the music papers read, Futurama's greatest benefits were apparently felt at the low end of the billing: Soft Cell's first-ever press mention resulted from their short, nervous set; Altered Images' first stride towards stardom was taken on that stage. For the headlining bands, Futurama was just another show, and the Furs, for their part, had their sights set on other adventures even as they ran through their set. They had a London Lyceum gig the following week, and then they were off to America again.

They'd already prepared a new single, heading into the studio to cut 'Mr Jones' with Ian Taylor, and it sounded great, driving and insistent, a switchblade riff over metronomic percussion, tougher and sharper than anything they'd cut with Martin Hannett. Released in October, within a deceptively Pink Floyd *Wish You Were Here*-style, overtly Magritte influenced picture sleeve, it was the band's hardest-hitting release yet, a frantic blur of energy which had no chance of breaking the band's radio duck, and probably didn't care. The band wasn't going to be around to watch it, whatever it did.

Back in New York, Columbia had done its level best to dissuade the group from coming back. Although one cut from the album, 'Sister Europe', had been placed on a double album showcase of the label's New Wave-and-related catalog, *Breaking The Rules* (alongside Elvis Costello, the Boomtown Rats, the Beat, the Hitmen and others), there was no perceptible market for the band, no apparent demand for them.

Sales of the just-released album were still being measured in handfuls, radio interest was less than zero. Even the cities which had offered some encouragement – Boston, of course, LA and San Francisco – could offer scant guarantee that anyone actually cared beyond a handful of DJs. Neither was there any way the label could put money behind a tour. Because the band was signed directly to the UK branch of CBS and were more or less on loan to the American wing, they recouped a far smaller royalty than a group which was signed to Columbia itself. To put it bluntly, they were an extremely low priority.

The Psychedelic Furs would not be put off, however. The first reviews were in and seemed unanimously enthusiastic: 'a post-hippy band who satirize hippie fatuousness,' mused Robert Christgau in the *Village Voice*. The Mudd Club crowd, too, had eventually been turned around. Thanking Columbia for their concern, the group shrugged the label's advice away. Tim Butler: 'They said, "Don't come over, there's no market for you yet." But we came over anyway, and paid for it mostly ourselves.'

Their reasoning was sound, if not exactly practical. British rock history has always taken a dim view of the United States, painting the country as little more than a graveyard which dangles untold riches in the face of Europe's superstars, drags them round the country on never-ending tours, usually on utterly inappropriate bills, then hurls them back across the ocean the moment their first headlining tour belly-flops. And there's a lot of truth to that view.

American history, on the other hand, paints a very different picture of things. There, the likes of Humble Pie, Savoy Brown, Ten Years After, Peter Frampton, Fleetwood Mac and Foghat had a commercial and cultural presence that their homeland never even dreamed of – and why? Because they'd worked their balls off, flying over for a two week tour, then stretching it out for months at a time, piling into a rented van and hitting every backwater hick town that had a stage and a power source, then coming back a few weeks later and hitting it again. American audiences have no time for foreign fame and continental success, couldn't give a damn about your three Top 10 singles and *Crackerjack* pencil. You're on their turf and they want to see what you can do. Those bands showed them.

It was still happening, as well. The first time the Police appeared on *The Old Grey Whistle Test* in 1978, around the time of their debut album, host Anne Nightingale introduced them by saying they were already bigger in the States than at home. What she didn't say was that, the first time they flew to America to tour, they took the budget Laker Skytrain across to New York, carrying their instruments as hand baggage. That was the approach the Psychedelic Furs intended taking. Get to New York, get into a van – and drive. With no help from their label, Columbia.

'One important reason we were able to break America was Ronald Reagan's deregulation of the airline industry,' says Les Mills. 'Suddenly it was possible to pick up incredibly cheap flights all across the country and then rent an econoline van wherever we landed. We had an English road manager at that time called Steve Wood. He had previously toured with 999 and had worked out that if you slipped the check-in clerk $50 you could usually sneak most of the backline equipment on as 'baggage'. It was amazing to see all of these huge flight cases winding their way along the baggage carousel amongst the legitimate suitcases. '

Mills had signed up the band with the FBI booking agency, owned by the Copeland brothers, who had established a network of small clubs all over the country.

'I had met with them and signed up to do the first tour with them when we came over for the Mudd Club shows in June,' he explains. 'I had also met with Columbia in New York at that time but the sum total of their contribution was to say "You should have waited until we told you to come." Fuck that, we'd still be waiting.'

Resigned to the band's stubborn intentions, Columbia at least hooked them up with a reputable booking agency, ITG – Ɪᴏme, at that time, to both Peter Gabriel and David Bowie. But, even the Psychedelic Furs' staunchest supporters couldn't quite believe what they were letting themselves in for. Renting a nine-seater minibus, the group hit the road in the dead of winter – with the majority of shows in the most wintry places of all. If they thought New York was extreme in the middle of August, wait till they got to Buffalo in the depths of December. Bruce Dickinson: 'They were out playing Boston, Rochester, Indianapolis, Columbus, Minneapolis, Chicago... and every city as cold as it could be.'

The tour was torture, a gruelling routine of tiny clubs, bars and student hangouts, some of which were so minute that the band had trouble even fitting onto the stage. The original plan, a month of dates opening and closing in New York City fell away, as the *New Musical Express* put it, through the booking agency's practise of 'adding "one more date" to the itinerary – a new spot on the map to be tried out, a return engagement somewhere else.'

'It's not even like going through a tunnel,' Ely sighed. 'Cos you can never see any light at the end of it. The end keeps getting further away, and you don't know what you're doing it all for. A treadmill. If they tell us that this is the way we've got

to do it to get anywhere in America, then I'll go along with it. But I don't have to say I'm enjoying it.' One night, somebody asked him how he was enjoying the United States. 'Well, you've heard of the Iranian hostages – we're the English ones.'[12]

'But of course it's fun,' Tim Butler reflects, 'because you're doing what you want to do, and you're lucky that you're able to do that. The first time in America, it was "Oh my God!"'

Discretion and modesty have drawn a veil over whatever shenanigans occurred as the tour progressed – Tim simply smiles and enthusiastically namechecks Ian Dury's first single, 'Sex and Drugs and Rock and Roll.' His bandmates, too, remain coyly silent over such matters, although Duncan Kilburn still smiles as he recollects one show, where the Furs found themselves being supported by A Flock Of Seagulls, 'real muso types' who were already outraged to find themselves opening for a group that clearly cared little for such niceties.

'Richard was into destroying mike stands during every show. It became such a problem that it actually showed up as a line item on our tour budget. At the end of the set, he would whirl around and smash the stand (hopefully without the mike) into the stage. I would keep my saxes at the back of the stage out of range but, one night I had to stand them under my mike, I think because the stage wasn't that deep. At the end of the set, Richard spun around and the stand hit both saxes across the necks, destroying them entirely. They actually opened up like a couple of tulips.'

Kilburn picked up a couple of replacements the following morning, but he still had the wrecked saxes handy. 'So that evening we were soundchecking and Flock of Seagulls were going through their warm up routines, like arpeggios and little triplets. Our road crew had fixed up the trashed alto and placed it in the stand. I pick up the horn and toss it to our roadie who of course misses it and it lands in pieces in front of Flock of Seagulls….' The look of horror and outrage that passed across the Seagulls' beaks remains one of Kilburn's most cherished memories. Elsewhere, too, whatever physical and psychological benefits the attentions and attractions of America might have offered, they certainly weren't doing the band any harm.

The Psychedelic Furs' first target was local – which quickly translated as 'college' – radio. A catch-all term for the (usually) short-range independent radio stations operated by, or within the catchment area of, the huge number of college campuses which dot the American landscape, 'college radio' has become something of a cliché over the last decade or so, its principles and practices hijacked by mainstream concerns as little more than a marketing slogan. As an alternative tag for, indeed, 'alternative,' 'College Rock' is today considered as viable a generic term as Punk, Industrial, Metal or Goth.

Throughout the 1980s, however, it operated almost wholly beneath the commercial radar, subsisting on a diet of predominantly imported left-field rock acts who would never be heard on more commercially oriented stations. Record companies were aware of it, naturally, and they targeted new signings accordingly; taking a ruthlessly parochial view of the decade, today one can credit college radio for the initial American breakthroughs of U2, Depeche Mode, the Cure, Nick Cave, Billy Bragg, the Chameleons, the Smiths, Robyn Hitchcock, Love and Rockets, Peter Murphy, the Sisters Of Mercy and so many more. One can credit the Psychedelic Furs, in turn, for opening the door to all of them.

It was, however, a tough nut to crack. Bruce Dickinson: 'Despite what people think now, there was real resistance to the Psychedelic Furs at college radio.' No less than their counterparts at the mainstream stations, many college radio program directors were steadfast in their musical tastes, with their own firm opinions on what was and wasn't good radio, or even a good band. Especially at the beginning of the tour, the Psychedelic Furs needed to play a town before local DJs would even look at their album. Only as word spread and playlists were swapped could the band hit a city to find their music already in rotation, and an audience with some idea of what to expect.

Dickinson continues, 'It really was the traditional way of doing things. You go out there and play and you find an audience. And they gradually won them over and the album started to sell, bit by bit every week, especially as they crossed the country.' By December 1980, *The Psychedelic Furs* had cracked the US LP chart, ultimately rising to #140, with US sales of 60,000 – an all-but-unprecedented quantity, at that time, for a band whose label had basically left them to sink or swim.

Not every show passed off incident-free. Finding themselves without a support band, one night deep in the American heartland, Roger Morris led Tim Butler, Duncan Kilburn, and three of the band's crew on stage, heavily disguised and bearing one another's instruments, under the spontaneously Pythonesque name, the Dead Gumbies.

'Our musical theme was about the bond that exists between man and beast. The bond that dare not speak its name,' Morris explains, a notion illustrated by the Dead Gumbies' repertoire of classic pop and soul songs, each with a pertinent lyric replaced by the word 'donkey.' The Supremes' 'Donkey Love,' Percy Sledge's 'When A Man Loves A Donkey'! 'You get the idea,' he continues. 'Unfortunately, so did the audience. Maybe we touched a nerve.'

A few disconsolate grumbles from the sides of the crowd quickly transmitted themselves throughout the room. Insults flew, threats, glasses... finally, faced with most antagonized audience they had ever seen, the Dead Gumbies curtailed their set and scurried back to the dressing room, fervently praying that when they emerged, unmasked, to perform their own set, the crowd wouldn't recognize them. They were lucky – it didn't.

Other shows, however, were absolute triumphs. David Bowie, then midway through his run in the Broadway production of *The Elephant Man*, dropped in on one New York performance; in the same city a month later, Led Zeppelin were guest-listed for another.

In Austin, Texas, during October, they took over the nightclub Rauls for two nights, fitting an in-store record signing appearance in between, and made a couple of local fans stars for the night, by letting them jump onstage to sing along with 'Flowers.'

Arriving on the East Coast, Boston, too, saw the band play a phenomenal set, followed the next morning by the Psychedelic Furs' American TV debut, as they traipsed down to the TV38 studios to pre-record a performance of 'Sister Europe.'

Disc jockey Oedipus, whose pioneering support of 'We Love You' had so influenced Bruce Dickinson a year before, accompanied the group to the studios. The band members had stayed over at his apartment after the show, sitting up all night while Oedipus and Richard Butler discussed the forthcoming broadcast.

'This was before MTV, before videos really took off,' Oedipus remembers, 'but we were talking about the handful that were out there, and Richard and I hatched the idea of turning the TV appearance into a video-style performance, the sort of camera angles they should use, that sort of thing. My vision was for them to keep a close-up on Richard because he looked so good; instead of shooting the whole band, they should just shoot Richard and only cut away to the band during the instrumental parts. By the time we left for the studio, very early in the morning, we'd worked out this entire "video", that I was going to direct.

'Of course, we arrived at the station, six unknown English musicians and a purple-haired Punk rocker, and all our planning went out of the window. They didn't want to know, they didn't pay any attention to anything I said. It was a one-take performance, they started with a wide shot and never got close to Richard. They'd cut away to the guitar when there was a sax break; I'd be screaming "go to Richard!" and they'd go to Tim. It was terrible, they didn't have a clue.'

Of course, none of that mattered when the clip was broadcast.

'One little acknowledged fact was the importance of HBO at that time,' says Les Mills. 'The fledgling cable channel did not have their own programming content at that time and they were in the habit of showing rock video's as fill-ins between programs. Bizarrely, they chose to show 'Sister Europe' in heavy rotation for a number of weeks.'

Also of huge importance was another TV broadcast, a few weeks earlier when Richard was dragged into NBC's *Live At Five* to face such scintillating questions as 'How long does it take you to get your hair that way?' and 'Are you Punk Rock?'

'The NBC *Live At Five* – a nationally networked news show – equivalent to the six o'clock news – appearance was interesting because we didn't realise at the time how wide an audience it had,' says Mills. 'John had been scheduled to do the interview but when it came time to leave for the studio he was nowhere to be found. So I went to Richard's room, where he was still sleeping. After waking him up it was by now nearly airtime and we rushed to the studio – only about five minutes from the Wellington hotel they were staying in around the corner – where, despite a severe case of bed-head, he eschewed any assistance in make-up and went straight on the air. Under-prepared is not the word for it he had literally fallen out of bed, put on a dishevelled old raincoat, refused any make-up and stumbled onto the air half-asleep to be interviewed by a bemused Sue Simmons – a well known TV journalist. We only became aware of the impact of the appearance the next day when people like the air hostess kept coming up to Richard and saying they recognised him from the show. This was a key event in building the band's US profile – their first US national exposure. "Naïve waifs airdropped into the goldfish bowl of the US media." '

For an unknown band from another country, any TV exposure was worth its weight in gold and, watching from New York City, Dickinson's colleagues at Columbia could only marvel at the Psychedelic Furs' tenacity. With next to no financial support beyond what they earned from actually playing, and no more merchandising than a somewhat tasteless array of psychedelic, furry badges, the band hadn't simply sustained a back-breaking cross-country schedule, they'd made a success of it.

'They weren't great every night,' remembers Dickinson, 'but when they were great, they were as good as anybody. And they went from being great one night out of every three, to two out of three, and they just got better and better.' Finally, as the tour entered its last few weeks, the label made its move. Tim: 'They begged us to go on tour with the Talking Heads.'

The band refused. 'We're like, "No, we've had enough, we want to see our girlfriends".'

Les Mills told the record company that the band were exhausted and just desperate to go home and would only do the Talking Heads support tour if they were treated extremely well. Now the band were finally selling some records, Columbia had the bit between its teeth. '"What do you want?" they asked the band,' Tim remembers. '"We'll pay for your tour bus, we'll get your girlfriends over, whatever it takes, we think you should do this tour." '

Desperate to keep the band out in the US, Columbia agreed to fly their girlfriends over, supplied a luxury coach and invited them out to a big dinner at the Russian Tea Room – an exclusive US restaurant equivalent to London's legendarily exclusive celebrity eaterie The Ivy.

'When I arrived with the band you could see the look of mortification on the face of the head waiter,' Mills recalls. 'We were immediately shown through to a private room where the executive throng were already assembled. This was just as well as most of the band were at the end of their tether. Duncan was particularly fractious and spoiling for a fight. Finally he took exception to something that was said and turned over his bowl of bright red borscht on the table, leaving a bright beetroot stain across the white lace tablecoth, had a brief rant and stormed out closely followed by the rest of the band. Astonishingly the bemused senior executives, far from being outraged, loved it and the whole evening became a part of label folklore. I thought the band would get dropped for the incident, instead they became a cause celebre and the label executives would dine out on the story for years to come. It gave a feeling that the band could do no wrong.'

In fact, the band only had to join the Talking Heads outing for two weeks as Kid Creole and The Coconuts were already in place for the rest of the tour, after which the band finally returned home; returning, too, to the sophomore album they'd left behind. Immediately, the experiences of the last couple of months came flooding out. Back at the BBC's Maida Vale studios to record another Peel session on 2nd February, 1981, the Psychedelic Furs lashed through three new songs, brittle assaults on 'All Of This And Nothing', 'On And Again' and the literally locomotive 'Into You Like A Train', a lyric Richard hatched on the tube one day, as he headed for a rehearsal. 'It just came to mind. I was looking for an "Into you like... something" and maybe the fact that I was on the [underground] made me think of "train".'

All three songs were clearly formative, newly written and barely demoed, and the Peel session howls its bare-boned birth pangs. But the make-up could be slapped on later. The heart and soul were already in place.

CONFIDENCE IS IN THE SEA

THE SEARCH FOR A SUITABLE producer was leading nowhere. Ian Taylor was again unavailable, Martin Hannett was unsuitable, there was an excuse or an exemption for every name the band came up with. So, the news that Steve Lillywhite, having insisted that he'd never make more than one album with a band, had now recorded follow-ups with both U2 and XTC was a good portend. Also, Lillywhite's management office was next door to that of Les Mills.

'We shared a connecting door that was often kept unlocked,' Mills explains. 'One day Steve walked in and said "if you haven't found anyone to do the album yet, I'd like to do it".'

Talk Talk Talk was our best album for me,' John Ashton enthuses. 'It definitely showed a band that had been playing together for a while, and had honed itself to the point where it had created a unique sound. Whereas the first album... some of the songs had existed in one shape or form for a while, the next album was all written with everybody in the same room at one time or another. For that, I think it's the best journal of a band in progress that I can think of.

'It was very English, all guys together, it was just a really fun, fun time. It was crazy, because we were kind of broke still, but it was more than we'd ever got before, so it was just this great way of being, getting a weekly wage, playing our shows, writing songs, meeting people, and having a great time doing what we wanted to. We became friends, did a lot of hanging out, and that's how *Talk Talk Talk* became the album that it is. Because we all got on really well, musically it just somehow locked all together. The first album was just the first album, you just do it. But the second one, for me, it was great, we felt very comfortable making that album.'

Ensconced within John Henry's rehearsal studio, dividing their time between playing and visiting the pub round the corner, the band had learned how to write songs. Tim Butler explains, '*Talk Talk Talk* is still aggressive and passionate, which the first one was as well, but the songs are more sculpted, more songlike, they're not jams. Things like 'India' and 'Blacks'/'Radio' you go into a studio and jam them. Whereas on *Talk Talk Talk*, we spent some time actually formulating the structures. Once we had the structures, then we said, "let's go for it," did two or three takes of each one, and that was it. So, it's got the aggression of the first album, but moving towards the melodic sort of songs that we peaked with on *Forever Now*.'

His brother agreed. A full year earlier, Richard told *Zig Zag*, 'I wanna do songs that are about something more definite, like when John Lennon brought out an album with songs like "God" and "Mother". They were really to the point, more positive.' On the first album, he reflected on a later occasion, 'It was more a case of just liking the words, liking the image they created, liking the way the words fitted the music,' then jotting them down in his notebook, without really worrying whether they meant anything.

For *Talk Talk Talk*, he focused more on substance than style, on meaning rather than motive. And if, occasionally, the listener yearns for a return to the open-ended imagery of *The Psychedelic Furs*, still the new record had some magnificent moments, lyrically and otherwise.

'We really dived headfirst into that album and got lost in it,' says Ashton. 'Musically, it just somehow locked all together.' *Talk Talk Talk* comprised a diverse set of songs, but they somehow shared a unifying sound, from 'She Is Mine' and 'Pretty In Pink', which effortlessly operated on a personal, poppy level, to a fresh re-recording of 'Mr Jones,' which was simply a full-tilt charge, to 'I Just Want To Sleep With You', a roughshod sexual lyric draped over a seething instrumental known as 'This Girl'. 'We were highly prolific, everybody had ideas, and it worked well. And Steve [Lillywhite] had become seasoned in the studio from working with a lot of bands over the last two or three years. So it was a really good mixture, he was up-and-coming, and so were we.'

Received wisdom today paints *Talk Talk Talk* as the Psychedelic Furs' masterpiece, the touchstone by which their entire future output should be judged. In fact, it really isn't: the first and third albums are, overall, far superior. But it's certainly

André Huckvale collection

an easy mistake to make. *Talk Talk Talk* does indeed pack an energy and excitement which none of their other albums can match, while simply placing the needle on the opening tracks, the relentless punch of 'Dumb Waiters', the insatiable beauty of 'Pretty In Pink', leaves you wondering whether any other album could start with such an immortal one-two.

The American magazine *Goldmine* once called 'Pretty In Pink' 'perhaps the best dark-pop song ever composed. A perfect guitar riff, sublime keyboards courtesy of Kilburn, and an unforgettable melody made this song a classic.' It was also the most archetypal song on the record, possibly of the Psychedelic Furs' entire career: edgy and rough, but sleek and sophisticated; hopelessly romantic with no romance in sight.

And it was also one of those magical flashes of inspiration which tend to arrive when they are least expected – in this instance, at the end of a long and fruitless day in the rehearsal studio. Richard Butler and John Ashton were simply messing around, talking half-heartedly about trying to capture the kind of effortless vibe that made the Velvets' 'Sweet Jane' such a jewel. What was it, a guitar line that simply rolled along, a vocal which simply tripped off the tongue, it sounded so easy… and suddenly, there it was. 'We were just hanging out,' recalls Ashton. 'I was playing the riff, Richard started singing, and there you have it.' The entire exercise was completed in 10 minutes.

The title, of course, refers to nudity; the lyric to the loveless self-abasement through which the protagonist, Caroline (revisited, perhaps, from the first album's 'India') searches for romance. But it has a lazy sensuality which words simply cannot replicate, and an tight melodic swagger which defies all attempts at categorisation. It does indeed share a mood with 'Sweet Jane', but other people have compared it to 'The Year Of The Cat' and, if you can dismiss the more mawkish connotations of that, they have a point. The same sexuality, the same inevitability and an opening line (and a titular chorus) which grabs the attention from the outset.

Ear-catching, too, is its enigmatic finale, as Butler wraps up the performance with a lengthy, wholly improvised spoken-word passage taken deep into the fade-out, a story-teller coda which convinces the listener that the song itself only told half the story. 'The whole idea was a kind of rant buried in the mix, so people would be going, "What, what, what?"' he explains. And, in answer to everyone who's ever asked him what he's actually saying… he doesn't have a clue. 'The thing is, I knew that one day I'd end up listening to it, and wondering the same thing!'

While 'Pretty In Pink' was being held up as the Psychedelic Furs' first classic song, 'Into You Like A Train', later in the song cycle, was reviled as one of their nastiest, a brutally sexual song which, following on from the so-casually off hand 'I Just Want To Sleep With You' brought a ton of anti-sexist rhetoric down on Butler's head – and continues to do so to this day. A decade and a half later, penning the liner notes to the Psychedelic Furs' BBC sessions collection, a pseudony-

Steve Lillywhite during the recording of *Talk Talk Talk*, 1981.

Bradley Stuart Berlin

Tim and Richard Butler in the studio, 1981.

Bradley Stuart Berlin

mous 'Mr Jones' still felt moved to apologise, 'Richard at this point was ranting a stream of consciousness… [but] just listen to the lyrics and it's obviously a put-on. Richard was and is a strict monogamist.' One wonders what one has to do with the other, but the point is made, regardless.

Such a defence, of course, buttered few parsnips for the forces that rallied against the song, especially when its sentiments were allied to the prickly aggression which permeated the entire album. Richard Butler: 'The time when *Talk Talk Talk* was made was immediately post-Punk' – a violent time in music, but an even more violent time in Britain. While the Psychedelic Furs worked in the studio, the first American nuclear missiles were being targeted for Greenham Common. In London, Brixton had exploded in flames, a presentiment of the rioting that would wrack the country all summer long. The IRA hunger strikes were nearing their tragic denouement, and unemployment was soaring towards a 3 million high.

'You tend to be affected by the aggression that was around,' Butler continued. 'The hostility you're feeling towards what's happening. All these things like being planted with drugs, they kind of make you hostile as well. It was very much us and them.' The chemistry of the album was further stirred, however, by the fact that the 'us' side of the equation was, itself, frequently splintering.

'I can remember making *Talk Talk Talk*, and it being all rowing, fighting and drinking,' Butler reflects. 'We all believed passionately that it should be a certain way, and we all argued passionately for that certain way. The result that you got on *Talk Talk Talk* was, six people arguing and fighting every inch of the way to find a common ground. It's what made the music so busy, such a wall of sound, and so much going on, because everybody wanted input on it, and they kind of got it.'

He's at pains to point out that 'we weren't a dissolute band, the music we were making was the most important thing.' But the alcohol certainly loosened tongues and, if the group did avoid dissolution, it probably wasn't from want of trying. Neither was their belligerence completely directed inwards – Butler's regular visits to CBS's Soho Square headquarters were an object of dread among his hosts, especially on those occasions when he'd arrive with a bottle of wine, then sit and get progressively drunker and increasingly ruder, in whichever office he'd slumped into first.

Of course, his mood only darkened as the first reviews of the album came in. Indeed, if the British music press of the era was renowned for its policy of 'build 'em up and knock 'em down,' the Psychedelic Furs were about to discover that the knocking can often prove even more effective than the building. Released in May 1981, *Talk Talk Talk* would emerge the band's worst selling UK release of the 1980s, stalling out at #30 on the chart and indubitably slowed by such pronouncements as delivered by the hitherto loyal *Sounds*. 'A hellish pastiche of everything that has been wrong with rock music throughout the last ten years,' growled reviewer Dave

Duncan Kilburn

Duncan Kilburn and Richard Butler, 1981.

Les Mills

The Furs in the back of a Texan pickup truck, USA, 1981.

McCullough, awarding the album a mere one star out of five, and he was not alone in his rage.

Nothing seemed acceptable, from the vaguely Warholian sleeve design, to the tumult of energy within. Searching for a reason for this overnight turnaround (the Psychedelic Furs were, by no means, the only recent press darlings to be suddenly skewered) has sent pop's psychologists scurrying down some alarmingly creative avenues of thought. But the one to which they most often return does seem to pack some substance.

On 18th May 1980, Joy Division's Ian Curtis hanged himself; less than two months later, on 14th July, the Ruts' Malcolm Owen OD-ed. Two very different people, two very different bands and two very different deaths. Throughout the British music press, however, vague recriminations echoed as critics pondered their own part in precipitating such tragedies; ruminations that may have dwelled on utterly unrelated themes, but that manifested themselves with remarkable consistency.

Where additional artistic commitment had once been encouraged, now bands were taken to task for taking themselves too seriously. Where further heights of personal expression were once demanded, now a backlash awaited anyone who dared strive above their station. In spring 1980, *The Psychedelic Furs* was the answer to a maiden's prayers and a band like U2, fresh on the record racks with their bullish debut single, were but a gaggle of uncouth rabble-rousers. A year later, the standings were completely reversed. U2 were the standard bearers of raw honesty and naked integrity, keeping it simple, keeping it thick; the Psychedelic Furs were art snobs and outcasts. If *Talk Talk Talk* had been called *Bellow Bluster Yell*, all might have been well in the world. Unfortunately, it wasn't.

The Psychedelic Furs remained unswayed and, for a time, their stance appeared justified. In April, the group scored its first hit single, when 'Dumb Waiters' drifted to #59; in June, 'Pretty In Pink' ascended to #43 and would, no doubt, have climbed even higher had Prince Charles and Lady Diana not chosen to wed at the end of July. The Psychedelic Furs were scheduled to appear on the following evening's *Top Of The Pops*, only for the BBC to revise the evening's schedule, to cram in another report on the happy couple. The show was cut short and so were the Psychedelic Furs.

They did, however, record another BBC Radio session, their third in little more than a year, airing 'She Is Mine', 'All Of This And Nothing', 'Dumb Waiters' and 'Pretty In Pink' for Richard Skinner's early weekday evening show. Their latest tour was sold out as usual and, when they hit London at the beginning of June, not even the charms of the opening Depeche Mode, then high on the chart with the fluffy 'New Life', could blunt the Psychedelic Furs' stoic roar. They simply turned everything up even louder than usual and drowned Depeche's memory with mayhem.

Besides, though *Talk Talk Talk*'s sordid fate was indeed a disappointment, still it was no disgrace. For all the critical plaudits which attended them, U2 were still awaiting their first ever album entry (the nine-month-old *Boy* finally charted in August 1981). The long-awaited and much-heralded debut by Pete Wylie's Wah! (the opening act at that ill-fated Eric's gig) stalled at #33; even the critically sanctified Joy Division's last album, the posthumous *Closer*, had barely made the Top 75. Plus, the Psychedelic Furs had a secret weapon which few of their peers could even dream of. America was gagging for their return.

Talk Talk Talk was released in the US in June, just weeks ahead of the band's arrival for their second full tour of the country. It entered the pop chart at the end of the month and slowly began to climb. By mid-summer, it was standing at #89, while the album absolutely dominated the "new music"-oriented CMJ chart, spending eight weeks at #1.

Still plying the club circuit, the Psychedelic Furs were nevertheless beginning to attract full houses wherever they ventured, with a number of shows additionally broadcast live on local radio – indeed, the opening night of the outing, at Boston's Metro on 30th June, was aired live by both WBCN and a couple of local college stations, WERS and WZBZ.

750 fans packed into Santa Cruz's Catalyst Club to catch them on 25th July 1981, and that was only one of the band's triumphs. Columbia, still reeling from the unexpected success of *The Psychedelic Furs*, remained uncertain of precisely what they should be doing with the band, but at least now when somebody made a suggestion, someone else at the label was willing to listen.

André Huckvale collection

Headlining above Depeche Mode

Bruce Dickinson: 'Talk Talk Talk really began to break through. We made major inroads into college radio, but we also got 19 or 20 commercial AOR [Adult Oriented Rock] stations as well, which was important because AOR at that point had been very resistant to new bands, especially new British bands. I had one very prominent programmer tell me that if any of his DJs played the Clash, it'd be their jobs. It took the Clash three albums, until London Calling, to start breaking the door down. So that was the big difference between the Furs' second album and the first. From the get-go, we got great college radio and, at the end of the day, the AOR stations started to come in.'

Such successes, however, were countered every step of the way by the band members' own, increasingly fractious, temperaments. Arguments were no longer an unconventional means to a creative end – circumstances put paid to that. Tim Butler: 'You always say you can write at soundchecks and stuff like that, but you get to a soundcheck and the soundman always says, "Why don't you play something you're going to play tonight?" Okay, and then you say, "Right, now let's get some new stuff sorted out," and the tour manager comes up and says, "Well, sorry, but you've got to do these interviews," so again, you can't do it.'

The bellicosity that they'd once been able to work off through the music, channelling disagreements and grievances into jams and songs, now had nothing to do but fester through the interminable hours spent driving or waiting, gathering strength with every fresh petty gripe and, then metastasising around the most insignificant incident – so insignificant that nobody even remembers what they were any more: misguided remarks, misplaced plectrums, misheard cues.

John Ashton: 'the band, at its best, was this powerhouse of fun and frivolity. We'd have drinking competitions, for God's sake, and stupid stuff like that.' Now, however, the competition became more important than the drinking – if the six couldn't out-do one another with their instruments, they'd do it with their gullets instead. Gradually, 'the drinking competitions became a way of life, and it was down to seeing who could do more than the next person. It made for a really bad mixture of too much drinking, too much partying, and not really concentrating on being professional.'

Alcohol clearly didn't agree with the Psychedelic Furs, but the band continued arguing with it regardless.

Other factors were causing internecine strife in the band too.

'In Los Angeles, Richard and Vince were having an affair with Bebe Buell... ' says Kilburn. 'And it was this affair that brought Todd Rungren, (Bebe's ex husband), into the picture. Richard obviously won the battle, although I think it was Vince that knew her first. It caused a lot of problems within the band though. Funnily enough, with John mainly who always came across as the more mild mannered amongst us. In protest he trashed his hotel room on Sunset, managed to get the wallpaper off the walls and remove the bathroom, everything. Billy Idol was in the hotel and even he was impressed, actually a bit shocked.'

On stage, 1981.

Duncan Kilburn and Richard Butler, 1981.

The band continued to drink and snarl their way across the United States, then flew straight to Europe to continue the quaffing and quibbling there.

Across Europe, the arguments and infighting continued. It wasn't even a matter of taking sides any longer – the Butlers were as likely to be at one another's throats as anyone else – while the appointment of a tour manager whom none of the band got on with only added to the tension. CBS let them down even further, failing to deliver on the tour support the band felt it deserved and, just when things seemed to have reached their nadir… they kept on getting worse.

A string of shows during October placed the Psychedelic Furs in direct local competition with U2, who were poised on the edge of their own European breakthrough, playing many of the same venues, to much the same kind of audience, but usually doing it just a day or two earlier. Ticket sales were suffering, airplay and critical response were muted and when the Psychedelic Furs were finally offered the chance of reasserting their supremacy… they blew it.

After too many weeks of playing second fiddle to U2 on the road, the Psychedelic Furs now found themselves expected to do it on the same stage, opening for the Irish band at the Fabrik nightclub in Hamburg, Germany, on 3rd November.

'Technically the two shows we did with U2 were 'co-headliners' and that was how it was billed on the posters,' Less Mills explains. 'However Duncan complained that their name was bigger than ours on the posters and I had to point out that this was because they only had two letters in their name!'

Worse was to come when they arrived at the venue, as the headliners stretched their own soundcheck out to infinity, leaving the Psychedelic Furs simply hanging. Finally, they'd had enough: 'We walked out and decided to go to the next gig,' says Ashton.

The group's morale was at an all-time low. The next show was in Berlin, where they turned in what all concerned remember as a disastrous, 50-minute performance on German TV's *Rockpalast*.

'It's true that the Rock Palast show with U2, didn't go well,' recalls Duncan Kilburn, 'and after the show Richard hit the bottle heavily, and it was JW Black.' Later an incident with an unpaid cab driver spiralled into a fist fight, claims Kilburn: 'Of course all hell broke loose. The cab driver was being treated in the lobby and somehow the Tour Manager smoothed it all over by paying a large amount of money, and we got out of Germany the next day.'

Richard does not remember this incident, indeed he swears it didn't happen. Les Mills doesn't recall all the details, but believes it indicative of the chaos of the time. On the ferry home, all the bitterness and rage that had been building up within the band finally exploded. Ashton: 'There were a lot of arguments, and they culminated with Duncan tipping his beer over Richard's head. And that was it for Richard. He couldn't handle it anymore.'

9

WAITING ALL NIGHT FOR SOMEONE LIKE YOU

HAVING RECORDED TWO ALBUMS with Steve Lillywhite, it was the Psychedelic Furs, not the producer, who believed it was now time to move on. 'We wanted a change,' says Richard. 'We'd already established that kind of a sound for the band. After we'd done those records, a lot of other bands were coming out that were starting to sound like that. So we figured 'let's go somewhere else, let's make an album with somebody that nobody would expect'.'

The Record Company's initial suggestion for producer was David Bowie and, it seemed, Bowie was equally enthralled by the possibility. He'd remained a staunch supporter of the band, attending a handful of shows on the *Talk Talk Talk* tour and he did express some interest in working with them when he dropped by to see them in New York. Unfortunately, Duncan Kilburn alone appears to have truly comprehended what a magnificent combination it might have made.

'I spent hours trying to persuade the band, but there was a definite hostility between Tim and Richard, and Bowie. I couldn't get to grips with it. David was gracious enough to come to see us in New York, and provided tickets to see the Elephant Man. And was charming and accessible. [But] Tim had fallen out with David at a backstage party in London. Very, very drunk, he walked up to Bowie and said, literally "problem with you is you can't fucking act" (Tim probably picked it up from some review), to which DB responded "well that's probably because I didn't take your advice", Tim, "I never gave you any" "Oh, that'll be it then". And Tim collapsed backwards onto the shag pile....

'Its hard to imagine what the third album would have sounded like if it were to have been produced by David Bowie. And as a progression from *Talk Talk Talk* after six months of hard touring songs like "President Gas" it would have been interesting to say the least. I think from an historical perspective its clear that the remaining members of the band saw themselves as rock or even pop stars and some of the great material that emanated from that lineup like "Love My Way" and "Heaven" are a great testament to that ideal. But they became a different band when that happened and the rest is in "what if" land.'

Tim' s brittle exchange with Bowie is considered apocryphal by some Furs insiders, not least Richard, who is keen to set the record straight about the issue. He insists that there was 'no hostility' between The Furs and Bowie: 'The reason we didn't use Bowie as producer was that the media were already making lots of comparisons between our music and his and we feared that this one influence was becoming too apparent. We felt we might be pushed in that one direction, when we wanted to steer off using all our influences, from Dylan to The Sex Pistols, and make something new.'

Bowie's non-recruitment was not simply a musical decision; there were practical considerations as well. The Psychedelic Furs wanted an album out by spring 1982; Bowie, on the other hand, would commence shooting his next movie, *The Hunger*, in March, with the weeks before that spent learning his lines, or whatever. Leaving him to his vampiric studies, the band moved on.

Their next choice was Todd Rundgren, a name pushed to the top of the list by Vince Ely, a long-standing fan, and readily grasped by Howard Thompson, who already knew Rundgren's manager, Eric Gardner. This time, Kilburn was the lead dissenting voice: 'Todd seemed a bizarre choice. Bearsville was cold and uninviting, and there were other undercurrents which were unhealthy and difficult to accommodate...'

For Richard, Rundgren was also not an obvious favourite. Vince remembers an earlier radio interview he did with the Furs singer. 'The DJ asked what kind of music we liked. Richard said, "I like Dylan ..." Before I could say anything, Richard interrupted me with the words, "Vince likes shit like Todd Rundgrun."' There was also, of course, the fact that Richard had been seeing Rundgren's ex-wife Bebe Buell.

Nonetheless, the decision was made. The group were still touring Europe when the invitation went out to Rundgren; a budget was agreed and the arrangements were finalized within days. By the time Steve Lillywhite caught the band in Germany, on the very last leg of the outing, and fell head-over-heels for a new song, 'President Gas', his offer to break all his rules and produce the Psychedelic Furs' third record was politely turned down. Rundgren it would be.

With the benefit of hindsight, the recruitment of Rundgren to the Psychedelic Furs' cause was a no-brainer, no matter how surprising it seemed at the time. Whether at their most densely experimental, at the height of Beautiful Chaos, or spiky and harsh through *Talk Talk Talk*, the underlying theme behind the group was of a wall of sound, the progressive layering of instrument upon instrument, noise upon noise (even the vacuum cleaner counts), with only the band's personal technical deficiencies standing in the way of a full-blown symphony – or a full-blown symphonic massacre.

Rundgren understood those deficiencies, and how to overcome them. Doing his homework with the band's first two albums, he saw his task less as a matter of piecing together the composite parts, so much as dissuading everyone from simply firing on all cylinders and calling the resultant mélange a take.

Furthermore, his own career was built around handling acts that other producers might have called difficult. Beginning with his days as the self-sufficient wonder-boy behind his own teenaged project, the Nazz, Rundgren had been producing records since 1967. It was no accident whatsoever that most of what are today

John Ashton at Bearsville, NY, during the recording of *Forever Now*, 1982.

Les Mills

Tim Butler at Bearsville, NY, 1982.

Richard Butler at Bearsville, NY, 1982.

Les Mills (2)

Richard and Tim Butler in Muswell Hill, London, 1981.

Bradley Stuart Berlin

John Ashton in Muswell Hill, London, 1981.

Bradley Stuart Berlin

ranked among his most satisfying productions are, in fact, those that could scarcely get arrested at the time.

The first album by Sparks, cut while they were still known as Halfnelson, but were already renowned as stubborn idealists; the scratchy street swagger of the New York Dolls' debut; the bombastic grandeur of Hall & Oates' *War Babies*; the other-worldly psych of Steve Hillage's *L*: these were the records on which Rundgren's reputation was built, because there are times when art does matter more than commerce. Even Meatloaf's *Bat Out Of Hell*, today ranked among the most successful albums of all time, needed more than a year to sink in to the psyche before it started out-selling hotcakes.

'I always hoped for success, but I've never really demanded it,' Rundgren once admitted. 'I always consider that the music people listen to is a matter of taste, and everything I've done has been for musical reasons and not necessarily for commercial reasons. I figure it'll either be a challenge or it'll be musically satisfying to do.'[13] The Psychedelic Furs, he believed, would fall into both categories.

'Rundgren liked us,' Ashton reflects. 'But, of course, he didn't know what he was letting himself in for.' Awaiting the band's scheduled arrival at the guest house he'd built alongside his converted barn studio in Bearsville, in upstate New York's Catskill mountains, Rundgren had already acquainted himself with the Psychedelic Furs' history and dynamic, and the fact that he'd be working with a tight, cohesive sextet. The arrival of only four musicians caught him completely off-guard.

Richard Butler was himself in the US, taking a break in Boston, when he decided it was time for the axe to drop. The European tour had concluded with a short swing through the UK in early November, ably supported by the rising A Flock Of Seagulls, and wrapping up with a sensational show at the Tottenham Court Road Dominion on 9th November. But, once he returned to the UK, the Psychedelic Furs would have just a month in which to demo up an album's worth of new material before they headed over to Bearsville and, frankly, he wondered how the hell they were going to do it. His own thoughts revolved constantly around the forthcoming sessions. But, in conversation with his bandmates, he was beginning to wonder whether everyone else was feeling the same way?

Ashton: 'Richard called me up and said, "I don't want to work with Duncan anymore, are you in or are you out?"' Ashton was in. Then Butler announced, 'I don't think Roger's pulling his weight either,' and Ashton agreed with that as well.

He'd been feeling increasingly constricted on stage lately, boxed in by the presence of a second guitar. 'So I said, "Yeah, I wouldn't mind having the room" – and I sunk his ship as well, which I regret to this day.' It was, he now mourns, 'the one time that two people, over the telephone, as opposed to a bar full of people, had a conversation that sealed the fate of the rest of the band.'

In 1983, Ashton elaborated, 'It was crossroads, really, at this point. "We work together or we don't work together, this is it. I'm not going on with this any longer." It was either working with Richard, or with Duncan and Roger. And I felt I would get more working with Richard. I felt I could at least come across with a raunchy minimalism, fill up the gaps where he wanted. And could also impart a little bit of my interpretation.'[14]

Communicating the coup to Tim Butler and Vince Ely, the executioners nevertheless discovered that they were in full agreement. Ashton continues, 'Everybody went along with it, thinking everything would be fine and, in a way, it was. In the real big picture, though, it stank. I feel awful about it, and it should never have happened. We thought we were together, but we weren't, because the "we" thing got thrown out by not thinking, not being honest, not looking into the future.

'It was not a decision we should've made on the spur of the moment, and it was not one that would have been allowed to happen, if we'd had some proper counselling on the whole matter. Les [Mills] or the record company should have stepped in.'

'It is not true that I did not 'step in',' Mills maintains. 'Richard and I had been having long discussions about the increasing difficulty of working with Duncan for several weeks and, whatever he may say now, Tim was also fully aware of the situation. Ultimately, I believe that if Duncan had not been fired the band would have self-destructed. When I relayed the decision to Muff Winwood at CBS he was fully supportive. After all, this was not the first time a band had changed personnel and gone on to greater things.

'Muff wouldn't have seen it as his role to intervene; Duncan was becoming confrontational for the sake of confrontation. By this point he was always on mine and Richard's case.'

Certainly, on paper, the group's decision appeared sound. Two less people meant two less arguments, which in turn meant two less battles to be fought before anything could be accomplished.

But it also meant two less opinions to be weighed on the things that did matter; two less bricks in the wall of self-determination that had hitherto been the Psychedelic Furs' first defence against the world. Six voices are louder than four and, no matter what personal difficulties might have come and gone, when it came to the welfare of the band, all six were of one mind. There is more to being a band than simply making music.

Les Mills, of course, was delegated to drop the bomb, calling Kilburn to inform him, 'the band's taking a different direction and it doesn't include sax …'! Yet he was telling Kilburn nothing that he himself had not already determined. Six months earlier, as the US tour hit the upstate New York town of Rochester, the saxophonist had himself determined that he no longer wanted to remain a member of the band – and had already told his bandmates as much.

For several months already, Kilburn had been tiring of the record company's attempts to single out one member of the band... inevitably Richard... as spokesman, a process that not only saw the singer alone scheduled for many of the group's most prestigious interviews, but even saw him spirited away from his band-mates to appear on radio and TV – Kilburn remembers 'We would be told of the outcome occasionally, and naturally felt we were becoming marginalised by the process. I believe this happens a lot. I think that it destroys most bands who don't have the enormous artistic input of someone like Richard.'

The media of course tend to favour a single spokesman for a group. 'They natu-rally gravitate to the lead singer,' maintains Richard. 'CBS were not alone in this.'

The final straw, that night in Rochester, came when the label chose to remove what Kilburn calls 'a great band, and great friends of ours, New Math, from a sup-port slot, in order to accommodate a stable mate.' Duncan was infuriated by the label and it brought to a head issues he had with Richard and Les. Duncan now felt that the music, art and any creativity at all were now out of the window.

'So I quit. Simple as that.

'I refused to play another show unless certain activities by the record company were reversed. CBS refused to budge, so I stayed over night in Rochester whilst the band traveled down by tour bus to gigs in the city. The following day we had vari-ous discussions with CBS in the UK and it was agreed that I would play out the tour, which included a U2 co-headliner, which I honoured. I flew down for the gig, and as we were soundchecking Richard sneered "… we can do it without you …" but I stuck it out until the last date, at The Dominion, Tottenham Court Road, London. It was a massive sell out, and an extraordinary gig, and after maybe six months on the road, I bowed out.'

So far as he was concerned, then, the 'sacking' simply allowed the remainder of the band to place a brave face upon what was in fact a walk-out, although it was some months more before he realised that the time that had elapsed between his announcement and his actual departure were, in fact, heaven-sent to the PR department, a grace period during which any number of new 'reasons' could be devised. Kilburn continues, 'they immediately begin to re-write the history of the band. One of the manager's gofers was engaged in writing various articles and his-tories of the band and it was all annoying bullshit. You'll notice that photographs of the band from that lineup have Roger and me cropped out! Its always amazed me that they would go to the trouble; and, of course, the number of shots they couldn't use because either Roger or I were standing in the middle….'

Richard is keen to contradict accusations of Stalinist revisionism: 'We'd already done the pictures with the old line-up. When the band was reduced in size, initially there was no budget for new photos, so we had to use the ones we had. As Duncan and Roger were no longer in the band, it didn't make sense to have them in the press shots, so yes we did crop the photos where we could. When we had the budget, we got more photos done.'

Still, even the so-called flashpoint aboard the ferry, that left Richard Butler dripping in beer, struck Kilburn as very small beer – indeed, until he read Butler's own recollections of the incident, he did not even remember it. 'It probably did happen,' he concurs. 'But it was just one of many drunken brawls that took place at the end of that tour. We were all getting a bit of a handful by that stage after months on the road. However I'd decided and agreed with CBS, our real paymasters, that I'd leave in an orderly fashion at the end of the tour. So whatever was said was rather irrelevant to me.'

If his own departure still leaves Kilburn feeling angry, however, he refers to the simultaneous removal ('shafting,' as he puts it) of Morris as nothing short of a 'great tragedy. I was very content with what we'd achieved up to that point with the first two records, but really couldn't reconcile myself to the fact that Roger had suffered as a result of my stand.'

In a way, Roger's exit was a matter of geography. By now, there were three factions in the band, based partly on where they lived.

When the band were recording in London, Tim lived with Richard and Tim and Richard and Les would walk home together and discuss how impossible Duncan had been all day – for weeks this situation continued… John lived in Fulham and would travel home with Vince; Duncan lived in Kingston and Roger lived in Tolworth so they'd head off for the train together – this meant the two were often lumped in together.

On stage at the Joyous Lake, Woodstock, NY, 1982.

Credit Les

Morris, for his part, still feels uncomfortable discussing the manner of his removal from the group: 'It was a long time ago and, however it was handled, I think is best kept to those involved.' But he, too, can reiterate Ashton's regret that, for the first time in the band's history, a major decision was not made face-to-face; for the first time, the unity that the Psychedelic Furs had hitherto placed above all other considerations was allowed to shatter on a simple whim. And he, too, is unable to account for precisely what happened.

Outside observers might remind themselves that the Psychedelic Furs, for all their musical and creative abilities, were spectacularly inept at actually communicating with one another; that "a problem shared" was not a proverb that had any place in their code of conduct. They might remember also that for all his protestations of democracy, the Psychedelic Furs was, and remains, Richard Butler's baby; that once he'd made his decision on a matter, it was highly unlikely he would ever recant, no matter how much his band mates protested. Both of these explanations might vaguely pass muster – indeed, in one of Kilburn's first post-split interviews, he reportedly admitted that he could no longer tolerate Richard's ranting.

And there are other considerations, regardless of whether or not they fit into the band's immediate calculations. Money, for example. As a band, the Psychedelic Furs had always regarded songwriting as a six-way split – as Robert Fripp once so wisely put it, 'if one person thinks of an idea, sooner or later, someone will play it. This is how a group works.' But, it is also how a group remains poor.

'We've always credited albums as being by the Psychedelic Furs,' Richard Butler told *Zig Zag*. 'But some people were putting more work in than others, songwriting-wise.' Not once during the sessions for *Talk Talk Talk*, he said, had Kilburn or Morris contributed a usable tune to the proceedings; almost every riff on the record sprang from either Ashton or Butler himself. In terms of the actual creative process, what was once a vibrant collusion suddenly seemed on the verge of total collapse. Still, Tim Butler insists to this day that both he and Roger Morris played a major role in the creation of the songs for that album.

Indeed, where does songwriting end? When the words have been written and the tune's been hummed out? Or when every instrumentalist has had his say, and every instrument has been laid down? Would 'Pretty In Pink' have been half as dramatic without the guitar tones that Morris drove in? Would 'Mr Jones' have sounded half as aggressive without Kilburn's sax to rally the melody? Were the Furs still Psychedelic with the basic rock instrumentation of guitar, bass and drums? Obviously they weren't, which is why every album they cut thereafter drafted sax and guitars in from other musicians (so much for the former instrument having 'no place' in their immediate vision!). But they never physically replaced the players; never committed to welcoming another musician into the heart of the band; never plugged the void that yawned where Morris and Kilburn had once stood. Indeed, in 2003 Richard Butler would take pains to insist that the writing was not just he and

John. 'Tim was involved in the writing,' he maintains, 'and all six people in the band were all putting in equal efforts."

Years later, the departure of Morris and Kilburn still haunted the group. 'I do sometimes wonder what it would've been like if they'd stayed with us,' Richard mused in 1997. 'It was stupid. It was just a stupid argument, basically, that got out of control.'

'It was a very, very bad decision all around,' Ashton agrees. 'And that, in a way, for me and for a lot of people, was really the beginning of the end. Even that far back, once the original band was split, it was a very different beast altogether.'

Today Ashton is keen to ensure that Roger and Duncan get their due respect. 'I spoke with Richard recently,' he says, 'and we both agreed that no one should dismiss Roger and Duncan's contribution to the Furs and the first two albums in any way whatsoever. Period. To do so would not only be unjust but also factually wrong. There is no denying the indellible mark they left. Those first couple of years I was lucky enough to spend in their company along with Richard, Tim and Vince were some of the best times I've ever had. I miss them very much.'

Tim Butler alone was not so fast to condemn the decision. 'Who knows, in retrospect, what would have happened? I think what *did* happen was pretty cool. I don't think it affected us that much. If we hadn't got rid of them, we wouldn't have had the space in our songs to have things like cello and other instruments. We'd have been stuck with two guitars and a sax player who couldn't really play, although he could come up with some nice lines. Who knows if we would've progressed as much as we did after they left?'

Les Mills is philosophical about the situation. 'It's not what they would have been if they'd carried on as a six piece,' he insists. 'There's no way they could have continued. They'd have split up tomorrow. '

Neither Kilburn nor Morris would remain full-time musicians following their departure, although both would form new bands in the aftermath. In Los Angeles on the Psychedelic Furs' last visit, Kilburn had been introduced to the then-unknown American singer-songwriter Toni Childs. Since that time, Childs had been relocated to London by her music publishers, Island Music, and was rehearsing a new band with ex-Masterswitch guitarist Stephen Wilkin and future Waterboy Martyn Swain. With Kilburn now free to come on-board, Nadia Kapiche (named for a pseudonym Childs had recorded under in LA) kicked off in early 1982, gigging around London with the Europeans, U2 and others.

He recalls, 'She's such a lovely lady with a great voice, a very talented musician and the consummate professional. We toured the suburbs for a year and it was great to be back in the venues we'd played in the early days of the Furs, and Island gave us some great rehearsal space at their offices. So I was in like the best of both worlds, club gigs with a big budget. Sadly no album resulted, and she had to return to LA, but she went on to make some great records.' By the end of the year, Kilburn had moved on.

Returning to his former career with Reuters, Kilburn drifted into session work, guesting on a couple of tracks on the *Same Mistakes* debut album by former Ultravox guitarist Steve Shears' new band, Faith Global. By the mid-1990s, however, Kilburn had left both professional music and, indeed, Britain far behind. 'I finally retired, and my wife and I now build restaurants. The main design feature is that they include a stage where I indulge myself with Velvet Underground covers and a version of 'Pretty in Pink,' taught to me by Jim Cruikshank of The Cruel Sea.'

Morris, meanwhile, relocated to California in February 1983, where he formed Castle Bravo with ex-Berlin keyboard player Richard Larsen and drummer Fred Drake. Named for the most powerful (15 megaton) thermonuclear device ever exploded by the United States, during tests in March 1954, Castle Bravo 'sputtered on for a couple of years,' before running out of money and folding. A talented artist, Morris moved on to Los Angeles' other major industry, working as a scenic painter on the set of *Twin Peaks*, before he and his wife opened their own art business.

For the Psychedelic Furs themselves, it didn't take long for the enormity of the split to sink in. Tim Butler: 'When it first happened, we thought, "Oh my God, we've got to do an album, there's only four of us left, what the hell are we going to do?" But, as we edged into *Forever Now*, we became more confident. We were forced to evolve into a much more melodic playing style, which was cool for me, because there was more room. John and I both had more room, which helped because it forced us to completely rethink our playing styles.'

Indeed, Ashton certainly seemed to benefit from the loss of those other instruments, opening his playing out as wide as it could spread, rather than forever pushing at the walls which a second guitarist and a showboating saxophone built around his instincts. That much was apparent from the very first set of demos which the band recorded as a quartet in December 1981.

Five songs were completed in those earliest sessions: the already formulated 'President Gas', plus 'Forever Now', 'Merry Go Round', 'Angels' (a working title for 'Only You And I') and 'Fire Engine'. Ashton and Richard Butler cut two more, 'Alice's House' and 'Silent Spring' alone, working with a drum machine at Ashton's flat one day. Yet another number, 'Sleep Comes Down', was slowly gestating around a bass riff Tim Butler came up with during soundchecks on the last tour.

New material was flooding out, then. But it wasn't only the songs that excited the band. It was the size of the canvas they had to work on. Richard Butler: 'The problem with having a sax in the band is that you have to have a sax on every song, whether you want to or not. Otherwise the sax player is just standing around, "Well, what do I do?"'

Now, they could recruit the musicians that the songs demanded, rather than the other way around, and even the demos revelled in this new-found freedom.

Les Mills

Richard Butler at Bearsville, NY, during the recording of *Forever Now*, 1982.

Les Mills

Ed Buller with Fairlight music computer, Melbourne, Australia, 1983.

Where once the horn would have loudly honked, they recruited a cellist from the Royal College of Music to send a cascade of classicism through 'President Gas' – Richard had been listening to Stravinsky's 'Rite of Spring' and wanted to recreate 'that same sort of chugging cello.'

The group also determined to insert fully-fledged keyboards, where once Kilburn might have added a minimal flourish to fill in round his riffs. Ed Buller was working at the little music shop that stood beneath the CBS offices in London's Soho Square when John Ashton first met him; the pair hit it off and, within days, Buller was sitting in on the demo sessions. He would remain the Psychedelic Furs' preferred keyboard player for much of the next six years although, when the group finally flew to Bearsville to meet up with Todd Rundgren, it was the Butlers, Ashton and Ely alone.

Expecting six and meeting four, Rundgren made no attempt to disguise his shock, but he was not to be wrong-footed for long. Playing through the Psychedelic Furs' pre-production tape, the gathering of songs they'd already accumulated, Rundgren dropped his own bombshell by announcing, 'I'm not hearing a whole album's worth of songs yet.'

Did he expect to? So far as the Psychedelic Furs were concerned, albums came together in the studio, built upon the ideas they'd formulated as demos, with the producer there to ensure that everything came together at the end. The idea of actually working everything out beforehand was anathema to the quartet. Where was the spontaneity? Where was the art? Where was the Beautiful Chaos? Besides, they'd brought more songs to these sessions than they ever had before. 'That's not how we work,' they ventured to reply.

'Well, that's how *I* work,' Rundgren curtly responded. End of discussion.

'Todd really didn't *like* a couple of the songs,' Ashton recalled. 'He said, "Aw, it's *Punk rock*, y'know?"' The group returned to London to heed their new master's voice, writing and demoing as much as they could, until Rundgren was finally convinced they had an album to record.

The painstakingly pieced-together demos were dissected and, sometimes, discarded. 'Silent Spring', a song which Ashton once described as 'very much the essence of what the Furs are about,' was abandoned. 'Fire Engine' was thrown away, passed on to a band called the Dangerous Bananas, to see what they could make of it. 'Newsbeat' was reworked; the ballad 'Hollywood' wound up fragmented, spread between two new songs, 'Only You And I' and 'Merry-Go-Round'; 'Merry-Go-Round' itself would ultimately be recorded twice, first as a mildly psychedelic piece whose swirling accompaniment absolutely matched its title, then as a more straightforward number, which the band retitled 'Yes I Do'. Somewhat confusingly, both versions would see the light of day, on the UK and US pressings of the album respectively.

The group had hoped to complete the record for a spring release. In fact, they didn't even return to Bearsville until Easter 1982. 'Forever Now was a strange time,' Ashton recalls. 'It was the first time we'd recorded out of England, there was a different producer, we were a different band. Plus, we were meeting all the crazy people in Woodstock, and just getting into a different mindset altogether.' By the end of the sessions, that mindset would have precipitated yet another shock amputation.

Arguments remained part and parcel of the Psychedelic Furs' chemistry – battles between the Butlers in particular scarred much of the experience, with several onlookers, unaccustomed to the group's methods of working (and the brothers' own relationship), convinced that it was Tim who'd be departing the band any day. In fact, it was Vince Ely who was approaching the end of his tether.

While Ashton and the Butlers spent their spare time together, exploring the town and hitting the bars (Rundgren had already banned them from taking off for anywhere further afield), Ely, in Ashton's words, 'kept himself to himself. Vince really wasn't a big part of our family at that point.'

In fact, the drummer was growing increasingly unhappy within the band. Never a heavy drinker, he was first alarmed, then discouraged by the amount of time his bandmates spent on the booze – and horrified by the consequences that their outbreaks of inebriated rashness laid them open to. One evening, the night before they were scheduled to record 'President Gas', Ashton and the Butlers took themselves out on the town, just as the heavens began dumping three foot of snow onto it. 'I woke up the next day without the faintest idea of how I got home,' Ashton shuddered. 'Apparently, I tried to drive us all back.' Fortunately for all concerned, one of Rundgren's friends spotted what was going on, and escorted the trio to the studio himself. 'Had he not,' Ashton acknowledged, 'I'm sure we'd all have been history.'

Rundgren heard about the incident and summoned Vince, threatening to send the band home. This was like a body blow to Vince. Vince guaranteed they'd behave and work hard, he'd dreamed of working with Todd – this was his dream come through and he didn't want to blow it…

The arrival in Bearsville of Howard Thompson, newly transferred to Columbia's New York office, restored some sense of normalcy to the proceedings, while Rundgren's own circle of friends also moved in around the band. Mark Volman and Howard Kayman, former members of the Turtles but now the legendary Flo and Eddie, were drafted in as backing vocalists and installed in the same house that the Psychedelic Furs were staying in.

They made an immediate impression. One evening, very early on in their stay, the pair returned to the house with an entourage of young, willing ladies. Volman still smiles at the memory of the band's response, particularly Richard Butler's. He made his excuses and left to go fishing. At 5 o'clock in the morning.

It was Rundgren's idea to recruit additional backing vocalists to the project, and one that he apparently kept to himself.

'Flo and Eddie,' Richard reflects. 'Todd mentioned them but I was really against using them. Todd said, "We'll bring them in and try 'em and if you don't like 'em we won't use them." So my hands were tied – under those conditions I couldn't really refuse. So, we used them and I liked what they did so we kept it.'

Kayman recalls the initial hostile reception, 'We got up there and those guys, the Furs, didn't want a note from us at all. Not at all. They took Todd aside and said, "What is this, why would you bring guys in to sing on our record? We're a self-contained group." And Todd said, "Yeah, but you can barely sing your own vocals, let alone background vocals."

'He had all these grand ideas about what could make this a distinctive record, but when we first went into the studio, it was really an uphill fight. They didn't want us around at all, they did everything they could to discourage us. They were rude... in that very English way, which is not to say "screw you guys," but you got the picture. They fought it, they really resisted it for the first day.

'But that evening, we hung out with them at the house. We sat around and sang classic R&B songs together, and they got to know us a little bit. We stayed up most of the night and, by sun up, we had them convinced that not only were we "the guys," but we *knew* the guys that knew the guys. We sat around and told stories, they wanted to know what it was like working with Lennon and Bolan and Zappa, and, when it was time to go back into the studio and record, there was a whole different atmosphere, it was way better. They were into us as singers and they were into us as an historical thing: "These guys have done this and this and this, and now they're going to do it with us".' The result, says Kayman, remains one of his all-time favourite albums.

Recreating the same magical harmony blend that they'd layered onto so many classic albums of the past, from the early 1970s best of Frank Zappa to T Rex's *Electric Warrior* and 'Hot Love,' Flo and Eddie completely altered the timbre of the sessions. Songs that once seemed dry suddenly exploded into life, passages that might have sounded hollow were suddenly bursting with life. Volman remembers, 'we ended up singing on about six or seven of the tracks. There was a lot of background singing.'

Neither were the backing vocals – and the backing vocal*ists* – the end of Rundgren's innovations. The sessions cried out for a saxophone – Rundgren introduced Gary 'call me "Sax Giant"' Windo, a renowned jazz musician whose past flirtations with rock had seen him work alongside Robert Wyatt, Ian Hunter and Pink Floyd's Nick Mason. Over the next few months, both in the studio and later on the road, Windo established himself among the group's most loyal companions – in fact, it was he who'd come to their rescue, that drunken night in a Catskill blizzard. 'Gary was a long-standing friend of the long-suffering Rundgren,' laughs Ashton, 'who would always bounce in to annoy him, so Todd palmed him off to us. And I still thank him for that.'

Although they were certainly more refined than the mad sounds that his prede-

Les Mills

On stage at the Joyous Lake, Woodstock, NY, 1982.

Les Mills (2)

Ann Sheldon, USA, 1982.

Gary Windo, Woodstock, NY, 1982.

cessor unleashed, Windo's contributions to *Forever Now* completely overcame any deficiencies that might have been laid bare by Kilburn's departure. Elsewhere, however, completely fresh dimensions were layered into the brew. A second horn player, Donn Adams, was recruited from NRBQ, one of American roots rock's most distinguished combos; upon Windo's recommendation, the classically-trained Ann Sheldon was brought in to recreate the cello that haunted the 'President Gas' demo, and then layer more into 'Yes I Do' and 'Only You And I'.

Plans to bring Ed Buller over to play on the album, however, were dismissed when Rundgren himself began layering in keyboards (he also tossed a sax solo into 'No Easy Street').

'I think Ed was very badly treated by the band by not being allowed to play his parts on *Forever Now*,' says Les Mills, who went on to manage Buller and felt the keyboardist should have been offered a permanent position in the band. 'Much as I respect Todd it would have been a better album if Ed had been on it.'

Still, as the record took shape, so it became increasingly clear that not only was it about to escape the Psychedelic Furs' traditional gravitational field, it was heading towards new heights altogether.

Mark Volman explains, 'I think the big difference on that record is Todd and the style he uses in terms of production. There wasn't a lot of huge, demonstrative equipment. Bearsville was kind of an unsophisticated recording studio, it's a nice one but it's not up to the records you'd have made had you been in New York City or Los Angeles. It really was an upscale home recording studio, inasmuch as you were pretty much making the album in a barn. The production booth was on the second floor and you could only see the band through video. But all that played a major part in the way the record sounded.'

'Todd works like no-one else I've ever seen in the studio,' Kayman continues. 'We've worked with everyone from Roy Baker to Tony Visconti and their styles are radically different. But I've never seen anybody work like Todd. If you're doing the background vocals and he hears in the back of his mind a little bit of echo and a bit of delay and a bit of filter, he'll slap all that on it while it's being recorded.

'He records everything he's going to do, he lifts the fader up to the halfway line on the board, locks in everything – sound, balance, EQ – and then records it, so when it comes time for the mixing part of the session, all Todd does is slide every fader up to the halfway point, presses "record" and leaves the room. It's unbelievable and it works, because he knows what it's going to sound like. He doesn't play around with the mix, he doesn't shove things around, he doesn't punch things in and out, it's already there.'

The band, too, were impressed by the producer. Richard Butler, on the *Interchords* interview disc, recalled, 'It was good working with Todd. You get different stories about him, you hear that he goes in at night while you're asleep and does ghost guitar parts and stuff like that, but we didn't find it like that.'

'It was a memorable album for all of us, I think,' Ashton reflects. 'We were able to joke Todd as much as he was able to joke us, and we all got on pretty well. Before, we all used to gang up on each other, now we all ganged up on Todd!'

Even the rows that were part and parcel of the recording process were readily smoothed over. Ashton: 'I had some bad arguments with him, where I got really drunk-assed and obnoxious, but he'd always forgive me. I look back on the times with him and, after the fact, I'd always learned something. Todd had this way of making you feel okay for being a dick. He's talented in more ways than people realize!'

Tim Butler agrees. '*Forever Now* is my favourite album out of all of them. I think it was the peak of our psychedelicness. Some of our biggest influences were psychedelic and, finally, on that album we got psychedelic. I just thought the use of the cellos, and the horn section on some parts, was so great. And I enjoyed working with Todd. I'd been a Todd fan before that, and he's a real character. It's just fun memories, as well as the music. It's just fond memories of that entire time.'

10

MR CLEAN AIR JUST WENT PAST

THE ALBUM COMPLETE, the Psychedelic Furs returned to the UK to await its September 1982 release and, faced with a little downtime, amuse themselves with other projects.

It was an interlude prickled with impatience and anticipation. 'I remember getting home to London,' says Richard, 'and Tim and I were playing it all the time. We'd go down to the pub during lunchtime, get somebody drunk, then drag them home and tell them, "You've got to listen to our record." These poor people were probably bored out of their minds, but we made them sit and listen.'

The opportunity to road test the new material on a larger audience arrived on 15th July 1982, with a more-or-less unofficial, and certainly inadvertent, preview at the Camden Palace – as the Psychedelic Furs' old haunt, the Music Machine, was now known. Now more of a nightclub than a live venue, the one-time cinema nevertheless continued to attract a trendy rock'n'roll clientele (the Butlers themselves were regular patrons), while it had also set itself up as the first choice for PAs – 'personal appearances' – by bands that weren't, for whatever reason, ready to mount a full live show, but wanted to debut their new records regardless. Three or four songs and a backing tape to sing along with – it was a mug's game.

Or so Richard Butler thought, as he chatted one night with the Palais' owner, Mick Parker. So, when Parker asked him if he fancied putting on one by himself, Butler quickly agreed. It was only the next morning, when the effects of the evening's alcohol intake had been replaced by an oddly unshakeable feeling of dread, that he realised quite what he'd let himself in for.

Of course, it was a fiasco from start to finish. Unwilling to simply yank Butler out from his drunken commitment, Les Mills instead concentrated on trying to limit the potential damage. In conversation with Parker, he won an agreement that the performance would not be promoted outside of the Palais, lest someone should get the wrong end of the stick and advertise a full Psychedelic Furs show in the music press that week.

Again at Mills' insistence, a disclaimer was posted on the main door, stating Butler alone would be appearing – only for the singer himself to start getting cold feet the closer he came to show time. He'd never appeared onstage alone before and, though he'd rehearsed with the tapes for hours on end, he still wasn't sure he'd be able to now. In the event, he put on a fine show, showcasing four songs and turning in such a convincing performance that, out in the audience, his near-perfect vocals seemed as canned as the accompaniment. One girl at the front even tried to take the microphone from him, convinced that he wouldn't even notice. Needless to say, he did.

Backstage afterwards, he was less composed. 'I hated it. It was horrible, it just didn't work. I knew people had done things to backing tapes, so I thought I'd try it. It was a mistake… but only because I did it so badly. It should have been better.' The pledge he made that evening, never again to gig without a full band behind him, is one he's kept ever since.

Performed that evening, of course, was what was scheduled to become the first taster for the new album, the group's next UK single 'Love My Way'. A bittersweet pop song, memorable for its lush keyboards and insistent xylophone-led melody line, the future epic was conjured by Richard from two notes he'd been playing with on his Stylophone. He'd just finished listening to David Bowie's *Scary Monsters* album, and his choice of instrument was probably no accident. That album's 'Ashes To Ashes' revisits Major Tom from the early hit 'Space Oddity' – famously, that song, too, was composed on a Stylophone.

Out drinking one evening, hungover when he awoke, but in desperate need of something to play to Ashton when they got together later in the day, the two notes stuck in Butler's head, while the lyrics came tumbling out, relayed into the Dictaphone he kept by his side. As potential blockbusters go, the resultant skeleton was scarcely impressive and Ashton, for his part, was deeply unimpressed. But Butler loved the song regardless – and so, it transpired, did a lot of other people. At demo stage, Ed Buller added the distinctive marimba sound; in the studio itself, Todd Rundgren admonished Richard to sing, not shout the lyric. The singer recollected, 'When we first sent it over to Todd, I was virtually shouting the lyrics. Then, when we went into the studio, he said, "Hold on, Richard, I think this could be a beautiful song and you're absolutely destroying it with this anger, it doesn't feel like it has to be an angry song." So I sat and thought about it and he was right. It's funny, when you've written what you think is an angry song, you kinda get used to it being angry.'

One of the other key elements in the finished song, however, was not originally even scheduled for inclusion.

As far as Flo and Eddie were concerned, their part in the sessions was over, and they were preparing for their return home. That final morning, as they were saying their goodbyes, Rundgren asked if they wanted to hear the projected single. 'He played us "Love My Way",' says Volman, 'and it had no backgrounds on it at all! We told him he had to put us on that record – of all the things we did, we said that song, more than any of them, had the potential to be a big hit. But it needed to showcase the sound. There was a sound coming out of those other songs that the Furs had never had before – there was that same ambient track that they were known for, that wall of tracks, but there was more going on and the backing vocals were a major part of that. "Love My Way" had to have a similar treatment.'

Kayman picks up the tale. 'We had a quick conference – we were all but walking out to our rental car at that point; we thought it, we came up with an idea of what we should do. So we showed the group, before we even showed Todd, what our idea was, we ran through it with them and it was magic, I am so, so thrilled that we got a chance to do it, because I listen to that record now and I can't imagine it without.'

Rundgren did not need to be told twice, not only unleashing the duo across the soul of the song, but even granting them a virtual solo, a ten bar section where Flo and Eddie alone take over. And his judgement proved perfectly placed. 'Love My Way' remains one of the Psychedelic Furs' best-loved releases to this day and, in climbing to #42 that summer, it became their biggest British hit yet. But it should have been bigger.

While Richard mourned what might have been, and wished he'd never even heard of Camden Palace, John Ashton, too, was keeping himself busy, heading into the studio to produce the Sisters Of Mercy, a Leeds-based Goth band whose vocalist, Andrew Eldritch, was himself a long-standing Psychedelic Furs fan, and who were now managed by Les Mills. Titular similarities aside, he even borrowed (deliberately or otherwise) the distinctive echoed intro from the John Peel version of 'Into You Like A...' for the Sisters' own 'Train'.

'I had been recommended to the Sisters of Mercy, who were looking for management, by Howard Thompson,' says Mills. 'Howard had wanted to sign them before he went to Columbia in New York and felt that I could help them. I arranged for them to record with John as I felt it would benefit both parties as the Sisters' previous recorded work had been dire and John wanted to get into production.'

The two groups had shared a stage in Leeds earlier in the year; now, following a week of pre-production at Andrew's flat in Leeds, over two weekends spent sequestered at Kenny Giles' studio in Bridlington, Ashton oversaw four songs: two destined for the Sisters' next (third) single, 'Alice' and 'Floorshow'; the definitive version of the oft-recorded (but still unreleased) 'Good Things'; and a distinctive cover of the Stooges' '1969', which would finally turn up on a 12-inch the following spring.

At Ashton's own suggestion, the Sisters Of Mercy were one of several support bands recruited as opening acts for one-off shows on the Psychedelic Furs' next British tour – Scritti Politti and the Passage were among the others.

It was in readiness for that outing that the Psychedelic Furs themselves reconvened in early August 1982, to begin rehearsing – and acclimatize themselves to the fact that they no longer had a drummer. The day before rehearsals began, Vince Ely announced he was quitting the group.

'I don't think Vince was really into touring,' surmises Tim Butler. 'He was a bit of a delicate thing. That's why he quit.'

Considering the estrangement that the band first felt while recording in

Bearsville, Vince's departure was not completely unexpected – just the abruptness of it.

Ashton, however, believes there was more to Ely's decision than simply a dislike of life in the back of a bus. The drummer had never truly adjusted to the departures of Kilburn and Morris or the absolute shift in the group's mechanism which it precipitated. Ashton explains, 'When it was six in the band, it was the perfect mix. When it was four, it became a little distraught, and that's why things went the way they did, and Vince left. [He used to] start arguments, then stand back and watch the fireworks, he loved that. He wanted excitement, he was always winding everybody else up. But it only really worked with the six.' As the group contracted, so did Ely's enthusiasm, and the common ground that he shared with bandmates.

The group's alcohol intake remained a recurring bone of contention. Alone amid the quartet, Ely didn't aspire towards the abandoned nights of sozzled hedonism which they apparently dreamed of; unlike the others, he didn't think that a backstage party was the universal panacea for every thing that could go wrong in concert. 'Tim equated being "delicate" with not being a big beer drinker,' Vince insists. The drummer enjoyed aspects of touring, he just didn't like the band's on-tour lifestyle. In cities such as New York, Vince would spend any spare time taking in galleries, museums and shops, while his bandmates would remain in the nearest bar...

Vince Ely, Asbury Park, USA, 1982.

Richard Butler fooling around in a borrowed wig, Melbourne, Australia, 1983.

Les Mills (2)

And, of course, Vince's objections to their lifestyle often precipitated another round of arguments – Richard Butler, in particular, could grow extraordinarily defensive of his drinking, especially when he was in the midst of it. Ashton isn't being cruel when he muses, 'I think Vince was a little too prissy for Richard's tastes.' Anybody who questioned the singer's intake fell into that category.

Ashton: 'Things just got too crazy, too strenuous, for him. After a while of living this party life, you find it difficult to make a sane decision, so it's easy to get pissed off with the whole thing. Maybe that's what happened with him.'

If that was the case, it was an exasperation that Ashton, at least, could readily identify with. 'I did it many times. I thought, "I'm just going to quit this band, it's crazy." Because you had to argue for anything you wanted, that was the way things worked. But, after a while, I learned to argue only for the things I thought were worth arguing for, and forget the rest. That's the way it worked.'

'It was left to me to try to convince Vince not to quit,' Les Mills recalls. 'I do not think it had as much to do with chemistry as John implies. The way Vince explained it to me was that he had an opportunity to establish his career as a producer on Ministry's debut album. He had a strong belief in Al Jourgenson and Arista wanted them to record immediately. For Vince it became a simple choice: Touring for the next nine months or production. For him it was a no-brainer. So I wished him well and he left. Although I wouldn't be surprised if Richard's antics at the 'Love My Way' video shoot didn't have something to do with it.'

The 'Love My Way' video was shot by director Tim Pope, at that time best regarded as the eye behind a string of gracefully assaultive films for Soft Cell and Altered Images – his award-winning and precedent-setting sequence of Cure videos would not be ignited until later in 1982. Pope had known the Psychedelic Furs since their earliest days when, as a teenager working for a political image consultancy in High Wycombe, he regularly turned up at their shows armed with a camcorder 'borrowed' from the office.

It was the show reel he developed from such raw footage that prompted Stevo, head of Soft Cell's Some Bizzare label, to employ the otherwise untried unknown during 1981 with spectacular results. In the year since, the lanky, amiable Pope had done as much as anybody to drag video into realms of creativity that were no less spectacular than the music they accompanied – and sometimes, even better.

The Psychedelic Furs, too, were pushing hard to add a string of classy videos to their résumé. Following that maiden exploration with Don Letts and 'Sister Europe', they linked with director Terry Bedford – cinematographer on *Monty Python & The Holy Grail*, among other things – to coax a disconcertingly colourful jewel out of 'Pretty In Pink', a fast-moving blur of furniture, art and instruments, and the disorientating sense that the sometimes-jacketed, sometimes-patterned shirt-clad Richard Butler was in every corner of the house.

The same director also turned in 'Dumb Waiters', a grainy, stroboscopic throwback to the band's own early days with a view that was as unreal as the sound. All over-exposed film and aircraft hanger chic, the video was topped off with an overload of colour which, aping the *Talk Talk Talk* LP sleeve, settles selectively on a face, shirt or odd random rectangle, but never tries to paint the whole picture.

Of course, things rarely went smoothly in The Furs' world, and though Tim Pope was extremely professional, the 'Love My Way' shoot was another chaotic flashpoint. During the filming of the video, which involved the illusion of Richard walking on water by stepping on Perspex blocks which were kept just under the surface of the water in a large tank, the band were nearly electrocuted!

'Richard was heavily fuelled on vodka – you can see how drunk he is in the close-ups,' says Les Mills. 'He missed his mark and stepped off one of the submerged blocks in the water tank that the band were filming in. Richard, in an attempt to stop himself falling out of the tank, instinctively reached out and grabbed a lighting stand which supported a high voltage lamp. Richard as a result avoided falling into the tank, but the lamp looked like it would. Time stood still as the lamp toppled toward the water and electrocution beckoned for the three remaining band members still stuck in the tank: Tim, John and Vince. Then, at the last moment, a technician reached out a hand and caught the stand.

'The crew were ashen-faced and the band remained shocked. I was appalled; Vince was appalled…

'Astonishingly, Richard remained oblivious to the situation as an electrician came up to me to complain that Richard was trying to put his bare wet toe into a lighting socket. The electrician had had to go over to him and say, "Are you trying to get yourself killed?"'

Richard is rueful when he recalls the incident, though he believes it has been exaggerated. 'I wasn't drinking spirits…' he protests. 'I was much more of a beer drinker. The story is mostly true, but it wasn't as close to death as it seemed. When I pretended to poke my toe into the socket, I knew it was not plugged in and was just kidding around.'

Neither Les nor Vince saw the funny side!

'When Tim Pope commented on "the excitement of a little bit of danger," Vince, who was sober throughout the incident, was not happy,' says Les. 'Maybe this incident had something to do with Vince's decision to leave the band a few weeks later.'

Relocating to the United States, Ely threw himself into sessions and production work. He'd already stepped outside of the Psychedelic Furs once before, guesting on four tracks on Robyn Hitchcock's *Black Snake Diamond Role* album in early 1981 (Hitchcock subsequently repaid the group for the loan, with a luminous cover of 'The Ghost In You'). Now, teaming up with Ian Taylor, co-producer of 'We Love You', 'Mr Jones' *et al*, Ely duly took the helm of the first ever Ministry album, the undisguised synthi-popcorn of 1983's *Work For Love/With Sympathy*.

Infamously, the entire album has since been roundly disowned by frontman Al Jourgensen but, once past his (with musical hindsight, understandable) bitterness, it remains a rather superb early-80s period piece, produced with all the sheen that the material merited.

The following year, Ely produced the major label (Elektra) debut by Shrapnel, a band featuring the then unknown Daniel Rey; and, that October, he was recruited by the Cure to stand-in for recently dismissed drummer Andy Anderson at 11 shows on their latest American tour. Coincidentally, a review of one of the shows, by the *Toronto Globe & Mail*, namechecked Ely and then continued, 'the Cure often brought the Furs to mind, not so much in sound as in the direction it has taken in demonstrating how a cultish English group can make selling-out look good. Both bands have exchanged inventive, but limited exploratory styles for greater popularity and, in the process, have pushed mass taste in an interesting new direction.'

1985 saw Ely play on and produce five tracks on former Go-Go Jane Wiedlin's eponymous maiden album, but he never fell out of contact with his erstwhile bandmates for long. Ashton: 'I remember him coming along to one of the shows on the *Mirror Moves* tour and telling me how much he loved the new stuff, and he was happy we were doing so well'

For all the Psychedelic Furs' experience with the revolving drumseat, Ely was always going to be difficult to replace. No matter what else was occurring on stage, he was the one musician who could be relied upon to keep things firing, a relentlessly powerful drummer whose timing was so precise that, no matter who else lost their grip on a song, his beat always pulled them back into place. It was a loss that fate, and miraculous serendipity alone could make good – and the Psychedelic Furs were lucky. Just like Ely, their timing could not have been better.

Australian Phill Calvert was the butter-probably-wouldn't-melt blonde who had materialized in London three years earlier as a member of the Birthday Party, and then proceeded to terrorize the incipient Goth scene with his contributions to a live show that remains one of the most cataclysmic displays ever unleashed on an unsuspecting stage.

'I had been turned on to The Birthday Party by The Sisters of Mercy,' Les Mills remembers, 'as they had played a number of shows supporting them. I played their albums to Richard and he picked up on Cave's lyrics right away. I remember him being less than impressed by the band live though.'

Sufficiently down-to-earth to become one half (with guitarist Mick Harvey) of the newly arrived band's organizational strength, making sure the vans were up to scratch and the hired equipment arrived on time, Calvert was a man possessed when he got behind his kit. Remove vocalist Nick Cave's barnstorming yodel from the mix, and the drums and percussion are the Birthday Party's most dominantly hellish component, a monster mash of incredible precision, a whirlwind that drove

Tim Butler and Ann Sheldon, Australia, 1983.

The Furs on stage in Sydney, Australia, 1983.

the band like a demonic Casey Jones.

He departed the Birthday Party when Cave announced that the band was quitting London and decamping to Berlin, but that Calvert wouldn't be accompanying them. 'Fuck, that's fine,' he replied. 'I don't want to live in Berlin.'[15]

The drummer played his final show with the Birthday Party at London's Venue on 16th August 1982, a bone-crushing performance which many observers reckoned was one of the best London shows the band had ever played. Richard Butler was one of them, eye-catchingly resplendent that evening in a bright yellow shirt and nasty pink trousers, and clearly having a whale of a time.

His attempts to communicate his excitement to the band, however, fell on characteristically surly ears. Even as the Birthday Party were absorbed into the prevalent English musical landscape, the group had consciously set itself apart from its contemporaries, via a studied combination of disdain and arrogance. Mere weeks after they arrived in London, in March 1980, the Australians descended upon the Lyceum, to catch the *crème de la crème* of the local underground, the Psychedelic Furs/Teardrop Explodes/Echo & The Bunnymen behemoth bill – and they hated it. 'They all just stood there and played their guitars and sang,' complained guitarist Rowland Howard later. 'It was lame, bland.'

The release of *The Psychedelic Furs* a couple of months later did revise the Birthday Party's opinion somewhat – Cave even admitted that he at least admired the lyrics, 'largely,' Howard continued, 'because of the repeated use of the word "stupid".' But the appearance of the lyricist backstage at the Venue was no time to acknowledge even that much. Howard: 'He came up to Nick and I and, in his thick London accent, he "Fawt that Nick and I, and himself and possibly Elvis Costello, are the only literate songwriters in rock." Nick's response to this was to grab the cigarette out of his mouth, have a drag out of it, grab the can of beer out of his hand and have a swig out of it, put the cigarette in the can and hand it back to him. Then he walked off. In other words, "No! You're wrong! There's only three of us!" I mean, what are you supposed to say to that? "Yes, you're right?"'[16]

Richard Butler is adamant that Howard's recollections of this incident are fundamentally flawed.

'I was backstage talking when Nick dropped his cigarette in my pint glass and then he reached into the glass to retrieve the cigarette, causing the beer to overflow and go everywhere,' he explains. 'Someone chastised him saying, "That's the singer with the Psychedelic Furs." Nick said, "No, Richard Butler is the singer with the Psychedelic Furs." I said, "Yeah, I'm Richard Butler." Nick then bought me another pint and we chatted for a while.'

'I didn't make that comment – I didn't even know Roland wrote lyrics... and I wasn't a big Costello fan... I'm not even sure I ever met Roland Howard.'

'It's not true that Nick Cave deliberately snubbed Richard as Roland Howard contends,' Les Mills confirms. 'Richard, his brother Simon and I went backstage after the show where Nick was being besieged by the usual sycophants you'd find after a London show. Richard went up to him and Nick Cave, assuming Richard to be a ligger took his own cigarette and dropped it in Richard's beer glass (not can). When it was explained to Cave who Richard was he apologised and a brief conversation ensued.'

Nonetheless, Richard remained true in his admiration of the The Birthday Party, however; with Calvert's exclusion from the Party now official, Les Mills called him up, inviting him down to the next Psychedelic Furs rehearsal.

Calvert wasn't immediately certain. 'I felt like I wasn't very good… I had a poor self-image because the guys I'd worked and lived with, done everything with for the last eight years of my life, had said, "We don't think you're the right guy to be in the band".' No matter that he agreed with them, it was the first half of the equation that stuck in his mind.

He needn't have been concerned. The Psychedelic Furs were already well aware of what he was capable of, they just wanted to make sure he could do it for them. Almost without even consulting one another, at the end of the rehearsal, the band asked Calvert if he wanted the gig. They'd found their new drummer.

With Calvert joined on stage by *Forever Now* guests Gary Windo and Ann Sheldon, plus the returning Ed Buller, the Psychedelic Furs hit the road hot on the heels of the album release. Calvert actually made his live debut on 10th October 1982 at London's Hammersmith Odeon, with a show simulcast across the country by Radio One – and was promptly mistaken for the absent Ely by *Smash Hits*' reviewer, Deborah Steels.

He got off lightly, though, compared with some. Describing Richard Butler's blue suit as 'straight from the cover of Bowie's first live LP' (which it could have been… not a sartorial tri-

Andre Huckvale collection

umph), Steels then delivered the unkindest cut of all, a comparison with the most annoying segment of Britain's most irritating radio show. 'I always used to wonder who Steve Wright's Horrible Voice was. Now I know...' It was an unflattering review, to say the least. But maybe, she did have a point.

For witnesses and listeners alike, it was an altogether different experience from any the Psychedelic Furs had offered up before – and an altogether tamer one. Even at the end, during those fractious final dates through Europe and the UK, the six-man Psychedelic Furs remained masters of the unexpected, capable of stunning spontaneity even within the tightening strictures of a 'conventional' set list.

New material may have been restricted to 'President Gas' alone, but nightly the song seemed to evolve a little more; older songs might have been falling out of focus, but 'We Love You' remained a *tour de* improvisational *force*. No matter what was happening on stage, six musicians understood one another intuitively, and adapted accordingly.

There was no room for that now, no wide open spaces for one instrument to colonise, no broad passages of sound for the others to follow. An arrangement rehearsed was a song set in stone.

So, the old frisson of danger was absent. But it was replaced with something that might have been just as worthy and was certainly a lot more saleable – a tight, programmed show whose dynamics were laid out from the off. You paid for a show, and that's what you got.

Somehow, though, that was no longer enough. *Forever Now* was easily the Psychedelic Furs' most commercial album yet, but it barely made the British Top 20 – and that despite a crop of reviews that at least toyed with forgiving the group for *Talk Talk Talk*. 'Love My Way' was one of their finest singles ever. It couldn't even crack the Top 40.

The same week that the Psychedelic Furs played London, Depeche Mode, Simple Minds and Bauhaus were lining up to go on *Top Of The Pops*. If that was to be their station in Britain, playing second fiddle to a bunch of bands that might never have existed without the Psychedelic Furs to light the way for them, then maybe Britain was not where their destiny lay. CBS was still to release the group's follow-up single, a sharp remix of 'Danger', when the Psychedelic Furs departed for their next US tour. Two of the group would never return.

ON EVERYTHING BUT ROLLER-SKATES

FOR THE HANDFUL OF Columbia Records staffers who'd championed the band for so long, persistence was finally paying off.

Bruce Dickinson: 'Breaking a band to the public is a military campaign, but the first battles are won within the record company itself. I often wonder what might have been if we had had their full belief and, maybe, even support, from the beginning.'

The gang was tiny: Dickinson and Peter Philbin; Joanna Spock Dean, a West Coast staffer who was so enthusiastic about the Psychedelic Furs that, along with Ricki Ostrov who was now working for the band, she'd paid her own way to New York in 1980 to catch the band's Mudd Club debut; Linda Kirishjian and her boss, Paul Rappaport, in the East Coast AOR promo department, Phil Sandhaus in artist development; and Howard Thompson, once he arrived in New York.

But they were effective, a tiny coterie of devout supporters who won out against… not the machine *per se*, but at least that segment of the machine that simply jogs comfortably along, happy to maintain the status quo and looking askance at anything that threatens to rock the boat.

The public tends to regard a record company as a single corporate entity, bent on success with every act it signs. In fact, just like any business, there are the acts that are priorities and those that, bluntly, aren't. More pertinently, there are factions within the corporate hierarchy that support those priorities, which regard other factions (and other priorities) as a threat to their own way of life.

This bunch of not quite kids, but certainly not seasoned industry veterans either, running around with their 'Psychedelic This' and 'super Furry That', were such a faction, ruffling feathers, demanding the impossible, refusing to take a categorical 'no' for an answer. Wheedling, insisting, demanding, breaking every unwritten rule in the unpublished book, they flew beneath the policy radar to make sure that *this* radio station got to hear the new album, *that* journalist was granted an interview, *this* fanzine got some exclusive photographs, *that* record store got a box of free posters.

They preached to the converted and let word of mouth do the rest. And now, confronted by US sales of around 90,000 apiece for both *The Psychedelic Furs* and *Talk Talk Talk*, the label was preparing, finally, to begin actively and aggressively marketing the Psychedelic Furs. They weren't top priority, of course – that honour remained the territory of the established giants, the Barbra Streisands, Neil Diamonds, Totos and Kenny Loggins of this world. 'But at least they were on the list,' as Dickinson puts it.

Dickinson himself knew the time had come when he overheard a prominent West Coast sales rep insisting that, if the label intended digging into the coffers, any extra promotional budget should be spent on the proven big-shots. Quietly, but very firmly, he was told that he'd get the money for those acts if and when they needed it. But he was also going to get money for the Psychedelic Furs, and he'd better spend it wisely.

'The thing about the sales for each album is that, to the higher-ups, the band hadn't made sense until now,' explains Dickinson. 'They still didn't understand the music – in fact, they felt threatened by the fact that something they didn't understand could sell. It didn't fit their preconceived notions of what would sell, yet they saw that it had. Maybe more importantly, they saw that it had sold with very little support from them, while they had thrown millions at cookie-cutter AOR artists that just weren't good enough to get the public's interest. No amount of money was ever going to make it work, yet here was this band from England that wasn't a priority because they weren't a direct signing, whose albums weren't really supposed to have even come out, doing everything that those other bands hadn't.'

Despite its low British chart profile, 'Love My Way' was the inevitable first choice for the disc that would lead the charge. It would be issued as the group's first-ever American single on the eve of their next US tour. It swiftly proved to be the correct decision, soaring to the edge of the Top 40 and, at a time when the most recent British Invasion of fresh-faced fops and New Romantic clothes-horses had finally run out of magical mascara, serving notice that a new force was preparing to land.

André Huckvale collection

Out now
Their great new single is 'Love My Way'

Music press advert for Love My Way single

That summer of 1982 was a confusing one. The late 1970s/early 1980s was the age of the One Hit Wonder, at least so far as what the American media quaintly termed the 'New Wave' was concerned. Soft Cell, M, the Flying Lizards, the Boomtown Rats, Devo, Tommy Tutone: all had apparently broken through on the strength of one major single; all would spend the rest of their careers trying fruitlessly – and increasingly desperately – to follow it up, ruing the day they ever allowed the marketing department to sell them as 'the "such-and-such a song" boys.'

Of the bands that had established a less tentative foothold, U2 – once every American critic's tip for the top – were now frantically trying to claw back the ground they'd lost when their second album, *October*, completely failed to crack the American Top 100 – just six months earlier, their debut had climbed as high as #63. The Cure were still searching for an American record company that actually knew what to do with them, and had just seen their best albums yet, *17 Seconds* and *Faith*, bundled together as a budget-priced double album. Depeche Mode seemed to be digging a deeper pit every time they released another record, and the Gang Of Four threw everyone for a loop when they abandoned scratchy, funk-fuelled pettiness for well-produced dance-friendly prettiness.

True, Billy Idol looked like cracking it, flexing his sneer and forgetting there ever was a time when he looked like he meant what he sang. But all that really proved was he'd figured out the kind of records that American radio wanted to hear.

Les Mills (2)

Ann Sheldon and Phill Calvert, New Zealand, 1983.　　Barney Bubbles with painting of Richard, London, 1983.

The Psychedelic Furs were making the records that they themselves wanted to hear, and that was the crucial difference for listeners, fans and the record-buying public.

It was also the key to Columbia's masterplan. For the Psychedelic Furs, a hit single was simply an introduction, and the album a quick consummation. The label was not interested in simply selling the records, it wanted to sell the band, brand them as a name that listeners could trust, so when people went to a record store, they didn't simply ask for the latest hit song by name. They asked for the new Psychedelic Furs.

It was an approach with which Richard Butler, reflecting on his own youthful record-buying practices, was in complete accord. He explained, 'When I would buy, say, Bob Dylan records when I was a kid, it wasn't just buying a Bob Dylan record, it was buying this "character" that you were interested in. You wanted an update on his life, an update on what he was thinking, and you didn't care if they were going to be hits. I was more interested in Bob Dylan the person, as I was with Lou Reed, and, to a degree, David Bowie.'

A decade later, it seemed that fewer and fewer bands commanded (or, perhaps, deserved) that loyalty, and people were simply buying 'the hits'. Later in the 1980s, any number of bands would have reversed that trend, U2, the Cure and Depeche Mode among them. No less than they opened the airwaves to a host of other bands, it was the Psychedelic Furs who paved the way. College had found its first superstars.

Radio was not the Psychedelic Furs' only ally, however. MTV, too, proved a vital friend. Less than one year old at the time, but already establishing a blinding presence on the greater American music scene as more and more homes were hooked up to the network, MTV scooped up the 'Love My Way' video, maybe raised an eyebrow at its less-than-Technicolor sheen, but slammed it into rotation regardless. At a time when most bands were still staring at the camera, looking totally lost and utterly gormless, the Psychedelic Furs' presence and performance were nothing less than captivating.

In spite of the near-death experience during its making, the 'Love My Way' video was stylish and classy with just a soupçon of gentle intensity, calmer than its predecessors. That was its magic. No budget-choking location shoots, or hi-tech computer trickery, the Psychedelic Furs returned to visual basics. A sepia print in an odd shade of blue, a band performance dominated by a full-size glockenspiel, a young Mick Jagger wearing David Bowie's pants, the video studiously avoids anything that could be construed as a gimmick – anything which might distract the viewer from performer or performance. And that was enough.

Richard Butler: '"Love My Way" was the point when I really noticed the change. All of a sudden, there was a lot of girls in the audience.' As the Psychedelic Furs set out on tour, every city they visited had been primed for their arrival – little things mostly. 'Marketing 101,' as Bruce Dickinson calls it. But they mattered and they made a difference: album ads on local radio, point-of-sale posters and life-sized art, concert previews in the daily paper, personal appearances at neighbourhood record shops. By the time the tour reached the West Coast, the band had even grown accustomed to the alien art work that had been slapped on the album.

For the British release of *Forever Now*, the group commissioned a sleeve from Colin "Barney Bubbles" Fulcher, visionary genius behind a slew of classic Hawkwind artwork in the early 1970s, and no less remarkable as in-house designer at Stiff Records later in the decade.

Bubbles was in a bad way when the Psychedelic Furs contacted him – commissions were still coming in, but they were mainly from his older contacts.

Other designs were falling on blind eyes; few major record companies accepted his submissions, while he was also fighting desperately against a voracious Inland Revenue chasing taxes dating back more than a decade. His personal life was in disarray; he was prone to massive bouts of depression. The Psychedelic Furs' approach offered him one of the first independent lifelines he'd been flung in far too many years. He turned in a jewel, a moody shot from the set of the 'Love My Way' video taken by Graeme Attwood, stills photographer on a number of Bond films, with the band's name picked out around it in stars. The band loved it, CBS were happy with it – and then the design arrived in America. Columbia threw it away. It didn't match the market.

For a replacement, a handful of recent photos were thrown onto a backboard, coloured in and printed up. A head-and-shoulders of Richard Butler, taken by Marcia Resnick up at Bearsville, dominated; his bandmates (Tim also shot by Resnick, John and Vince by Antoine Giacomoni) were scattered insets. Even the group's name had been quietly subverted. 'Psychedelic' only if you looked real close, the band was, to all intents and purposes, abbreviated down to 'the Furs', a deafening tribute to the American industry's absolute inability to comprehend the notion of irony. 'Why call yourselves "psychedelic", if that's not what you are?' they'd ask in interviews, and there really wasn't an answer to that. At one time, Richard himself mused on the day when the group's name might need to some serious surgery. But seeing it as a virtual *fait accompli* was a jagged cut too far.

The cover was ghastly and the first time the singer saw it, he said, he actually burst into tears. It was that bad. But Columbia wouldn't be swayed. Bubbles' masterpiece was thrown on the scrapheap – he would not be designing another. A little over a year later, on 14th November 1983, Bubbles killed himself.

Whatever its faults, of course, the new sleeve certainly pushed the band members' faces further into the spotlight, conspiring with the 'Love My Way' video to give American youth a new set of pin-ups. Richard: 'While we were touring, we did an in-store in Seattle and, when we came out, we were actually mobbed. That was when we thought, "Hey! We're becoming more popular," which was a very strange feeling. Then we got into the limo and started back to the hotel, and the driver said, "Hey guys, we're going to have to take a detour here, so we can lose some cars following us." We thought, "Wow, this is very strange".'

Seattle was just one stop on a tour that neatly traced both American coasts, a month-long outing which was destined to sell out at almost every halt. Rarely hitting venues that held less than a thousand souls, frequently packing halls two or three times larger than that, the Psychedelic Furs pulled almost 1,500 into Toronto's Concert Hall, over 2,300 into New York's Beacon Theatre. When they got to the Santa Monica Civic, a capacity 3,500 fans greeted them, and that was a thrill in its own right. One of the most famous David Bowie bootlegs of all time was recorded on that same stage almost exactly ten years before and, though the white concrete building itself could scarcely be less romantic, actually reaching it was nevertheless an achievement to be cherished.

Reviews of the tour were ecstatic. *Musician* described Richard Butler as 'a genuine rock'n'roll spectacle, seducing the audience with the melodrama of Bowie, the androgyny of Jagger and the sneer of Sex Pistols-era Johnny Lydon. He sings pointedly to one girl in the audience, touches the hand of another, then leaps offstage onto the floor, enticing the screaming, energized crowd with his charismatic proximity.' In Atlanta at the end of November, he even recreated one of *the* great moments of rock concert imagery, stepping onto the outstretched hands of the audience, *à la* Iggy Pop at King's Cross Cinema, and walking over their heads. 'It was really wonderful,' Phill Calvert recalled. 'They all held him up.'

Tim Butler: 'That whole tour was cool, because I can't think of many bands that would tour with a cello mixed into a maelstrom of guitars and stuff. With the older songs, we actually had interesting ways of adding the cello into it, which updated them. And that had sort of a shock value – people would come to the show, they'd see a seat being set up at the front of the stage: "What's happening down there?" And they'd see someone walking on with a cello. "What the...?"'

In fact, the cello quickly became a *de facto* extra member of the group, at least according to the band's travel arrangements. Tim Butler continues, 'We had to buy the cello its own seat on the plane, because Ann

Forever Now era show at The Beacon

wouldn't put it in the baggage hold.' It travelled under the name of Mr Cello, but repaid the band's forbearance every night, raising the first wild cheer of the evening with a solo during 'President Gas'.

Sheldon, too, blended perfectly with the group, to the point where there was even talk of her joining the Psychedelic Furs as a full member. Ultimately, it didn't happen, just as a handful of songwriting collaborations between cellist and band never truly came to fruition. But still, Ashton was moved to enthuse, 'Ann's going over to more "head" music, as it were.' Ashton raved, 'She's throwing away what she's been trained in for *feel* – which is where we come from. We're a feel band, you know? She's great, she's got lots of good ideas, she's not like actually working with a session player.'[17]

Neither was that the end of the band's expansion. Another musician had joined the party in November 1982, after it was discovered that an old drug bust left Gary Windo unable to complete the Psychedelic Furs' full worldwide itinerary. At Windo's own suggestion, they recruited Mars Williams, at that time a member of the Akron-based New Wave act The Waitresses, but once a bandmate of Earth Wind & Fire's Rob Lee in a high school funk covers band and, from there, a key player in the New York No Wave scene, gigging alongside Fred Frith and Bill Laswell in Massacre.

The Waitresses had scored their first major hit, the compulsively caterwauling

Richard Butler and John Ashton doing an interview in New Zealand, 1983.

'I Know What Boys Like', earlier in the year, but were now taking a short break. For the workaholic Williams, the Psychedelic Furs' offer, when it came, arrived at just the right time.

Mars Williams: 'I knew of the Furs, although it wasn't like I had all their records. But I went to hear them at the Ritz in New York, and Gary introduced me to everybody, "This is Mars from the Waitresses." Richard was, "Oh yeah, cool, I've heard that band, sounds really good." But we just hung out and talked. Then, the next day, I got a call from Gary. "I can't leave the country because of some old bust; the Furs are going to Australia and New Zealand in January, and they were wondering if you could do the shows?"' Williams accepted immediately and, anxious to find his way around the set, joined the Psychedelic Furs just days later, doubling up alongside Windo onstage for the remainder of the American tour.

Back on the East Coast in December, the tour broke for the Christmas holidays, the entire group holing up at the Gramercy Park Hotel in New York, meeting the press and local media.

'The band also made a number of videos over the Christmas period,' Les Mills recalls, 'with a director called Bill Price: 'Sleep Comes Down', 'Goodbye', 'Danger' and, I think, 'No Easy Street'. Bill had been the video DJ at the Ritz in New York and had made an early composite video of 'We Love You' to show in the club. Unfortunately we couldn't license the clip because it contained too many copyright images but I made a note to use Bill at the first available opportunity.'

The New Year then put them back out on the road, opening on 3rd January 1983, with their first national radio broadcast, when their return to the New York

Daytime crowd at Sweetwater Festival, New Zealand, 1983

Ritz was aired on the legendary King Biscuit Flour Hour. (Five songs from the show became the group's first ever bootleg, the ever-impressive *File Under: Psychedelic Furs*; the opening, squealing 'President Gas' was then lifted for the band's next B-side.)

Then, as the band bid Windo goodbye, Williams made his first appearance as sole saxophonist when the Psychedelic Furs headlined the opening night of Auckland's Sweetwater festival at the end of January 1983. 'Love My Way' had ended 1982 as New Zealand's second biggest-selling single of the year (Barbra Streisand's 'Evergreen' edged it out) and 60,000 fans were camped out to hear the group perform it. Williams: 'It was amazing! It was at night, and on the hills around the festival site, everyone was holding torches. I got so pumped up, totally hyped. It was unbelievable!'

From New Zealand, the Psychedelic Furs shifted to Australia. There, too, 'Love My Way' was tearing up the chart; there, too, the band was greeted with scenes of pandemonium they could never have imagined back in Britain. And, for the first time, they seemed to be enjoying it, leaving the musical and creative arguments behind as they concentrated solely on making the most of the madness. Thanks to his then-girlfriend Cheri, Richard Butler had even sworn off alcohol, finally tiring, as he put it, of having to get drunk every morning, simply to cure the hangover from the evening before.

Though, according to Les Mills, the reality behind such public pronouncents of abstinence was quite different. 'Richard was still drinking heavily all through the Australian tour,' he insists, 'ably abetted by Mars and Tim. He didn't quit until we returned to the USA where he knew Cheri would leave him if he didn't quit.'

Williams: 'We had the best time, the most fun. Everyone was partying, we were wild and crazy, we were trashing dressing rooms, it was a blast. We really got along well, and became really good friends.'

'Early on that tour we were befriended by an eccentric chemist who had found a way to refine MDA (the natural form of Ecstasy) from the bark of a Brazilian tree,' Mills adds. 'He became our personal tour chemist and travelled around with us until we left Australia.'

The Psychedelic Furs returned to the United States on 6th March 1983, for another month-and-a-half's worth of shows. Most of them had been arranged back in the autumn, which meant few were anywhere near as large as the band now merited. Demand for tickets in Pasadena was so huge that the band was forced to add on two further shows; other venues sold out in near-record time. *Forever Now* was peaking. Although it climbed no higher than #61, it was already on course for a gold disc. While the group's latest single, the odd choice of 'Run And Run,' didn't chart, a new video, for 'Sleep Comes Down', quickly stepped into 'Love My Way's shoes.

Gary Windo rejoined the band for this latest round of gigs, but his continued involvement remained completely untenable. 'We were feeling very awkward about the situation with Gary,' Richard Butler admits, 'because we liked him. But we came back to America, and then we were going to Canada, which Gary couldn't do, so it just became [too difficult].' Williams had already returned to the Waitresses by this time, only to discover the band on the verge of total collapse. When he was asked if he was interested in rejoining the Psychedelic Furs once this latest round of gigs was over, he accepted on the spot. Like Ed Buller, he would never become a full-time member of the group. But he was to remain alongside them for the next five years regardless.

Williams' recruitment was not the only decision that the group would make as the *Forever Now* tour wound down, however. Discussing their plans for the immediate future, the Butler brothers realised they really weren't looking forward to returning to England. Richard's girlfriend, Cheri, was a New Yorker; the city itself seemed more like home than London ever could. Finally, the singer voiced the thought that had been on his mind for the last few weeks. 'I said, "How about staying over here then?"; he said, "Okay, great. Let's get a place." So we did.'

It was not a spur of the moment decision. Even before the tour, Butler had been ruminating on the possibility, telling *Musician* magazine, 'Everybody over here has got this image of England as being a great place, but we're pretty bored with it. It rains all the time and it's gray and everything closes at 11 o'clock. It's great for us [in America], we love it. People understand the music more.'

But a change of scenery wasn't Richard Butler's only motivation for getting out of England. He wanted a change of culture, too. He had remained faithful to his Australian resolution of cutting back on drink but knew that, if he was going to continue, he needed a new social life as well, one which didn't revolve around the traditional English custom of meeting at the pub, then staying there till closing time. In New York, bars can stay open all night, but it's a very different scene, and serves a very different purpose. At home, you go down the pub to socialise. In America, you go to the bar to get drunk.

It was time for a completely clean slate. With the drink, he also threw out recreational drug-taking, and he laughed a year later when journalist Johnny Waller informed him of the latest London gossip: that the only reason he'd moved to New York was because he kept being given free drugs.

'That certainly would be a reason,' Butler mused. 'But I don't take drugs now [either]. Coke was the only drug I ever took when I was on tour, but it got to the point where you'd take it and just feel immediately anxious and depressed – and if you've got a show to do, you can't go on because your voice goes and your mouth feels dry.' Like the booze, 'I just figured I'd give up when I got back.'

Ashton, too, was tempted to remain in New York, but ultimately decided not to. His girlfriend of the time was pregnant with daughter Sophie, and the prospect of the upheaval was simply too daunting. He returned to their home in Tonbridge, Kent, the Butlers remained in New York City, and work on the next Psychedelic Furs album became a transatlantic affair. 'Richard had met a new girl, and he was very together with his life. He'd changed it around completely; he was clean for the first time in many years, and he began to see things very differently.'

It was only as the logistics of that new album began to tangle that Ashton realised that a lot of other stuff needed to be treated differently as well. 'I was in England doing my thing, they were in America doing theirs', and that was the sum of the parts. The way they came together was the way they came together.'

12

OUR DREAMS HAVE ALL GONE UP ON SALE

THE PSYCHEDELIC FURS HAD NEVER been renowned for pulling things together on schedule, far preferring to wait until the last minute or so before downing their pints and getting to work. Even in the days of Beautiful Chaos, the pub was always a brighter lure than the rehearsal studio – if they ran out of songs, they could always improvise. But if they ran out of drinking time, they might as well go home. There was always something in the fridge.

Drink was not an impediment anymore, although the problem was still made of liquid. There was an ocean dividing the group's three songwriters and, in those days before e-mail and affordable phone rates, it proved just as great an obstacle. Tim Butler: 'Richard and I would write a song and send it to John in England, and he'd send tapes over to us. Then we'd get together every few months, either over here or over there'. Time simply passed them by. Instead of taking a few months to come together as the trio had expected, by the time they were ready to reconvene the Psychedelic Furs, close to a year had passed since the release of *Forever Now* – and they still hadn't recorded a note.

Manager Les Mills believes it was the lack of alcohol that was to blame for this creative hiatus. 'Once he stopped drinking, Richard couldn't write. He'd never written a lyric or ever sang sober… It's no coincidence then that he dried up creatively once he stopped drinking. One night Richard called me up and told me he

André Huckvale collection

Various badges

was nursing a glass of whiskey and that maybe he'd get inspiration if he drank it…'

Richard disagrees, conceding only that he did drink when he was writing early on. 'It is not true at all to say I only ever wrote drunk,' he protests. '"Love My Way" I wrote in the morning before going to John's house. When I called Les I wasn't nursing a whiskey, I was in a hotel on Portobello Road which had a minibar and I was surveying the minibar desperate for a drink, which I thought would help the creative process. Now I haven't been drinking since the 80s. I've written all my lyrics since *Mirror Moves* sober and I haven't had a problem writing lyrics.'

In the meantime, Richard maintained his sobriety and the creative silence was deafening. Both CBS and Columbia were getting restless. There was talk of cutting an interim EP; Richard Butler himself pondered aloud the possibility of recording a solo EP, comprising favoured Jacques Brel, Edith Piaf and Charles Aznavour songs - sidestepping the writer's block - but baulked when Columbia started talking about expanding it to a full LP. 'And you could even use Sly and Robbie!' they enthused. 'I wouldn't want to,' Butler responded. 'I'm pretty content with Tim.' Sly and Timmy?

Finally, just to prove that the group was still alive, CBS put together a greatest hits EP. 'They were wanting to bridge the gap between new material,' Tim recalls. 'We did get to the stage where we took a long time between albums, and the record company would tear their hair out saying, "Where's the next album?" Oh, chill out. So they started bringing out a lot of weird packages.'

In fact, such fears were utterly groundless. By summer 1983, no more than three months after the *Forever Now* toured wrapped up, the Butlers alone had eight or nine songs in more or less studio-ready shape, including 'Here Come Cowboys' (Richard had at least coined the title for 'The Ghost In You.') Ashton, too, had been busy, while Les Mills could offer further proof of the group's intentions, in the form of the weekly retainers that the band was paying the otherwise inactive Phill Calvert, Ed Buller and Mars Williams.

Finally, however, they were ready for action, and it was time to start searching for a suitable producer. Again, the band was in favour of completely redesigning their sound; again, they wanted to keep one jump ahead of the chasing pack. But there were other considerations as well. *Forever Now* had succeeded despite not paying even partial lip-service to the kind of sounds then filling the American air-waves. Imagine what could happen if the group was able to embrace those sounds wholeheartedly, yet still retain the uniqueness that had always characterised their work. As Richard Butler muses, 'Melodies are like fingerprints. [A songwriter] definitely has a melodic style which is very difficult to change, if not impossible.' But there are different ways of treating that style, and different ways of presenting it. As the search for a producer began to narrow down, the Psychedelic Furs were beginning to formulate a very clear image of what that presentation should be.

David Bowie, once again, was an early contender. He turned up at one of the Psychedelic Furs' Australian shows and told them, 'You're getting better every time

I see you. I must produce your next record.' 'But he said that last time,' Richard laughed. In the end, Bowie contented himself by voting 'Love My Way' his third favourite single in a magazine poll.

It was Les Mills who suggested Keith Forsey, at that time riding high in the US as the sonic architect behind Billy Idol's ascent. The pair had still only scored a couple of minor hits at that point, 'Hot In The City' and the epic 'White Wedding', but already a trademark sound was established. Months before its 1984 release, Idol's next album, *Rebel Yell*, was being touted as one of the defining records of the year – and so it would prove.

There was considerably more to Forsey, however, than an ability to harness Idol's rock'n'roll heart. A drummer before he ever turned to production, the English-born Forsey's recording career dated back over a decade, to the days when he was regarded among the top session musicians on the German studio circuit. Freak favourites Amon Duul II, Ralf Nowy and Udo Lindenberg had all benefited from his presence, while he was also one of the unsung heroes playing on producer Frank Farian's Boney M project.

Forsey made his greatest mark, however, as a member of Italian-born (but Munich, Germany-based) motorik dance supremo Giorgio Moroder's Musicland Studios house band. There, his precision chops underpinned a string of Donna Summer albums, Sparks' *#1 Song In Heaven*, the Munich Machine's 'Whiter Shade Of Pale' and more. And the Moroder mood, if not exactly its sound, was in Forsey's mind when he did finally move into production in 1980, helming Generation X's genre-splitting 'Dancing With Myself' single. The record's breathtaking collision of Punk energy and disco sensibilities posited a musical future which few other bands had ever even dreamed of, but vocalist Billy Idol grasped it with both hands.

Since then, the Forsey/Idol team had continued to triumph, although Richard is insistent. 'Keith Forsey was just a name that came up. We weren't picking people for what they had done, but for what they were like. The basic thing about producers was that they knew how to work a studio, where we didn't. After that, it's down to personality, whether you're seeing eye to eye, whether they seem excited about it. He seemed excited by it all, was good to be around, and seemed to be in agreement with us. So we hired him.'

Last time the Psychedelic Furs went into the studio, Todd Rundgren had been dismayed to be confronted by less musicians than he was expecting. Forsey's first disappointment was to discover too many. The sessions were still in the pre-production stage when Forsey and Phill Calvert found themselves at loggerheads. And there was only ever going to be one winner.

Naturally, given his background – and obviously, when you hear his productions – one of Forsey's greatest strengths was his drum sound. It was that which prompted Mills to recommend him in the first place. It was how he went about achieving it that proved divisive. Calvert's own take on the dispute was simple: he wanted 'live' drums; Forsey didn't.

'It is not that Keith Forsey didn't want live drums,' Mills counters, 'he just did-n't want Phill playing them. Although I had originally suggested Phill for the band, by the time he finished touring *Forever Now* I had begun to harbour serious doubts about his ability – both as a time-keeper and as a creative force. Particularly when I found out that Mick Harvey had played most of the drums and percussion on those records by The Birthday Party. I felt that aside from Keith's obvious qualities as a producer, having him on board would provide a little bit of insurance where Phill was concerned.'

Calvert, not surprisingly, wanted to play his parts himself; Forsey wanted to bring in other players. Tim Butler: 'We were rehearsing, and Keith said to Richard quietly one day, "We could do this album in three months, or we could still be here in six months with that drummer." Richard, for whom the turnover in drum-mers now must have seemed as natural as turning over in bed, merely sighed. Here we go again.

His brother continues, 'the reason was – I think Keith Forsey had a thing against drummers, because he's an ex-drummer himself, so he likes to be in control of the bottom end of things. Most of the stuff he records with drum machines... even on albums like Billy Idol's *Whiplash Smile* and *Rebel Yell*, he did a lot of the drums on drum machine. Then he'd get Tommy Price [one of America's hottest session players] to come in and redo things.'

Mars Williams confirmed Butler's take on Forsey's working practices. While he was awaiting the Psychedelic Furs' own return to action, he accepted the invitation to guest on one of Billy Idol's Forsey-led sessions, laying down the sax line that dis-tinguishes 'Catch My Fall'. He was able to report back on precisely what the Psychedelic Furs could expect.

The surprise is that the band even tolerated Forsey's notions, let alone went along with them. Richard Butler remains adamant, after all, that 'We weren't into drum machines at all. Yeah, it would have disposed of the drummer problem that we always seemed to have, but it also would have disposed of a lot of the excite-ment as well. We wanted somebody that could go off and play something really god awful, while drum machines would just sit there and go "goo-kih-kih, goo-kih-kih".' That wouldn't have sounded good with the hoover at all.

But the group had already delayed the new album long enough. The studio – Westlake Audio in Los Angeles – was booked, the engineers hired, and the die, unfortunately, was cast. Tim Butler: 'So Phil was unceremoniously dumped which, with hindsight, I think we're all a bit ashamed of doing.' For Calvert, the timing couldn't have been worse.

'Keith had persevered with Phill throughout the pre-production rehearsals at John Henry's in London,' Les Mills explains, 'and then when the sessions had fin-ished Richard and Tim flew back to New York for a break before we re-convened to record the album in LA; this left John, Keith, Phill, Ed and I in London. Both Ed, whose judgement I trusted, and Keith had already made it clear to me that Phill just wasn't cutting it but that Richard, Tim and John seemed loyal to him. By now the band had toured with Phill and were reluctant to sack their friend. So Keith and I decided that we would have to sit down with John and try to convince him of the reality of the situation. They both came round to my flat and John was, reluctantly, persuaded. Over fish and chaps John accepted Phill's limitations, but he wanted to bury his head in the sand. Keith was adamant and John eventually accepted it. It was then left to me to convince Richard and Tim in New York. Unfortunately Richard procrastinated, saying he'd think about it. Three days later he was still thinking about it. Once he realised that Phill was on a plane to New York and that Richard would have to confront him, he told me he had to tell him on Phill's arrival. So I had the thankless task of calling Phill where he was staying to tell him he was out of the band. Phill had to fly straight back to Australia. I felt that Richard's indecision was unforgivable but was something that I increasingly had to live with. Whenever there was something important to decide then and there on the spot, it would take a month.'

Richard for his part insists sacking Phill was a band decision made in London: 'We were at the Portabello Hotel and I'd said I'd think about it. Les and John came to my room and we went downstairs and talked about it. Keith felt it was better to get rid of him now rather than when he had started the session. It would be less painful and awkward for Phill. It was agreed as a band.'

Either way, Calvert returned to Australia, rejoining Birthday Party compatriot Mick Harvey in Crime & The City Solution for a year, and subsequently working with the bands Blue Ruin and the Sunday Kind. The Psychedelic Furs, meanwhile, got to work on their fourth album.

It was difficult from the outset. Although all three members arrived at the sessions with songs, that was all they had. There was no heart and soul within the frameworks, no sense of self. With just one exception – 'Alice's House', an atmospheric invocation of life in a mental asylum, was resurrected from the *Forever Now* sessions – the album that would become *Mirror Moves* was written in a vacuum. Forsey's task, and the band's, of course, was to make sure that it didn't remain in one.

John Ashton: 'We'd stopped jamming together, that's what it was. Richard and Tim were in New York, they were playing with different people, jamming with different people and getting influenced by different people. I was in England, very much on my own, doing my own thing. I wasn't really hanging out playing with that many people, I was just doing it myself, so my writing totally came from me, and I bounced it off nobody.'

But, for all the differences in approach which the band members brought to the table – and which Forsey only emphasised – still the producer proved a pleasing

Les Mills

Tim, John, and Richard on the set of the 'Heaven' video shoot, London, 1984.

André Huckvale

Richard Butler on stage at Aylesbury Friars Club, 1984.

collaborator. After all the concerns about the writing divide, the band's own identity imprinted itself firmly across the nine songs, regardless of authorship, with only shades to separate the bulk of the numbers.

There were extremes, however. While the Butler brothers penned 'Here Come Cowboys', 'The Ghost In You' and 'Heaven', a hasty studio marriage between a bass line Tim was playing with, and a lyric Richard had socked away some place (each one lush, luscious and wholly accessible cosmopolitan pop songs that would duly take their place among the decade's all-time classics), Ashton was stuck in Kentish suburbia, pouring all his frustrations into his edgy, squawking rhythms.

Andre Huckvale collection

Cover of sheet music for Heaven

Andre Huckvale collection

Heaven-era advert for Furs merchandise

It was Ashton (with Richard supplying lyrics, of course) who came up with 'My Time' and 'Only A Game'; he who conceived the pounding urban triumph of 'Heartbeat'; and he who penned 'High Wire Days', the dark, beautiful ballad which, despite being chosen to close the album, was also singled out as the song which most echoed the band's distant past, and which would sustain long-time fans through the unfamiliar territory mapped. How ironic that 'High Wire Days' was originally composed for the 1984 comedy *Joy Of Sex*! It was passed over, perhaps surprisingly but, given the film's ultimate puerility, certainly mercifully, and Ashton handed it on to Richard Butler to complete.

The lyric is one of Butler's finest, a yearning ballad reflecting on the demands and downfalls of the very fame that the band was courting, wise *before* the event, as the repetition of the phrase 'tomorrow's papers' makes clear. As cautionary epics go, it's unbeatable, up there alongside David Essex's 'Stardust' and David Bowie's 'Rock'n'Roll Suicide' in its invocation of an incipient nightmare that the careers officer never warns you about. One should normally steer clear of songs that document life in a rock'n'roll band – do plumbers and estate agents sing about their jobs? – but 'High Wire Days', like most of Butler's best lyrics, is never overt, and never states the obvious. It simply hangs forebodingly at the end of the album, a natural cliff-hanger that time alone would resolve.

Today, Ashton himself refers to 'High Wire Days' as one of his proudest achievements, an opinion that is shared by Texan blues rocker Chris Whitley. Ashton: 'Whenever I bump into Chris, he's always giving me the thumbs-up on that one. That's how I met him, and it was quite a blast. He was like, "Oh yeah, you played in that band, I went out and bought that album, it has my favourite song on it, 'High Wire Days'." "Oh, I wrote that.' Wow, let me shake your hand." I was a real Chris Whitley fan, so it was really nice.'

Another admirer who surfaced around this time was Bob Dylan, who actually offered the band a song, 'Clean Cut Kid'. The group turned it down – as, so it transpired, Dylan himself had done. A version recorded during the sessions for his 1983 album, *Infidels*, never came close to making the final cut. He later returned to the song, sprucing it up for 1985's *Empire Burlesque* album, but still the Psychedelic Furs' own critical wisdom seems unimpeachable. In his multi-volume *Performing Artist* study of Dylan's career, author Paul Williams pulls no punches when he describes the song, succinctly, as 'charmless'.

True to form, Forsey programmed the entire album into his drum machines, with Tommy Price then coming in to punch up 'Here Come Cowboys' and 'Heaven'. The dreaded onset of modern technology wasn't as bad as it could've been, either. True, Richard fought tooth and nail against the keyboard sound that Forsey insisted on draping over 'The Ghost In You' (a battle that he eventually lost) but the drum machines opened the band up to an entirely new avenue of thought.

Sitting in the studio listening to the playbacks, Forsey suddenly announced that he wanted to do a dance remix of 'Heartbeat', a frenzied dance attack that had already been raised to new heights by an opening Mars Williams sax line. Tim Butler: 'We said, "A what? Dancing... what's that?" "Oh, it's a cross between disco and pop, you jump up and down, then do the odd John Travolta move." So he played us some dance remixes, and we just said, "Go for it".'

According to Les Mills, the dance mix of 'Heartbeat' was directly influenced by Frankie Goes To Hollywood's 'Relax'.

'I had flown in to New York from London for the re-mix sessions,' he explains. 'Keith, John and I were staying at the Mayflower Hotel on Central Park West. The night I got in Keith came to my room and I was playing a twelve-inch mix of 'Relax' which had just been released in England. Keith, who hadn't heard it before, got really excited and listened to it over and over again and asked to take it to the studio with him.'

'I had very little to do with that,' Richard says on the *Interchords* interview. 'It was so unusual to hear something like this coming from this band – there was a lot of cries of "how dare they!", but that was the reason we did it, to irritate slightly. We just wanted to try something different.'

The so-called 'New York Mix' of 'Heartbeat', dropped onto the B-side of the 12-inch 'Heaven' single, would become one of the biggest club hits of the year; a second remix, by Julian Mendelsohn – hot, then, from his recent dance floor updates of the Bob Marley back catalogue, but familiar to the Psychedelic Furs for his mix of the old 'Mr Jones' single – proved almost as successful. As Butler concludes, 'It's amazing what you can do when you use drum machines.'

Mirror Moves artwork

Andre Huckvale collection

Of course the British media was generally unhappy over such developments. *Sounds* approved: 'This is a real strong record that sees the band in a position to finally render many of their contemporaries impotent.' But, elsewhere, the accusation flew that the band had sold their souls to the Yankee dollar. And, in a way, they had – but only because British sterling had refused to buy them first. But, for even the most disapproving onlooker, there was one aspect of *Mirror Moves* that couldn't be faulted; which proved that, behind the high gloss and sheen of the music, the Psychedelic Furs at least retained some contact with their original, subversive roots.

The album's sleeve was Richard's idea, but it was, by no means, his concept. The titles rolled in a circle, there was a glorious surfeit of stars. It wasn't quite *Forever Now Revisited*, but it was close, and Butler wanted the world to know that. 'Design… After Barney Bubbles' read a note beside the credits – indeed Bubbles had also recommended the photographer Brian Griffin – and this time, there'd be no giving in.

Not that the subject was ever even raised.

13

HIGH WIRE DAYS

THERE COMES A POINT IN every band's story where the story itself slows to a crawl, when the characters become sudden caricatures, when what were once great events – a single, an album, a tour – become simple mundanities woven within the larger fabric of fame and celebrity. Like, what else do you expect them to be doing?

For the Psychedelic Furs, that point came in May 1984, with the release of *Mirror Moves*. Even before the record hit the stores, its success was assured; the only question to be answered was, how much bigger that success might become? Or, how badly it could be ballsed up. From the band's point of view, either possibility seemed easily in reach. 'We handed it to the record company on a plate,' reflects Ashton. 'We couldn't have gotten more pop if we tried.'

In Britain, where CBS first hit the streets with the all but hymnal 'Heaven', two months before the main attraction, the answer to that question was more or less academic. Both single and album peaked at best-yet highs, but neither did as

Music press advert for *Mirror Moves*

well as they could have. Reflecting on the UK chart in the weeks when 'Heaven' was gnawing the low end of the Top 30, all the handicaps of their homeland came home to haunt the Psychedelic Furs.

Ashton remembers, '"Heaven" wasn't at all well received in England… well, not well received as far as Radio One plays goes. There were other songs getting played much more – it was grim rock, the Cure ("Caterpillar") were way up there, U2 were doing better than us in England.' He could have added efforts from the Thompson Twins and Howard Jones, comics Alexei Sayle and Mel Brooks, the resuscitated Slade and

Les Mills

Richard and Tim Pope on the set of the Heaven video shoot, London 1984

a resurgent Special AKA. There was no shortage of either novelty or variety. But, even with a rare UK TV appearance on Peter Powell's *Oxford Road Show* to bolster its appeal: 'Heaven' was not to be part of it.

Again, the band had no alternative but to believe 'Our main strength was in the US. Even if we weren't charting, our tours were going well.' There, the word on the band was finally out. The years of hard graft were over. The corporate machine was taking over, and everybody wanted to get in on the act. Even if they didn't know what they were talking about.

The Psychedelic Furs noticed that change from the outset. John Ashton recalls a promotions man, John Fagot, 'a guy from Texas, who spent two weeks strutting up and down trying to pick the first single. He simply couldn't figure out what it

should be.' Both Howard Thompson and the band had made their own recommendation, but still every conversation took the same twisted course. The band would
ask if Fagot had decided yet, he'd ask them what their first choice was. Every time,
the group's reply was the same: it had to be 'Heaven'. They got 'Here Come
Cowboys'. 'So there you go,' shrugs Ashton.

'The label had always been pretty good,' Richard agrees, 'besides making a lot of
mistakes in choosing singles. We bowed to their will. We thought, "They're a record
company, they probably know better than we do about it." But releasing 'Here
Come Cowboys' was a big mistake – and one that was about to become even bigger.

The group had already shot a video for 'Heaven', returning to the pastures
tilled by 'Love My Way' and drawing Tim Pope back into the fold. His vision for
the new song was a delight, even if it was a bugger to execute. Taking over the old
London Transport bus garage in Willesden, north London, he filmed the band performing the song, while technicians dumped gallons of water on their heads. But,
of course, filming is never that simple.

The shoot lasted all day, with the band being brought back for take after take,
usually just a few minutes after they'd finally got dried and warm again. Then it was
time to squeeze back into the still-cold, sodden clothes they'd just climbed out of,
back into the increasingly glassy expressions of happiness which had felt so natural
at the dawn of the day, and back into the icy spray that gave the video its so-mem-
orable hook. The end result looked spectacular and, almost two decades later,
Richard Butler confirmed that 'Heaven' remains his favourite of all the Psychedelic
Furs' videos. It's also the only one that sent him down with a stinking cold.

Pope was commissioned to shoot a video for 'Here Come Cowboys', too. But this
one would wind up back on the shelf almost before it was out of the editing room.
Inspired by the song's title, Pope opted to film in the American South, emerging
with an impressively choreographed ménage of rodeo riders, evangelical preachers
and, because they happened to be there at the time, the Ku Klux Klan. The images
themselves were magnificent, but the implications were somewhat less than complimentary, at least so far as the preachers were concerned. They sought – and were
granted – a court injunction; the video was canned and the single, naturally, followed it. Strike one, as the Americans would say.

Unaffected by these scars on 45, Mirror Moves followed in May, a high gloss,
high production set which simply bowled you over the first time you heard it, and
demanded at least a dozen listens before the sonic shock wore off. Politely, you can
call it a child of its time. Impolitely, it's a bastard to listen to if you didn't like the
Eighties.

Tim Butler: 'Mirror Moves, I think, is the only album out of all ours that you
could actually put a recording time on, as being recorded in the Eighties. The other
albums sound like they could be recorded now, but with that one, you can hear it
and say, "production technique, mid-1980s" It still sounds like a good album, but

you can pigeonhole it in time. It was definitely radio-friendly.'

Radio, however, did not take the lure. The mainstream American step-forward which the band had spent so long teetering on the brink of, remained tantalizingly out of reach. With 'Here Come Cowboys' having slumped into the dumper, and the follow-up 'The Ghost In You' barely bothering the Top 60, *Mirror Moves* stumbled to #43 in the US. And there was no doubt in anybody's mind why it had all gone so wrong. 'The record company cocked it up,' condemns Ashton. 'I remember at the very end of the tour, one of the guys from the label coming up and going, "We fucked up".' Strike Two.

Les Mills though has 'a more sinister explanation for the records' failure at commercial radio.

'Ray Anderson was the overall head of promotion at Columbia. I remember having a meeting with Anderson and saying the single had to be 'Heaven'. To which he replied "What's the matter, has Richard got religion". I had taken this comment to be a further example of American literalism but a couple of years later I found out that Anderson had been indicted for his role in a wider payola scandal.'

Though Anderson got off after the Judge dismissed the case with prejudice due to 'outrageous government misconduct' as fully documented in Fredric Dannen's expose of record company payola, *Hit Men*, he was not cleared of the charges that he had been taking kick-backs from an independent record promoter named Joey Isgro on behalf of bands on the label to promote their records over other more deserving contenders.

'We had been one of the unwitting victims of this activity, that was apparently rife within the industry at the time,' says Mills. 'As nobody in the Furs' camp was

André Huckvale collection

paying independent promoters. The band were platinum in Canada but were not getting US airplay... *Mirror Moves*, should have been massive in the US, but the band didn't get a big US hit – perhaps due to my naivety in not getting independent promotion.'

The Furs' tribulations contrasted highly with the success of Billy Idol, whose Keith Forsey-produced glossy post-punk records made him a huge star in the US, and whose records were independently promoted by Ray Anderson's fellow indictee, Joey Isgro!

Opening in the UK in May, 1984, a nine-month world tour stretched into the New Year, with shows as far afield as

Cover of Furs' 84 tour programme

Australia and, for the first time, Japan.

The early shows were tentative and unpredictable. *Sounds*' Dave Massey was waiting in Chippenham and went home very impressed – 'the Psychedelic Furs are here in the forever now and I know damn well I'm going to see them again on this tour. I haven't felt that way about a band for a long time.'

But the ever-loyal *Zig Zag* caught the final night in Britain, a sold-out performance at the old Hammersmith Odeon and seemed to wish it hadn't. Dave Thomas groaned, 'Imitations of Christ? Or the real thing? Pretty in black, [Butler] emerges dressed for a funeral… swirling dry ice, a modern day Jack The Ripper come to mutilate those that we love – "India", "President Gas", "Sister Europe", "Love My Way"… and then, crouching on the drum riser, he conducts the audience through [a] tiresome little clap-along and the spell is broken. Beneath that ghoulish exterior there beats a heart of gold.'

The view from the centre of the stalls did little to disprove that assumption. In the almost-two years since the Psychedelic Furs last played in Britain, they had undergone an absolute transformation. Gone were the wired and weirdly worldly mavericks who still seemed forever torn between playing a set full of hits and bits, or simply thrashing the odds till the plugs were pulled; in their stead, the band was sharp, tight, choreographed, even. Oh yeah, and anonymous.

Only three faces were instantly recognizable, the basic core of Ashton and the Butlers. In the shadows, Mars Williams and Ed Buller offered a vague taste of continuity; second guitarist Mike Mooney was only familiar for filling a similar role with Echo & The Bunnymen; the group itself had only met drummer Paul Garisto on the eve of the first rehearsal. Tommy Price had been the Psychedelic Furs' first choice, especially when they heard that he'd just quit

André Huckvale collection

FRIARS MAXWELL HALL AYLESBURY

SAT. 12th MAY

THE PSYCHEDELIC FURS

with guests PASSION [P|P] PUPPETS

Tickets 4·00 From Earth Records Aylesbury Record City Luton
F.L. Moore Dunst · B&A Bletchley · Hi vu Buck · Bogarts Oxford &
Bicester · Happy Days Banbury · Strings 'n Things Amersham
Old Town Reds Hemel · Scorpion H.Wyc. · Virgin Milton Keynes
Buzzard L. Buzz or at door If Available
Minimum Age For Admission 16 · Life membership 25p

Billy Idol's band. By the time they were able to contact him, though, he was back behind the Peroxide Sneer, so they took Garristo after Keith Forsey had preferred him to the other drummers that had auditioned to backing tapes.

The set was tight, slick and unsurprising. But, even as onlookers chafed at the Psychedelic Furs' sonic ascension to a glossy new plateau from which they might never again descend to vacuum the carpet, evidence that a degree of rebellious mockery remained in their souls was served up by the evening's support act.

Video director Tim Pope had recently cut his first single, a Robert Smith-fired (and fried) piece of whimsy called 'I Want To Be A Tree'. The video had already been screened on the *Old Grey Whistle Test*; when the Psychedelic Furs invited him to play a short set during the interval at Hammersmith Odeon, he leaped into the fray. Convening a ten-piece band for the occasion, but pointedly refusing to rehearse them, Pope slammed out a four song set at unnatural volume. 'It turned into a fucking riot, and then I retired,' Pope reflected. 'But my annual royalties pay for a curry, so what else do you want?'[18]

Pope was not the only special guest at the show. Duran Duran were in the audience that night, reappearing backstage to buttonhole Williams. Oddly, he didn't recognise them. 'I think it was Simon le Bon and John Taylor. They said they'd come to check me out and were blown away, and we had a good time, we hung out afterwards. But I didn't know who John Taylor was. He's back there and he's saying, "You were really great, we really enjoyed the show," and I'm like, "Yeah, cool." And he says, "Well, maybe you could do something with us," and I said, "Yeah, if you can afford me," or something like that. And he's like, "Really?" Then, we hung out for a while, and after he'd gone, I said, "Hey, who was that guy?" And someone comes back, "Oh, that was John Taylor from Duran Duran."

Duran Duran did, in fact, offer him a place in the band and Williams admits, 'I was kind of in flux between going with Duran Duran or staying with the Furs. And around the same time, I was asked to do Tina Turner, so things were really happening. But in the end, I said "No, I want to do the Furs." With the Furs, I was a part of the project, I was contributing something to that band. Tina Turner, I'd do a couple of stupid little sax solos, I'd be way up in a spot in the corner. And that's not what it was about for me.'

Having shaken off the cobwebs in Britain, the show quickly began improving once the band moved onto the continent – early evidence of that was delivered by bootlegs of a Milan, Italy, radio broadcast in June. There, the suave élan of 'Here Comes Cowboys' becomes sinuous and seductive, the thumping rhythm and agitated guitars transforming the lyric from a casual observation to a statement of intent. There too, 'Sister Europe' is transformed, a slow funk growl crawling across the floor, sinister, sexy and sad. Indeed, by the time they reached the US, the group was playing some of the tightest shows of their careers. It was only natural, therefore, that they'd also be facing some of the biggest audiences.

Although American album sales were stubbornly refusing to go much higher than *Forever Now* (*Mirror Moves*, too, would eventually be certified gold), the accompanying tour saw the Psychedelic Furs' stature climb to another level entirely. Initially supported by the appropriately-named Talk Talk, themselves Top 40-bound with the mini-anthem 'It's My Life', the Psychedelic Furs kicked off on 18th July at Boston's 3,000 capacity Orpheum, then slowly wound their way towards California for a Greek Theatre co-headliner with Sparks – decade old British hit-makers whom the UK had forgotten, now enjoying renewed favour in the homeland that once scorned them. On paper, it was an unusual pairing. On the night, it was one of those shows that the Eighties were made for.

A short haul through Canada took the band out of September, with record sales there pushing *Mirror Moves* to platinum status; then it was back into the US to wind up, triumphant, at New York's Radio City Music Hall. Then they could begin it all again in another country.

The Psychedelic Furs finally came off the road in early 1985. The group's living arrangements had not changed. Ashton retired home to Tonbridge, the Butlers retreated back to New York, and the five months which could elapse before they needed start thinking about their next album stretched ahead like a welcome eternity – and then raced past in the blink of an eye. But, as Richard Butler allowed his thoughts to turn towards that next record, he was shocked to discover that the thoughts would not come.

'You hear about people getting writer's block, and you think, come on, I only write lyrics. It's not like I was writing a novel. But I did, I just kind of dried up for ideas for a while.' He forced himself to persevere and, with the benefit of hindsight, he stills hear the gears grinding dryly together when he thinks of the songs he would finally wring out. 'I think it really shows on the record...I think it's the worst album we ever made.'

Ashton, too, was suffering from the fall-out of the recent adventure, both at home on his own and on the occasions when he and Butler met up to write. 'It really was a very difficult time. We spent a lot of time together, but we weren't really working together. Whatever I came up with was too rock, whatever Richard came up with was too much of a rewrite of past stuff, and never the twain shall meet. That writer's block, it works both ways. I wasn't coming up with what he wanted to hear and, certainly, he wasn't coming up with what I wanted to hear either.'

The main problem, both men knew, but which neither had formulated sufficiently to voice, was that they didn't have a sound anymore. Or, rather, they no longer knew what sound they wanted. Ashton continues, 'U2 had just come out with *The Unforgettable Fire*, and we had kind of... we should have able to do whatever we wanted to do, and what we really wanted to do was, all get into a room and start playing. Because that's when the magic would happen. Except it wasn't happening.'

The reference to U2 was no idle comparison. For five years, the two groups had been running neck and neck, not only in chronological terms, but also creatively, matching one another step for step – they were even labelmates in Ireland, where U2's material was handled by CBS. For much of that time, the Psychedelic Furs had managed to stay just about a neck ahead: first to sign a record deal, first to release an album, first to work with Steve Lillywhite, first to visit and impact on America.

U2, however, had always made up the ground and then upped the ante. The Psychedelic Furs cut two albums with Lillywhite, U2 cut three. The Furs' first album made the American Top 140, U2's debut *Boy* went to #63. 'Love My Way' soared to #44, U2's 'Pride' had just peaked at #33. And no matter how high people's eyebrows soared when the Psychedelic Furs recorded *Forever Now* with Todd Rundgren, they shot even higher when U2 harnessed Eno for *The Unforgettable Fire*.

Released in October 1984, just as the Psychedelic Furs were wrapping up their American dates, the ensuing *The Unforgettable Fire* was suddenly all that anyone seemed to be listening to, blaring from even the most loyal college radio station, flickering from MTV. Now U2 were out on a tour of their own, hitting many of the same venues as the Psychedelic Furs had just played, but shifting tickets just a little bit faster. At Radio City Music Hall in mid-November, the "sold out" stickers were already up for U2, and they weren't due in for another two weeks. Now it was the Psychedelic Furs who were having to play catch-up. And, every day that passed without a fresh idea was another couple of miles they'd have to run.

Adding to their woes was Howard Thompson's departure for Elektra Records in mid-1984, where he would nurture the Sisters Of Mercy with the same care and decisiveness as he'd once lavished on the Psychedelic Furs. Alongside Peter Philbin, his hand on the rudder had always proven a steadying, even reassuring, influence. Left to their own devices, there was no guarantee the Psychedelic Furs would ever negotiate their latest roadblock.

The very last thing they'd wanted to hear, then, was that Columbia bigwig at the end of the tour, saying sorry for not turning the band into superstars. 'We fucked up.' Strike three and you're out.

WE PAID FOR THE CROSS AND THE NAILS

OF ALL KURT WEILL AND BERTOLT BRECHT'S contributions to the purposefully lowbrow people's operas of pre-war German cabaret, and those that habitually spun on the teenaged Richard Butler's hi-fi, few shared the immediate impact and subsequent imagery of *(Rise And Fall Of The City Of) Mahagonny*.

Threepenny Opera might be more instantly recognisable – who cannot sing along with 'Mac The Knife'? *Happy End* might be more notorious – who does not thrill to the image of Brecht's own wife appearing onstage to quote the Communist Manifesto in the Nazi stronghold of Berlin? But *Mahagonny*, the last of the duo's major collaborations, not only combines the musicality of one with the drama of the other, it also illustrates the sheer brutality of the then-incoming Nazi regime and the bully-boy petulance of its rank-and-file supporters.

Premiered in Leipzig in 1930, just a year after violent rioting had forced *Happy End* to an ignominious close, *Mahagonny* was targeted for disruption from the moment it was announced. Without even stopping to discover whether this latest offering actually contained anything of similar subversion, but assuming that a Jewish composer and a Marxist lyricist were scarcely likely to offer anything else, Hitler's henchmen descended upon the theatre *en masse*, buying out entire blocks of seats and barracking the performance with whistles, shouts, klaxons and stink bombs.

Mahagonny folded within the week. Scheduled performances throughout Germany were cancelled as nervous theatre-owners reacted to the threats of their own local Nazi cadres. Within three years, Weill's entire catalogue of works had been banned from the German stage. The composer himself fled his homeland, first for France, then America.

There, he was feted as a superstar; wrote four major Broadway hits, and ultimately was elected to that same realm of rock'n'roll mythos that only a handful of other non-rock iconoclasts – Jacques Brel, James Dean and Aleister Crowley among them – had ever attained. The Eighties, in particular, cherished him – the Psychedelic Furs made their own contribution to the legend with 'Mac The Knife'; David Bowie walked those same corridors with his own adaptation of Weill and Brecht's *Baal*; Bunny-boss Ian McCulloch snatched 'September Song' from the Broadway behemoth *Knickerbocker Glory*.

Mahagonny, however, rose above them all with one song whose rock pedigree needed no introduction. The Doors recorded 'Alabama Song' in 1967; David Bowie, once again, reinvented it in 1978. Now, 1986 was to bring a third major reconstruction as keyboard player Ralph Schuckett combined with Richard Butler to restore the song to its pre-rock sensibilities, even as they upped the volume on its portent and foreboding.

A founding member of Todd Rundgren's Utopia (he first worked with Runt on the legendary *A Wizard A True Star* album), Schuckett based his arrangement upon one of the earliest American recordings of the song, from 1929. Laconic and ponderous, sparse and spookily theatrical, it employs three lead vocals: Butler supplying the verses, Schuckett's wife Ellen Shipley contributing harmonies and echoes and Bob Dorough adding the choruses.

But nine other singers filter through chorale and effects, creating an unearthly backdrop to the performance. If Butler himself would later compare his own performance to David Bowie's earlier model, that was the only conceivable comparison, with Bowie, with the Doors, with any rock version. Nevertheless, Butler insisted, 'I was pleased to do "Alabama Song" because a lot of people have said my voice is like… Bowie's. They've only got to put that version of the song next to his to see how much we do sound alike.'[19]

'Alabama Song' was recorded for inclusion on the 1986 album *Lost In The Stars*, producer Hal Willner's all-star tribute to Weill; Butler was joined by an almost lunatic gathering of artists drawn from almost every conceivable modern musical discipline, with absolutely unpredictable results: former Policeman Sting linked with Dominic Muldowney, the arranger whose own vivid eye for musical detail had completely transfigured Bowie's *Baal*, and turned in a superbly sleaze-drenched 'Mac The Knife.'

There was a pulsing, electro-whipped appearance from Rundgren and former Fur auxiliary Gary Windo; Lou Reed followed in Ian McCulloch's footsteps for a breezily stylised 'September Song'; chanteuse Marianne Faithfull teamed with rocker Chris Spedding for 'Ballad Of The Soldier's Wife'. 'I'd quite like to do a duet with Marianne Faithfull,' Butler mused in that same *Sounds* interview. 'I think our voices would sound great together.' Indeed, as he reflected on the project in other period interviews, Butler sounded as enthused and bedazzled by plans and possibilities, as he ever had in the past. Only when he returned to the band did harsh reality come steaming in once again.

The new Psychedelic Furs album was deadlocked and growing deader. Tim Butler: 'One of the most destructive things that happened to the band was Richard and I moving [to America], and John being [in Britain]. That definitely slowed things down, and it [created] a bit of a gulf between where our heads were coming from. Starting with *Mirror Moves*, we'd sort of painted ourselves into a musical corner, and it was very hard to break out of it.'

Desperately searching for some kind of kick-start, the band booked themselves into a studio, intending simply to jam. When that didn't work, they grew even more desperate and booked themselves a farmhouse. Mars Williamson and Paul Garisto, retained from the live band as Furs for the duration, simply tagged along whenever they were asked. And the bills started mounting up. 'For me, it was fine,' Williams admits, 'because I was getting paid a salary. So, if they wanted to go to a studio in England and try to write.... Or they'd rent a farm that had a recording studio, and have people cooking for us....'

'And without us realizing it,' Ashton acknowledged, 'that and a bunch of other things really drained our resources, and we ended up being really in the hole. The whole machine had become a bit of a dinosaur and, every time we wanted to resurrect that dinosaur, it cost a lot of money. You had to justify it, the clock was ticking, and it wasn't as carefree and simple as it had been before. But nonetheless, we really didn't care, we just sat around watching videos, hanging out, and trying to figure out what to do.'

What they needed to do, of course, was stop hiring musicians on a pay-to-play basis, stop trying to second-guess everyone else's expectations of them, and simply get back to being a full band again. No matter how loyal a sideman a session player is, he's still a session player, performing what he's asked to perform and happy to wait it out when he wasn't.

Williams himself admits he was horrified by the waste, but he went along with it anyway, at the same time as keeping several other options open. Back in contact with the Duran Duran contingent, he was briefly involved with the Power Station spin-off, completing their album but departing before the leviathan took the road. From there, he hooked up with fellow faux Fur Mike Mooney and Pete DeFreitas, Echo & the Bunnymen's newly-estranged drummer, in the Sex Gods, an ecstasy-addled outfit whose legend, best told in Julian Cope's *Repossessed* autobiography, is now far greater than the band's own renown ever was.

Mooney would not rejoin the Psychedelic Furs. Returning to his Liverpudlian roots, he next surfaced in Julian Cope's live band, touring Japan and, in Cope's own words, '[returning] to this magical place which had so adored him with... the Psychedelic Furs.' Today, he can be found with Lupine Howl. Williams, however, drifted back to the Psychedelic Furs whenever the occasion demanded and, by early 1986, he was shocked to discover the band readying itself for a return to the studio – shocked, because nobody, the band members included, believed they had anywhere near enough material to work with.

Richard: 'We should have taken a break at that point, instead of forcing ourselves to put out an album, because we still had no direction, we were just floundering. Les [Mills] was saying, "Ah, you gotta put out a record" – not the record company, our manager. So we spent ages in these bloody ridiculously expensive studios in Zurich and not enough time down the pub writing songs.'

'It is all very well for Richard to say that the band should have been down the pub writing songs,' Mills counters adamantly. 'There are a number of reasons why this would not have been very practicable: For one, they had already had over a year to work on songs and it was apparent, that without a deadline at least, new material would not be forthcoming. For two, the band had never written songs in the pub – especially as the pub was now more than three thousand miles away and Richard wasn't drinking anyway. For three, the ridiculous overheads we were now incurring to maintain the luxury of a stable of premier hired musicians and luxury residential studio's had overextended the band financially. In fact I had to take out a second mortgage on my flat in London to keep the whole edifice afloat.'

Booking into the Swiss city's Powerplay studios, the sessions were to be overseen by Daniel Lanois, Brian Eno's co-conspirator on U2's *The Unforgettable Fire* and, to many observers, the more powerful of the pair – indeed, when the group first contacted Eno, he told them outright, 'I don't want to produce right now, but there's this sort of whippersnapper here [meaning Lanois] who'd love to do it.'

Mills remembers things differently, maintaining that he 'had been keen to work with Lanois after hearing his collaboration with Brian Eno on *The Pearl*.'

Though not a Furs fan as such, the Canadian Lanois was enthused by his friends at home where the band were now huge.

'After further research I was convinced that he could tease out whatever ideas already existed from the various rehearsals and demo's we had already undertaken,' says Mills. 'After meeting him and seeing him work with the band at Barwell Court, a residential rehearsal studio in Surrey. I knew that he had the potential to deliver a great album. Daniel was at this time still in the studio with Peter Gabriel mixing 'So' at Gabriel's Real World Studio outside of Bath. However Gabriel did not work at weekends so I had arranged with Lanois for him to work with the band on these days off. The idea was that the band would work on their ideas all week and that Danny would come down and spend a few days licking them into shape. Every Friday afternoon I would pick up Daniel from Paddington station and drive him down to Barwell Court. Then on Sunday afternoon I would drive him back to the station again. I got to know him quite well on our trips back and forth and the more I got to know him the more convinced I became that he was the right man for the job.'

Indeed, hindsight screams that the French-Canadian wasn't simply the perfect choice for the Psychedelic Furs, he should have been the only choice. Exquisitely skilled at drawing texture and mood out of the most unpromising material, capable of transforming the ugliest rocker into a thing of beauty, and not averse to condemning music altogether to second place behind an atmosphere, if anybody was capable of making a silk purse from the self-confessed pig's ear of half-formed ideas and notions which the group presented him with, it was Lanois.

'Unfortunately we hadn't taken account of the lack of motivation from Richard, Tim and to a lesser extent John, says Mills. 'The band was not willing to give him a chance.'

'Lack of inspiration,' insists Richard, 'not motivation.' Asked if they themselves had an overall vision for the album, the Psychedelic Furs admitted only that they knew what they didn't want. Richard Butler: 'We were wilfully wanting to change things as we went along. When it came to [those sessions], it seemed *Mirror Moves* had simply been an extension of *Forever Now*, it was "let's make a real pop record." Now we wanted to get away from that. But we didn't know where that was.'

How did they want it to sound, then? Again, all they could tell him was how they didn't want it to sound – with *Mirror Moves* now at the top of the list. 'I don't think the production there did John justice,' Butler condemned. 'All that weird chording… he doesn't play like anyone else I've ever heard. I listen to *Mirror Moves* and I like it a lot. But it's not the way I'd like to hear the Furs presented. I'd like to make the ideal album that we could make, and our personalities didn't come through very clearly on that record. I miss the edge of the earlier records. It was as near to a commercial record as we'll ever make.' So, not so commercial, not so compromised – and poor Lanois was at the end of his tether, like a barber waiting for a customer to tell him how to cut his hair. 'Not too long, not too short, and I don't know if I need something for the weekend either.'

'Things got off to a poor start at the first meeting,' sighs Mills. Some band members simply didn't hit it off with Lanois and there were some childish jibes which created an immediate division between band and producer. 'Worse still,' continues Les, 'was the fact that Daniel was there to work. He would go into the rehearsal room after dinner and pick up an instrument and start jamming with whoever was there. This would usually be Paul, Ed or John. Daniel wanted to work and Richard wanted to do anything but… Mostly Richard would be hanging out in the pool room with Tim and Mars or watching movies on TV or listening to his current fave raves. In fact Richard was doing everything he could to mask that fact that he didn't have any ideas for either musically or lyrically. Ed confirmed my positive impression of Lanois but unfortunately the rest of the band could not see it.'

On one occasion when Richard was voicing his doubts, Les had to resort to calling Paul McGuinness, U2's manager, and asking him to have Bono call Richard to reassure him as to Daniel's abilities. This Bono duly did and so things limped along for a few more weeks, including a couple of days recording at Air Studio one, during which period they at least worked up a couple of songs. Finally exasperated, however, it all became too much for Lanois to handle.

'You need more time before you go into the studio,' he told the band. The Psychedelic Furs disagreed. Shuddering, Butler continues, 'We were, "Nah, bollocks. We've written the other ones when we're in the studio," so he said, "Well, I don't like working that way…"'

'He wrote me a lovely note,' Mills recalls, 'saying "I would really love to work with the band but unfortunately I believe that Richard is a 'tin pot dictator' who is intent on undermining the project". Sadly I have to concur with that assessment.'

The warning bells should have gone off there and then. Hadn't Todd Rundgren also told the band they had to finish the songs before entering the recording studio? And hadn't they knuckled down under his mandate and created *Forever Now*? Yes and yes. But times had changed, tempers were fraying, the band just wanted to get the album – any album – out of the way.

'We did the previous album with Keith Forsey – we went in with just ideas and wrote songs like "Heaven" and "High Wire Days" in the studio,' says Richard. 'Danny said to us "You don't have enough songs to go in the studio. I want to put the album back." Well, we didn't want to put it back. We wanted to get on with it. We said we'd go in the studio and work with someone else and that it would come together in the studio.

'This was foolish as we got in the studio and we were fairly bereft of ideas. Unlike *Mirror Moves*, good ideas did not come quickly.'

'[Daniel] was right, God bless him,' Richard now readily admits. 'Plus, it would have been a really interesting collaboration. And it would have been good for us.'

Les Mills goes much further: 'I believe that the failure to make the album that would subsequently become *Midnight To Midnight* with Daniel Lanois was the beginning of the end for the band. We just didn't know it at the time.

'There were two critical reasons the Furs never made it into the premier league and that was: one, payola; two, the fact that they alienated Daniel Lanois so much that he walked away from a project that he had his heart set on....

'When I heard U2's [Lanois-produced] 'With or Without You', I felt sick, I almost wept, because that could have been us ...'

From the potentially superlative to the somewhat ridiculous: while the Psychedelic Furs were trying to put their future in order, Hollywood was becoming acquainted with their past. For almost five years, teen theme actress Molly Ringwald had been carrying a torch for 'Pretty In Pink', convinced – like so many of the people who heard it and learned (almost) all the words – that there was a lot more going on in the song than ever met the ear.

She was in a position, however, to maybe winkle out some extra details or, at least, to posit some possible outcomes. Talking with director John Hughes, with whom she worked on 1985's *The Breakfast Club*, she brought up the song and the premise she'd deduced, and suggested he write an entire movie around it. Hughes, as intrigued by the song as the story's leading lady (for, of course, Ringwald would be the eventual film's star), agreed.

Of course, the movie that he ended up with, the kind of story that Ringwald herself originally envisioned, and the song that set the whole ball rolling share only the vaguest of common features: the film's lead character doesn't even have the same name (Caroline) as the original song's protagonist, while the plot unearthed themes of suburban adolescence and class distinction that the lyric surely never hinted at. Nevertheless, the deal was done, the movie was made and a suitable soundtrack was being assembled from the cream of the year's college rock superstars.

It was a proven format. Assembled by Keith Forsey shortly after he completed *Mirror Moves*, *The Breakfast Club* soundtrack had made American superstars of two quite unlikely oddballs – the doughboy denizens of Simple Minds, and the arty syn-thipop of Huang Chung (Wang Chung as they were now tagged to circumvent possible phonetic mishap). The queue around the block for this new one was extraordinary, but slowly it came together... the Smiths, OMD, Echo & The Bunnymen, New Order, INXS – and the Psychedelic Furs? Maybe.

'I only found out about the film when I was flicking through a copy of *Rolling Stone*,' Richard Butler told writer Ro Newton. 'We were quite flattered, to say the least.' There was one tiny little problem, you see. 'Could the band possibly re-record the song? The original is quite unsuitable.'

Tim Butler: 'The reason they gave was, on the original, the guitar was slightly out of tune, which completely eludes me. Maybe that was just the excuse. I've lis-tened to that track and I can't hear it myself. Maybe they wanted to clean it up a bit sonically for the movie. If they'd said that, "sonically, it's just not usable for a soundtrack," it would've been fine. But they went all round about it. They should've just said the original recording sucked! So, we went back into the studio and spent two weeks on one track.'

Co-produced by the band and Fabulous Thunderbirds engineer Charles Harrowell, the end result more than satisfied the movie moguls. But the Psychedelic Furs themselves are in full agreement with the fans who still murmur that the glossy re-recording of 'Pretty In Pink' thoroughly diluted the purity of the original. Tim Butler: 'The original has more aggression, it just sounds free-er. The second one sounds sterile, which is probably to do with the production. I guess the more into the '80s it got, the more polished the production became. If people want to go back and listen to the original, most would prefer that. But the only control we had was to say we'll go in and re-record it, and not someone else.'

Ashton was a little less dismissive. 'At the time, we thought, "Let's remake it, let's do the best we can." We got to be creative with it, and tried to be as 'on' about the whole project as possible. It was fun, we just did it. Hey, we were in the movies, we were pop stars.'

Elsewhere, of course, the clock was still ticking. Through the remainder of 1985, the band continued working up new ideas, even taking to the road early in the New Year for a ten-day tour around Spain and Italy, easing further rough notions into readiness. And finally, it was time. 'By the end,' says John Ashton, 'we had some really good raw material, [including] a lot of stuff that never saw the light of day.'

Shrugging off the notions that Daniel Lanois' recruitment had suggested, the Psychedelic Furs now approached Chris Kimsey, a veteran Englishman who started his career as an intern at London's Olympic Studios in the late 1960s, engineering and co-producing the likes of Ten Years After, Spooky Tooth and Mott The Hoople. Into the 1970s, he helmed Peter Frampton's multi-million-selling *Frampton Comes Alive*; through the early 1980s, he was the Rolling Stones' producer of choice.

The Cult's 1984 *Dreamtime* was a dramatic Kimsey production; so was Killing

Joke's *Night Time* the following year – indeed, Richard Butler later admitted it was the Killing Joke album that most recommended Kimsey to the band: 'We liked the sound of it, a good solid band feel that we wanted to get back to.'

According to Les Mills, Kimsey was something of a rushed choice. The record company were on their back and the band had to find a replacement for Lanois quickly in order to keep the record label's commitment.

'When Chris came to meet the band,' says Mills, 'he parked his huge red Ferrari outside. The thing that worried me was that the band were more impressed by Kimsey's Ferrari than his production credits…'

Nonetheless, Kimsey brought a well-tuned ear for a classic commercial sound to the party, and that, too, suited Richard Butler to a tee. Discussing his mid-1980s record-buying habits, he simply shrugged. 'I've been reduced to going back and buying things the second time around – Suicide, the Velvet Underground, even Led Zeppelin.'[20] Kimsey was an assistant engineer at the sessions for *Led Zeppelin I*. Cry havoc and let slip the Black Dogs of war. 'For us, this is our most normal rock-'n'roll record,' says Tim Butler. 'It's a guitar-orientated classic rock sound.'

Still struggling to find a sound and direction, without any firmly-held convictions of their own, the Psychedelic Furs were happy to allow the producer to take control, as Tim Butler also acknowledges. 'The problem was, we went in with so few song ideas. I do think Chris Kimsey had more of an influence than we did.'

So did what they all acknowledged was their primary target audience. The United States had informed Butler's lyrics since the band's very first glimpse of the place – who was 'President Gas', if not Ronald Reagan? But this time, that information provided far more than a mere launchpad for inspiration. Even the latest song titles, at least in their original form, dwelt on some kind of American preoccupation – 'Midnight To Midnight' was originally titled 'Drive In', 'One More Word' began life as 'Stars And Stripes'.

Only the choice of studio seemed likely to deflect the band from its manifest destiny. Eschewing the joys of American facilities, the Psychedelic Furs arrived in what was then West Berlin on April 5 1986, to take up residence at Hansa-by-the-Wall. David Bowie recorded the landmark *'Heroes'* there in 1977 – it was from one of the studio's windows that he saw the lovers whose embrace inspired the album's title track. Since that time, Hansa – indeed, the divided city of Berlin itself – had become a virtual byword for the moody sounds and atmospheric stylings that that album so unselfconsciously oozed. But any thoughts the Psychedelic Furs entertained of absorbing that atmosphere into their own new record were swiftly to be curtailed.

The band was still unpacking when news came through that the city's American Discotheque had been devastated by a terrorist bomb. A nervous tremble of apprehension rippled through Berlin's bustling nightlife. Three weeks later, that apprehension turned into total panic as word spread through the West about the disaster at Chernobyl. Radiation the equivalent of 30 Hiroshima bombs spewed into the atmosphere from the crippled Soviet nuclear reactor, and Berlin was directly in the line of fire.

The Psychedelic Furs' world constricted overnight – from hotel to studio and back again. Suddenly, it wasn't even safe to go out. Nobody really knew precisely what could happen, so they adopted a worst-case scenario. Nightly on the news, daily in the press, the authorities cautioned anybody who had to leave their house to make sure they took a shower the moment they returned home to wash away the poisonous dust. You couldn't buy food from open-air vendors, or fruit from markets and grocery shops. You shouldn't scratch your arm, then rub your eye… in fact, you shouldn't even scratch your arm in case particles entered your bloodstream through a scrape. It was like being back at school – except the playground was out of bounds.

It wasn't all bad news, of course. Just one week after the group started work in the studio, the re-recorded 'Pretty In Pink' edged into both the American and British charts, on its way to becoming their biggest hit yet. While the movie was a monster, and the soundtrack, following suit, became an absolute giant, 'Pretty In Pink 86' was positively epidemic and if its sudden elevation was a surprise to the band's British fans, who still liked to think of the Psychedelic Furs as their own little cult, past members of the group were taken utterly by surprise.

Duncan Kilburn only learned of the new life for the song in which he'd played such a major role when he read about it in the newspaper, 'on the 7.42 from Norbiton to Waterloo, in my *Guardian* if I recall. It was just a small piece about

Richard Butler and Mars Williams on stage at the Mean Fiddler, Harlesden, 1987.

André Huckvale

Molly Ringwold appearing in John Hughes latest movie, *Pretty in Pink*. I was pretty
incensed, as I assumed that he nicked it, so when I got to work (I think I was at the
Stock Exchange at the time), I called the record company and of course they say
"hasn't anyone told you ....." Oops.' Even more gallingly, though Kilburn was in
New York on a business trip when the movie opened, he was not even granted tickets for the premier. 'I was given my tickets by a fan!'

Disappointing though this was for Duncan, it is not really surprising. The band
and he were no longer in touch and it is unlikely they would have gone to the trouble of tracking him down in the hope he would be in the US for the premier of
someone else's film.

The single reached #18 in the UK; and, though it ultimately faltered at #41 in
the US, still airplay and MTV conspired to make it appear much bigger. Back in
New York, therefore, Columbia restructured their entire game plan. A new
Psychedelic Furs album had been tentatively scheduled for an autumn, 1986,
release, with a major American tour to follow.

The success of 'Pretty In Pink' turned that particular plan upside-down – the
tour would go ahead, soaking up the plaudits for one of the year's most memorable
hits, but the album could wait until the following spring.

Having completed the album in early summer, the Psychedelic Furs ignited this
latest round of live action with a stunning performance at the Glastonbury Festival
in June, turning in a dynamic set, and introducing a new set of players. Williams
and Garisto, of course, were still on board but, for the first time in five years, Ed
Buller was absent, departing to follow a career curve which, within half a decade,

had established him among the principle architects of Britpop – he produced essential early albums for both Pulp and, most notably, Suede.

In Buller's place came Roger O'Donnell – a former Thompson Twin, no less; with Marty Williamson, from the album sessions, coming in on second guitar, the swing through North America saw the band finally moving onto the amphitheatre circuit – the 20,000 capacity CNE Grandstand in Toronto – part of the Toronto Blue Jays stadium – the even bigger Irvine Meadows in California.

The crowds were rabid. 'I nearly got torn apart,' Richard shuddered afterwards. 'I jumped into the audience and it took the bouncers 20 minutes to tug me out. It was pretty scary. I was being swamped by so many girls… I was black and blue, my jacket was in shreds and my pants were around my knees. I'd do it again, though. It was a gas.'

And everywhere, the audience came kitted out in pink.

T-shirts, pants, hair, and lip-gloss… the view from the stage was of a sea of livid pink, as Tim Butler still bemusedly recalls. 'Everyone came dressed in pink. The words of the actual song went totally above their heads. You'd get people coming to our shows dressed in pink everything, and we helped the sale of pink clothes, worldwide. But, I think if we'd done a video, translated the lyrics, and had it played on MTV, we'd have been run out of town!'

In fact, Wayne Isham's video for the single was little more than a glorified trailer for the film, intercut with shots of the Butlers and Ashton – the newly super-styled Butlers and Ashton, their hair gelled sharp and pointing to the skies, their gestures reaching out to the back to the bleachers.

Of course, the mid-1980s were a time of sartorial absurdity and exaggerated coifs, broad shoulder pads and open-necked shirts, stud-studded cool and black-leathered abandon. And everybody got into it. But, compared to the Psychedelic Furs, the rest of the pack – from the Sisters Of Mercy and Love and Rockets, to Flesh For Lulu and even Billy Idol, the man who invented the look to begin with – had been dressed up for church by their mothers. Oh, how we laughed.

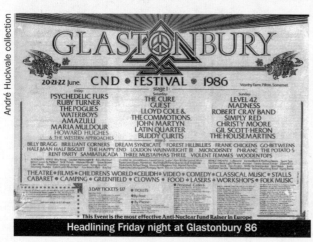

André Huckvale collection

Headlining Friday night at Glastonbury 86

It was a captivating look and an accessible image. Once again, the group was quivering on the edge of a major step forward and, for all its troubled, protracted gestation, *Midnight To Midnight* looked like being the album that ensured they took it.

MIDNIGHT TO MIDNIGHT

RELEASED IN MARCH, 1987, the first single from the now imminent *Midnight To Midnight* was 'Heartbreak Beat' (aka 'Over In A Look'), a well-chosen follow-up to 'Pretty In Pink'; a pounding taster for the main attraction; and a skilful distillation of everything America liked about the band's past work.

The remainder of the album could not help but follow in its footsteps. Around the core trio of the Butlers and Ashton, Williamson and Garisto blurted and pounded in splendidly cavernous style. Second guitarist Marty Williamson added flourishes and riffs to dart between those which Ashton was layering; keyboard player Jon Carin swirled atmosphere into every crevice he could find. It was an impossibly huge sounding record – 'as big as our hair!' Richard later joked – and, initially, its sheer sense of pomp and occasion bowled everybody over, the band most of all. British purchasers were even given another taste of 'Pretty In Pink', a thrusting Chris Kimsey remix that made the recent hit sound like a demo.

But behind the drama, what was there really? Richard admits to liking the album when it was first completed, but would dramatically change his opinion within a few months. Ashton was equally unhappy; only Tim Butler is adamant that he regrets nothing musically. It was the presentation of the record, and the subsequent tour, that left so much to be desired.

Following the album's completion, a period of reflection left the Butlers, at least, convinced that Chris Kimsey's final mix was too muddy. As Richard recalls, 'We specifically said to each other, and we were all pretty much in agreement, that the album had been over-produced.' Ashton, however, still believed that they ought to leave it as it stood; looking back a few months later, his bandmates agreed with him.

By then, however, it was too late. Producing a band called the Toll earlier in the year, Tim Butler had been introduced to Steve Thompson and Mike Barbiero, a pair of remix engineers with their own unique handle on what made a record sparkle. They were handed the tapes and given free rein – polish the drums, shine the guitars, punch up the vocals, iron out the ambiguities. Unfortunately, that wasn't what *Midnight To Midnight* demanded.

Richard Butler continues, '[Thompson and Barbiero] made it sound much too clean, very slick. It wasn't the way Chris Kimsey had mixed it. Wow! I wonder if those mixes still exist? Put the album out again! The Chris Kimsey mixes really were the ones we should've gone out with.'

Just as the album didn't sound like a Furs album, it didn't LOOK like the

André Huckvale collection

OUTLAW IN ASSOCIATION WITH PERFORMANCE
PRESENT

PSYCHEDELIC FURS

MIDNIGHT TO MIDNIGHT

TOUR

FEBRUARY

4 NEWCASTLE CITY HALL
£6.00, £5.50 – 091-261 2606
11 NOTTINGHAM ROYAL CENTRE
£6.00, £5.50 – 0602-472 328
12 BIRMINGHAM ODEON
£6.00, £5.50 – 021-643 6101
13 LIVERPOOL ROYAL COURT
£6.00 – 051-709 4321
15 MANCHESTER APOLLO
£6.00, £5.50 – 061-273 3775
16 BRISTOL COLSTON HALL
£6.00, £5.50 – 0272 291768
17 BRIGHTON CENTRE
£6.00 – 0273 202881
22 POOLE ARTS CENTRE
£6.00, £5.50 – 0202 685 222
23 NEWPORT CENTRE
£6.00, £5.50 – 0633 59676
25 SHEFFIELD CITY HALL
£6.00, £5.50 – 0742 735 295
26 BRADFORD ST GEORGES HALL
£6.00, £5.50 – 0274 752000

TICKETS FOR PREVIOUS SHOWS VALID FOR
NEW DATES

PLUS GUESTS
apple mosaic

Leather jackets and big hair –
Midnight to Midnight on tour

Psychedelic Furs. Art director Nick Egan and fashion photographer Michael Hasbrand had the band preening in big hair and designer leather jackets for the fashion-shoot style cover.

Not that such matters impacted the album in the slightest. While 'Heartbreak Beat' marched to #26 in America (singles from the album were steadfastly ignored in Britain), *Midnight To Midnight* itself broke them into the Top 30 album chart for the first time. A second single, 'Shock', rode MTV all summer; the tour kicked off in San Francisco, with full houses all the way.

And, at the outset of the adventure, confidence was high. 'We believed in *Midnight To Midnight* when it came out,' Richard admits. But, as the tour progressed, something maggoty stirred.

It is hard to say when the first cracks began appearing in the well-oiled machinery, the moment when the first sense of unease caused the members to sit back and take stock of the direction the band and its fortunes had taken. Richard Butler remembers the moment when it cracked, however. 'I woke up one day just hating everything about it. I woke up hating the way I looked on the album cover, thinking, 'God, that looks stupid.' And I hated the idea that people would buy that record and think that was what we were about, and not that it was just a *part* of what the band was about. It seemed like rubbish. I didn't like the whole glamour aspect of it all, I got very depressed. There's nothing like being halfway through a tour and realising you don't like it. I don't like the lighting, I don't like the places we're playing, I don't like this record.'

'Richard was totally into the sound and the look of the record,' says Les Mills. 'It was more his baby than anything he'd ever done. This is why it hit him so hard … When he realised what he'd done he virtually had a breakdown…'

At the height of their success at Merryweather Post Pavilion, a sold out 16,000-capacity show at the height of 'Pretty in Pink'-mania, Mills flew in from London. Straight from the airport he arrived in the dressing room and asked Richard how he was.

'Richard replied, "What the fuck am I doing here? Singing these songs? Wearing these clothes?" …This was the start of the crisis. Beware of what you wish for. Tim had modelled himself on Steve Stevens and Richard on Billy Idol and the *Midnight to Midnight* cover art director Nick Egan had encouraged it and now it was all unravelling.'

Richard is adamant that neither he nor Tim had these role models in mind. Personnel problems added their own weight to the strain. At the outset of the tour, and all the more so once the American shows hove into view, the group slapped a stern 'no drink or drugs' ban on their entire touring party. Of course, it was a notion that was easier said than done but, for the first few shows, it seemed to be holding. And then they were joined on the bill by the Mission. Suddenly, the gloves were off.

In just a few short years, the group – arch gothic rockers born via an acrimonious split within of the Sisters Of Mercy – had acquired a reputation for intoxication that made the Psychedelic Furs look like life-long teetotallers. And, from the moment the newcomers joined the tour, in St Louis on 29th May, it appeared that reputation was well-placed. The Mission's road crew arrived first, having driven non-stop from Las Vegas with only two bags of coke for company. Later

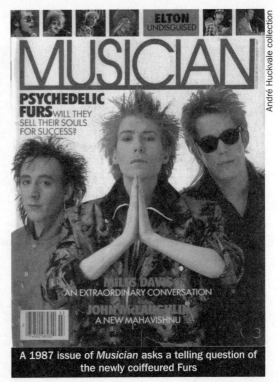

André Huckvale collection

A 1987 issue of *Musician* asks a telling question of the newly coiffeured Furs

into the outing, it was Mission drummer Mick Brown's turn to mortify the headliners as he staggered around their own road crew, hoping one of them would fill in for
him. He knew he was too drunk to actually play the set. At every turn and in every
corner, the Mission's love of the rock'n'roll highlife was on open, vivacious display.

The Mission were only scheduled to be on the tour for three weeks, after which
they were to be replaced by the Call. It was halfway through that stint that the
Psychedelic Furs' resolve finally broke. Mission lore still recalls the evening when,
as they sat backstage sorting through the evening's entertainments, first one member of the Psychedelic Furs' party, then another, crept surreptitiously into the
room, swore all onlookers to secrecy, then did a quick line of coke. By the end of
the evening, most of the band and their crew had imbibed, all secure in the belief
that they alone had been smart enough to break their own prohibition.

The Mission's final shows of the tour, two nights at New York City's Radio City
Music Hall, were their most memorable yet. At the first, they so trashed their dressing room that management outlawed them from ever appearing at the venue again;
when that proved not to be immediately enforceable, the group was simply banned
from spending any more time in the building than their actual performance
required. A special escort was formed to bring them in to the venue just minutes
before show time, then lead them out again the moment their set was over.

With the Mission's mischievous presence now behind them, the Psychedelic
Furs should have returned to their avowed course of the straight-and-narrow. But,

The Butler brothers on stage at the Hammersmith Odeon, 1987.

of course, it didn't work like that. To worsen matters, Richard Butler and Mars Williams were no longer seeing eye-to-eye: the saxophonist was in the throes of a drug habit, and he acknowledged in a 1997 interview with *Goldmine*, 'It just got sour between us [and] part of it was my… addiction.' But internal tensions of all descriptions were breaking out, as the band members each came to the horrific realisation that they were hating every minute of the tour.

A few stopgap remedies were executed – they stopped wearing the outlandish costumes that had seemed such a cool idea at the start; they stopped playing the songs that had once seemed so hot. As the World Tour drove into its final months, there was barely a single *Midnight To Midnight* song left in the band's repertoire, as though purging the show of any mention of their shame could, somehow, purge their consciences as well. It didn't work.

What was worse was the knowledge that there was nobody to blame but themselves, as Richard Butler explains. 'People always whine and complain about their record companies but we never had any of the problems. CBS were always really good to us. They left us pretty much to our own devices from the word go, there was never any of this "you gotta do this or that," pressure. They picked the wrong singles on occasion, and there was that business with the Barney Bubbles artwork. But, in general, It was just "get on with it," which is quite remarkable considering the number of shifts and turns the band made. And they were all our fault. We made those decisions ourselves.' That was how he preferred it, as well. 'I'm glad we made our own mistakes. I'm glad we were given that freedom.' It's just that sometimes, you can have too much of a good thing.

Keyboard player Roger O'Donnell quit long before the outing was over. The future Cure mainstay later admitted he'd rarely felt so miserable in his life as he did as the Psychedelic Furs tour ground on and on. He was hastily replaced by Joe McGinty, a member of Robert Hazard's band, and the tour continued. But the Butlers and Ashton, the ringmasters responsible for holding the entire mad circus together, were increasingly wishing that somehow, it could be stopped. 'It was,' as Richard Butler understates with such eloquence, 'a very tough time.'

He, in fact, was suffering from stark fears of his own, even as he tried to stop everybody else from falling apart. Offstage, he worried; onstage, he stressed. Then, one day, he noticed that his heartbeat seemed somehow wrong. Sometimes, it was simply drifting out of sync and, though that was worrying, he could rationalise it. On other occasions, though, it felt like a sparrow had flown into his chest, and was now flapping about trying to find a way out. And that could not be explained away so easily.

It wasn't the first time he'd suffered on stage, of course. In Glasgow, Scotland, he leaped onto a flight case positioned at the front of the stage, forgetting that it was on rollers. 'It started rolling away and I landed on the floor, flat on my back. I broke two ribs and I had to talk my way through the rest of that song, then I was carried off and the audience was smashing on the dressing room, really annoyed that we hadn't done another encore.'

This, however, was a very different experience, a very different physical sensation. 'It was doing it constantly on that tour, and I thought I was going to die. I'd be walking onstage sometimes, and my heart would just… it feels really strange when your heart does that, really strange. And I would think I was going to die, because it's a pretty good workout being onstage.' Suddenly, one of the lyrics to 'Shock', itself among the most energetic of the songs in the set, came home with chilling significance: 'I feel my heart beat black and blue.'

Pressed to explain his symptoms to the doctors he consulted as the tour rattled on, he was diagnosed with cardiac arrhythmia, literally an abnormal heart rhythm – as if he hadn't already deduced that for himself. What none of the learned men could tell him, however, was what might be causing it. Of course they had their suggestions and a few of them might once not have been out of the question – cocaine, alcohol, tobacco and caffeine are all known causes of arrhythmia. But not one of them applied in this situation, not even the cigarettes which Butler was endlessly consuming.

As the problem worsened and the tests grew more complex, he was fitted with a Holter monitor, a portable electrocardiogram which he wore beneath his clothes for a couple of days, to record information about the electrical activity of his heart. It confirmed the diagnosis, but shed no further light on the cause.

The search for a cure was equally hit-and-miss. One doctor in England recommended a course of digitalis, a drug that slows the transmission of the heart's electrical impulses, and thus reduces an overactive heart rate. Butler refused. He didn't want to simply camouflage the symptoms. He wanted to cure the problem. He wanted to know why his heart was behaving like this.

At one point, he considered cancelling the remainder of the tour, but ultimately demurred. It was not until the end of the tour, therefore, that he was finally free to submit himself to a full battery of tests. The answer had been staring him in the face all along. 'I came back to New York, and went to my doctor here. He did all these tests and said, "Well, actually you've got a heart murmur, but I don't think that's anything to do with it. I think what this has to do with is stress. And I suggest you take some stress reduction classes."

'So I went to stress classes, and that's what it was. It turned out I was just stressed about the record, just generally stressed. As soon as he told me what it was, and I went to a couple of classes, it went away and, knock on wood, it'll never come up again. It was a total over-reaction.' But it was also completely understandable. 'After years of working with a band, believing that you'd done great work all along, to suddenly wake up one morning and realise you've made a hellish mistake…' that's one hell of a shock to anybody's system. And, as for making sure it would never happen again, that, too, was simple. He was going to quit the band. *Midnight To Midnight*, the album that the Psychedelic Furs never really wanted to make, had become the album that ensured they would never do another.

Back home in Tonbridge, John Ashton, too, was tearing himself to pieces. 'So much was resting on that album, and we pandered as best we could. We went out and became this huge sort of rock band, culminating in the big hair, shiny suits, all that kind of crap. We really weren't being true to ourselves. I went through this period of denial of who I was, what I was, what I'd become. I know Richard did the same thing in New York, kicking himself, looking in the mirror each morning and saying, "I can't believe I made *Midnight To Midnight*, I can't believe I went from that to THIS".' But whereas Butler turned his fury inward and almost caused his heart to short-circuit, for Ashton, it all exploded out in one horribly drunk, horribly violent outburst during a fight with his girlfriend.

Everything came pouring out at once, every frustration, every failure, everything the band had dreamed of being and now would never become, until finally, out of words, out of patience, out of all the little failsafe devices he'd constructed around his emotions, he slammed his left fist through a glass-framed picture. The wounds he sustained in that one moment put him out of commission for the next six months.

The hired musicians were all let go, free to pursue their careers elsewhere. The Psychedelic Furs would not be requiring them again. Williams and Garisto stuck together for a while, planning a new band, Mars Williams – An Act Of War. It didn't pan out, though, and Garisto plunged into a brand new maelstrom, as part of Iggy Pop's latest band. Williams, meanwhile, left New York altogether, relocating to Chicago to clean up, and play some sessions with Ministry and their Revolting Cocks spin-off. Today, he leads his own highly-rated jazz-rock band, Liquid Soul.

While Les Mills tried to nurture the band, John in particular, through this difficult time and spoke to Richard on an almost daily basis, the label kept their distance. When CBS suggested that the Psychedelic Furs' next album should be a 'best of' compilation, what they really meant was that the group's final album should double as an epitaph. Nobody expected the Psychedelic Furs to return.

The irony was, for Richard at least, he knew precisely what had happened to the band; had, in fact, discussed it with *Sounds*, back in January. 'It's really easy for bands to get too involved in trying to get on the radio,' he said. 'You just lose your identity, end up doing music you don't like, get successful for a while and the next thing you know, you're dropped.' Back then, he was generalising – or, at least, he thought he was. Now he wasn't so sure, and his last thought on the subject had come back to haunt him. 'There's always a place for a band that's honest with its own sound. People respect a bit of character.' The Psychedelic Furs had lost that honesty. And he had lost his respect for them.

'I wasn't really very pleased with what we had become,' he condemned, a decade later. 'It felt like we'd become just a big Pop band. I'd never really thought of us as that. I'd always thought of us as being something a bit more important than that, or a bit more meaningful than that.'

16

GOODBYE TO YOU, GOODBYE AGAIN

MANY PEOPLE, JOHN ASHTON AMONG THEM, are convinced that the seeds for the Psychedelic Furs' eventual destruction were sewn in 1981; that the day that Duncan Kilburn and Roger Morris walked out the door for the last time was the day that the Psychedelic Furs, as the entity that the remaining members held the dearest, died. They'd retained the name and even retained some of the swagger. But the soul of the band was washed away with the drink that Kilburn poured over his lead singer's head.

They fought to fill the void, but it was a losing battle. Vince Ely realised that when he left just eight months later and, like Morris and Kilburn, he was never to be replaced, neither by the musicians who followed, nor the friends they became. How could it have been otherwise? Where once there were six very distinct personalities nursing the band and fattening its music; where once squalling arguments fed into sprawling jams, which refined themselves into cohesive music; where once the Six Musketeers had faced down the world; now it came down to three tired voices and a heap of hired hands, sitting on the sidelines with the meter ticking beside them.

Richard Butler, too, is painfully aware of the tumors that were gnawing away at the band. 'You don't notice things as they're going along, but certainly towards the end of the Psychedelic Furs' career, I missed the fact that it didn't feel like it was a band anymore. It felt like three members of a band with a bunch of other people. And that wasn't the way it started. I missed all those impassioned, heated arguments, because it meant there were a bunch of people around that all cared about it. Something was missing. It had all become watered-down somewhere.'

Even Tim Butler, the one member of the trio who has continually surveyed the upside of the downsizing, who dwells on all the magic that the group went onto create, rather than some hypothetical vision of six-sided wholeness, even he agreed. 'We had to get back to being a group. For three albums, we'd been using people who'd just turn up to play what we told them and then go on to the next session. We needed a working relationship with other musicians again.' When his brother told him of his intentions to quit, the bassist quickly began talking him out of it.

A little over a year earlier, on the eve of *Midnight To Midnight*'s release, Richard had remarked, 'We still haven't made the record where we can stand back and say, "Yeah, that's what we've been on about all these years. That's perfect."'[21] On another occasion, he insisted that his ambition was to make *the* 'ultimate, definitive, lyrical album' and then quit music altogether to concentrate on something else entirely... silk-screening, maybe, or literature. Tim reminded him of that now. 'He said, "Look, we've had a run of great records up until now. Why do you want to leave it on this note? You should leave it on a better note than this, if you're going to do that." And I agreed.'

Reconvening in the studio in early 1988, with Ashton healed from his physical injuries and Richard cured of his emotional ones, the Psychedelic Furs gratefully latched onto the label's "greatest hits" concept, envisioning a set that would sustain the commercial strides of the previous year, at the same time as informing their newfound audience that there was a lot more to the group than big drums, big hair and monstrously outsized shoulder-pads. It also brought them some much-needed breathing space. 'Whereas bands like REM, The Cure, or maybe even U2 had swept the world,' Ashton sighed. 'We felt we had fucked ourselves over, just because we didn't have our direction together as well as we could. So we paid the price for that.' Now it was time to start making amends.

Of course, the compilation more or less picked itself, mixing singles in with album cuts and presenting a well-rounded portrait of the story-so-far. Anxious to signpost some kind of future, however, the band suggested recording a new one-off single to coincide with the release. With only Joe McGinty remaining on board to remind the band of the times that now lay behind them, the return of Vince Ely reinforced the sense that, at last, the group was moving in the right direction again. The Three Musketeers were upgraded to Four.

Ely's reappearance was pure coincidence, absolutely fortuitous. By now The Furs' former fanclub manager Tony Linkin had begun working for Les Mills. He had remained friends with Vince, who had by now moved back to England. 'It was while Vince was in our office one evening visiting Tony that Richard popped in to see me,' says Mills. 'While he was waiting for me to finish a meeting Richard got to talking with Vince. Later, over dinner, Richard mentioned the idea of Vince rejoining the band.'

The drummer was in-between projects at the time and, when Richard voiced the possibility of a return to the Psychedelic Furs, the damage that surrounded Ely's original departure was remedied on the spot. Ashton: 'Vince felt differently because he wasn't doing anything, and Richard felt differently because we didn't have a drummer. So, Richard asked how he felt about coming back, and Vince said yeah. Which is how it should be.'

For the guitarist, Ely's arrival was a godsend. 'I was breaking up with my long-time girlfriend, the mother of my daughter, so it was a difficult time for me, emotionally. But Vince being back made it all a lot better.' Suddenly, all the nonsense of the last few years had been wiped away. It felt like a band again. All but overnight, Ashton resolved to pull his own life back together, 'to somewhat clean up my act.' He finally made that long overdue move to New York, taking an apartment in the East Village, close to Richard and Tim. There, almost immediately, he met his future wife, Catherine [the couple married in June, 1993]. 'So it went from very bad to very good during the space of that [period].'

The reunion was even better news for Vince. 'I loved being in The Furs,' he reflects. 'It was like a love affair and I was really disappointed with the end – I felt they could have done so much more and I felt like it wasn't resolved, so I was very keen to rejoin…'

With Vince on board, the group adjourned to Tears for Fears' Wool Hall studios in Somerset, to record two new songs with a new producer, former Smiths' mainstay Stephen Street.

'I was a huge fan of The Smiths,' says Les Mills, 'and had been approached to manage them early in their career. Although that did not work out I followed their development with keen interest. It was apparent that Stephen Street played a crucial role in their sound. When I met with Stephen to sound him out about working with the Furs it transpired that he loved the band and had seen them live on a number of occasions.'

Neither 'All That Money Wants', written by Ashton and Richard Butler during one of the singer's visits to England, nor 'Birdland' paid even token obeisance to the sounds of recent Furs – stripping back to the bare minimum of sound, the group sought not only to recapture its early flavour, but also to restore something of its early soul. And, maybe, re-establish its sound.

Rundgren, Forsey, Kimsey… even Lillywhite to an extent, all are producers with firm ideas of how a band should be presented, and characters strong enough to make sure that they comply. You listen to a record that Todd Rundgren has produced and, even before the first kitchen sink hits your brainpan, you can guess who's responsible for throwing it. Forsey, too – the stream of brilliant records he made with Billy Idol through the early 1980s remains the indelible Billy Idol sound. When the partnership parted and Idol struck out alone, he didn't even sound like himself any more. That honour went to Forsey's own next clients.

Stephen Street was different, viewed his duties in a different way. 'I like to think of recordings I've made as having taken an audio snapshot of the artist at that particular time in their career,' he explained. 'I certainly do not feel I should impose a sound on an act. It should be their talent that is being showcased, not mine.'[22] For the first time in a long time, then, the Psychedelic Furs were being forced to make some very tough decisions by a producer who asked them how they wanted to sound rather than telling them how he thought they should.

The group responded with a stately roar, a symphonic *Talk Talk Talk*-era rush pumped along by Ely's percussion, flooded by guitars that raged both melody and mayhem. As a postscript to the hits compilation, issued in August 1988, 'All That Money Wants' brought the band all but full circle; as a single, it went even further, reuniting the band with photographer Andrew Douglas who shot the photographs for the cover. One of Douglas' images had formed the basis of the half-tone screen on the front cover on the first album, as well as the live shot on the back. He also shot the photographs that were used on the covers of 'Sister Europe' and 'Mr Jones' and the portraits that were used on *Talk Talk Talk*.

'All That Money Wants' was never intended to give the group a worldwide hit single, and it didn't disappoint – the 45 struggled to puncture the UK Top 75 and sank without trace in America. But the experiment was a success nonetheless.

Equally gratifyingly, CBS themselves seemed content to allow the band to follow its own path – the label, too, had seen the damage that their brush with the big time had wreaked upon the band and, apparently, welcomed their decision to step back from the brink. Richard Butler recalls, 'We went in and said, "We want to make a record, and not have any singles on it," and they said, "Okay fine." They were always pretty good with that. Things had evened out, were a bit more even-keeled.'

Aiming to build on the success of the Stephen Street sessions, the band initially approached him to handle this next project. They managed to squeeze in a handful of new recordings in early 1989, but the producer's schedule simply couldn't flex to accommodate a full LP, not if they wanted to get it out this decade. Instead, the group approached Dave M Allen, at that time riding high on his work with the Chameleons (*Strange Times*) and the Cure (*Kiss Me Kiss Me Kiss Me*).

Richard Butler: 'We made up a short list. The conclusion that some people have come to is, "Ah, they used Dave Allen – they must like the Cure's production." Which really isn't the case at all. You look at the producers that are available. We wanted to work with an English producer, because we wanted to work in England. And when you look at the producers who are available, there really aren't an incredible amount. Not very many with the right attitude that we wanted, and not many people, personality-wise, that we liked. I mean, we met up with him and we really liked him as a person."

Allen's experiences with the Cure, however, were important to the final decision, in that he had already conspired to create an aura that the Psychedelic Furs themselves were now aiming for. *Book Of Days* was to continue in the sonic footsteps of 'All That Money Wants', bare-boned and simple, dark and atmospheric, low-key in every sense of the sound. Tim Butler: 'We decided to strip it back, and go back to natural sounds, no synthesizers and stuff.'

'Making *Book Of Days* was a hoot,' Ashton recalls. 'Vince was back, and he was taking the piss out of everybody, making up corny jokes. It was a very coherent album, it was a very inventive time – I think it was the most inventive time we'd had in a long while, and we were trying a lot of things out." From the moment the sessions got underway, in May 1989, every aspect of the project was designed to take the group back to an earlier and, in retrospect, happier time. They returned to the RAK studios, scene of their first two albums, and reacquainted themselves with the pub around the corner; in the studio itself, they simply jammed together, just to see what happened.

The songs flew out. Ashton: 'We were still watching a lot of videos and drink-ing, or not drinking, depending, and we were just getting into making music again. It had all the good things about the band in it – the songs were getting darker, the sonic feel, the kind of yearning. Richard was going through some changes in his personal life, and that was reflected. I had undergone a lot of personal changes, and I felt much more in tune with Richard for the first time in a long time. I really believed that things were on the up.'

With Ely naturally reinstated as a full member of the band, session guests were recruited on an as-needed basis: McGinty, of course; American guitarist Knox Chandler, recruited from, among other past projects, Gary Windo's *Deep Water* solo album (in later years, he would work with REM, the Golden Palominos, Siouxsie and The Banshees and Depeche Mode); cellist Emily Burridge, haunting the already nostalgia-riven 'Torch'; a startlingly well-chosen horn section compris-ing jazzman John Hymas and the Waterboys' Anthony Thistlethwaite – their flour-ishes during 'Should God Forget' are simply classic Psychedelic Furs; and the Pogues' Jem Finer, with his arsenal of banjos, mandolins, hurdy gurdies and more. It was a magnificent pot-pourri, the Psychedelic Furs' deepest, densest album and, as Tim Butler observes, their most English-sounding since *Talk Talk Talk*.

'Dave Allen brought us back to [that]. Oddly enough, the producers we'd used on the two previous albums were English as well, but Keith Forsey had been [in the United States] for a while, and Chris Kimsey was a global-type producer, he'd done that stuff with the Stones, so he was more into the American side of things as well.'

In fact what Ashton described as hired gun guitarist Knox's '"Americanisms" and guitar histrionics and "I've been to music school" smarm' brought out the English values in some of the other participants. 'It was Dave Allens idea for me to smash the guitar during the take for "Entertain Me",' Ashton explains. 'He also provided the lighter fluid! A sort of "Up Yours" if you will. So English.' The result-ing visceral destruction can be heard on the final take.

It wasn't a wholly retrogressive situation, though. 'We didn't say, "Let's listen to the early albums and make another record like that",' Richard cautioned the American magazine *The Bob*. 'Our songwriting has never been radically different. It's mainly been production differences with records. I think songs like "The Ghost In You" could have been off *Talk Talk Talk* or *Forever Now*. It's just the way that we treated them.' Or, on this occasion, didn't treat them. Dave Allen handled things in the best way imaginable, by turning in a record that didn't sound like he'd touched it. 'That's what we sound like when we're not produced,' Butler proudly concluded.

The album would not emerge perfect. For Les Mills, this was down to two factors: 'Unfortunately,' he says, 'both Dave Allen and the engineer Roy Spong were mas-sive potheads. The other mistake was that we recorded the album in studio two, which was really an overdub suite. I think the lack of a 'live', or ambient sound on that record is a large part of its failure for me. The songs were great, it just sounds dead.'

'To me,' says Tim Butler, '*Book Of Days*' production was a little *too* cloudy. I'd love someday to remix it. There's some very strong songs that are a real return to the Psychedelic Furs basics, but I think the production lets it down.' Ashton agrees. 'I remember having table-tennis matches with Richard and him saying, "I think this is our best album." And I said, "I think it's pretty good, but I think we can do better." I'm always like that, I think we've got more, more, more.'

The question was, how much more, more, more, did they really have?

The world which the Psychedelic Furs left behind in 1987, at the conclusion of the *Midnight To Midnight* tour, and that to which they returned in 1989, had changed immeasurably. Nobody had put that change into words, for it is only with hindsight that all but the most seismic shifts in pop culture can be identified. But, just as the American rock'n'roll of the 1950s had withered away by the end of the decade, to be succeeded by the beat boom of the British and the Beatles; just as the psychedelia of the late 1960s died on the vine, to be replaced by the metal and glam of the '70s; and just as Punk was superseded ten years later, so the end of the 1980s was being marked by a similar cataclysm – a cataclysm, that is, for the bands who fell victim to it.

Tastes shift like continents, slowly but inexorably. But once a bridgehead has been built, the invaders pour across like ants and devour everything in their path. It has always been that way: every decade has its signature sound, and 'Remember The Whatever-ies' compilations abound to reinforce that fact.

No matter that the latest Psychedelic Furs album had more in common with the Happy Mondays than Men Without Hats; that great swathes of the group's sound could be – and would continue to be – referenced by a slew of the bands that emerged over the next few years. Still the Psychedelic Furs were tainted by the decade they shaped, and the kids had moved on without them. Rave, shoe-gazing, the first stirrings of grunge – new bands created new fashions and there was no room in any of these exciting modern bags for a bunch of '80s oldies, no matter how cool they might once have been. Ecstasy was the new pink, because that made you look pretty in everything.

Aware of these swings, but confident that their name still counted for something – for not every concert-goer can be so forgetfully hip that they'd completely abandoned their oldest heroes – the Psychedelic Furs announced a two-month American tour, taking them through the end of the year and into the next decade. With only Joe McGinty added to the core quartet, establishing the most concise Psychedelic Furs touring party ever, the band launched their eighth American tour over Thanksgiving weekend, November 1989.

Book Of Days was released as the tour kicked off, and Columbia were true to their word. 'They let us do the record,' Richard Butler celebrates. 'They released a single, but they didn't work it very hard – no pop single push.' They just let the band be and didn't even say a word when the figures came in and *Book Of Days* had barely

Saluting 'President Gas' at Subterania, London, 1989.

Tim Butler on stage at Subterania, London, 1989.

scraped to #138 on the American chart. A decade earlier, after all, a similar (#140) ranking for the first album had been cause for wild celebration.

The less than sparkling commercial vistas that greeted the album were repeated on the road. The once-loyal Boston's Orpheum was little more than half-full, Washington DC's Charles E Smith Center somewhere under one-third capacity. The shows were good – especially after second guitarist (and cellist) Knox Chandler was added to the line-up, to beef up what had hitherto been a slightly thin sound – but the tour remained low-key, as it would be when, America out of the way, the Psychedelic Furs returned to Britain in February 1990, to tour for the first time in three long years – and record, for the first time in three times as long, a radio session for the BBC.

Broadcast on DJ Nicky Campbell's show, their set was dominated by three of the new album's songs, 'Entertain Me', the acoustic ballad 'Torch' and 'Book Of Days', but closed with a fascinating 'Pretty In Pink', unplugged and utterly naked. If any single song illustrated how far the band had stepped back from their mid-1980s selves – and how far forward they were now looking – that was it. It was, however, a deceptive vista. Before the tour itself got underway, Ely withdrew once again – 'on musical grounds – again,' as Tim Butler put it. The classically trained Ohio native Don Yallech, veteran of sessions as far afield as John Cage, Glenn Branca and Broadway, replaced him. He was also a Psychedelic Furs fan. 'He'd been coming to our gigs for years,' Tim Butler remarked, 'and was just waiting for the drum seat to be vacated.'

Commercially, the

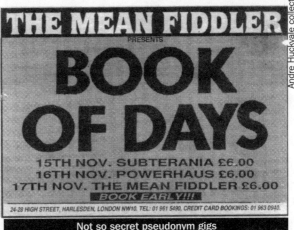

Not so secret pseudonym gigs

UK visit was little more encouraging than the American outing. Again, part of that was the fruit of the group's own decisions – just like Columbia in New York, their UK label kept to the agreement, and didn't pressure the band with a big press build-up; again, they knew – as Tim Butler put it – that 'we needed to get our heads together. Get some sort of sense of what had happened over the past few years.' But who was there to celebrate the Psychedelic Furs' successful return from the abyss? Highlighted by three pseudonymous London club dates, the tour proved that the Psychedelic Furs retained a devout audience. But the band's return to action made no headlines, and the album limped no higher than #74, then left the chart after just one week.

The Psychedelic Furs returned to the US in April for a last round of live shows, highlighted by a semi-secret six-night residency at New York City's CBGBs, the legendary birthplace of New York Punk rock and still a vital part of the city nightlife 15 years later.

Like the secret London dates, the CBGBs shows were intended to reacquaint the band with their small-time roots. Richard explained at the time, 'As much as people say certain bands can turn a theatre into a club atmosphere, I don't believe it. There's something about being in an actual club, and singing to people who are [in front of your face]. It was good to do shows without any kind of production at all, without any of the trappings of rock shows. [Plus], this just seemed like a good way to end the '80s, or begin the '90s.'

The shows themselves were a revelation. Though the set, predictably, drew from across the band's career (*Midnight To Midnight* notwithstanding), subtle rearrangement and reinvention created a seamless whole from disparate elements – 'Heaven' slowed and shrouded, 'President Gas' punked and riff-laden, 'Pretty In Pink' as spiky as it could be. 'It was pretty good,' Richard understated. 'It was exactly what I expected. It was a bit hotter than I expected and there wasn't as much oxygen as I expected. But besides that....'

Other gigs included a Rock Against Fur benefit for the charity PETA (People for Ethical Treatment of Animals) and two fabulous nights at Washington DC's tiny 9.30 Club, effortlessly recreating the thrill of CBGBs. Afterwards, they agreed that the next time they toured, they'd play even more shows like that – there would be a next time, on that they were all agreed. It was only a little later on, back home and getting on with his life, that John Ashton, at least, started wondering whether that really was in the band's best interests?

'I was very up on *Book Of Days* to start with, there were certain songs I really liked. But, to this day, I can't even listen to that album. I just felt it was not the highpoint that I was expecting at that time. Something was missing, and I just couldn't put my finger on what it was.' Only with close to a decade's worth of hindsight could he opine, in a 1997 interview, that '*Book Of Days* maybe should have been our last album.'[23] The missing ingredient, he realised, was the need for closure. And that was something that no amount of rehabilitation could bring them.

17

SPLIT LOVE SPIT

THIS IS ALL BEGINNING TO FEEL like the last months of a soap opera. You know the end is coming, and most of the cast believe it's already overdue. But nobody – not the stars, not the producers, not the writers, not the network – is willing to actually put the beast out of its misery.

New characters wander in and they spark a new plot line, old favourites return and old glories resurface. But nothing sticks, nothing lasts, and even a change of scenery – throw out the old set, wheel on the new – adds little more than a cosmetic glamour to the story. John has moved to New York City, a few blocks away from Richard and Tim, and built a little recording studio in one room of his apartment. Joe, Don and Knox have settled in for the duration and they're helping their friends demo new songs.

Les had renegotiated both the record and publishing deals to take account of the commitment that had been promised by the record company. 'We were now signed directly to the American label Columbia and there was a real expectation that the new president, Don Ienner, would make up for previous failings. Also the deal with [Atlantic subsidiary] East/West for the rest of the world meant we had an opportunity to make a fresh start in other territories that had long given up on us.'

Now read on.

From the outset, the new material looked even darker than the Psychedelic Furs' customary shades. Talking after the album was completed, but simply making public thoughts he'd already aired in private, Richard Butler acknowledged, "Lyrically... it's the most personal album we've made. It's more about relationships... involvement. I hate the idea of concept albums; if you sit down and plot what each song's going to be about, then you're dishonest. I want to concentrate on a song as it's happening, work on it then put it to one side and work on the next, and there's no vision of a full picture until the end, when you listen to the playback. But when I listened to the playback, I was struck by how much of a personal vision it was, how it didn't seem to be settled back or easing into the third person too much. It felt like I'd exposed a lot of myself, which means that it is basically an honest album.'

Perhaps, as it transpired, it was a tad too honest. At least one review, in the American *Alternative Press*, would comment, 'Butler does little but talk about himself and his all-too-common experiences with relationships' and, though one could certainly admire the obsessive honesty of a song like 'Until She Comes', still, as the review continued, one yearned for days when he preferred 'social commentary [to] social disclosure.'

Neither did Butler's bandmates seem especially comfortable within these new surroundings. Reconvening with the now-available Stephen Street, the Psychedelic Furs returned once more to Bearsville Studios in mid-1990, to begin work on *World Outside*, their seventh album in a dozen years. Recording would be completed in New York City at various studios. The album would be mixed by Street at Sigma Sound and several tracks, notably the singles, would be remixed by Hugh Padgham at Electric Lady.

'It was interesting,' says Mills, 'that we had finally caught up with Hugh on these sessions, which were to prove the final act in the Psychedelic Furs recorded output after being unable to work with him back in 1979 on 'We Love You'.'

Spirits were high when the sessions began, but they quickly took a turn for the worse. Edgy and fractious, the musicians suddenly seemed unable to gel – after almost every take of almost every song, they'd listen to the playback, then someone would speak. 'It's not as good as the demo.'

It was a strange sensation. In the past, the group had looked upon the demoing process as a way of sketching out the ideas they'd be filling in later, skeletons that would grow flesh in the studio. This time around, the demos seemed to represent an ideal that they were growing increasingly unable to recapture. And, in the end, they simply stopped trying. Ashton: 'We actually ended up using part of the demo for "Until She Comes" on the album. We took the drums, which were a drum machine, and looped it in with real stuff and the original acoustic guitar, and made the song.'

Nobody truly understood the malaise that was prostrating the creative process. But they all felt it, and all reacted to its malevolent presence. As usual, the basic band had been supplemented by extra musicians, but they were surrounded by friends nevertheless – McGinty, of course, and the returning Yallech and Chandler. But even when the band members were out on the town, away from the red lights and mikes of the studio, the tired eyes and weary expressions didn't go away.

John Ashton: 'I really didn't feel comfortable, and I think it showed, in my performing, playing, being, everything. I just wasn't happy with the album; something about it was so squeaky. It was weird; I enjoyed making the demos, but not the actual album. When it came to doing the album, I'd almost lost interest in it. It was like, "yeah, whatever." I was just kind of over it. I had just totally changed my life around, given up drinking, drugs and everything, and I went straight back to it during that album. "Fuck this." I guess I needed the excuse.'

Part of his own problem, he knew, was insecurity. 'Knox and Richard had struck up a real friendship and Knox, in a way, is a much more technically superb guitar player than I am. I guess I felt a little jilted and jealous – it was very hard for me to make my thing happen when I felt I was being overshadowed a little bit. I felt something was missing, the in-jokes were getting a little too much to handle, and I felt I was getting shunted further and further out.'

When he looked for someone to turn to, however, it seemed there was nobody there. Tim Butler: 'The whole thing that used to bug John was, he thought that because I was Richard's brother, I was necessarily on Richard's side. When it came down to the big decisions, he thought, "Oh, they're brothers, they're going to go with each other." I don't think he bothered to bring up a lot of his deeper thoughts about things, because he thought he'd get shot down.' So instead, he withdrew, from the music, from the band, from everything he'd once cared about.

Worse, his feelings were left to fester, to be joined by another awareness, one that was even less readily defined, but just as damaging. It was the slow realization that, in the world outside itself, very few people actually cared what the Psychedelic Furs were now doing – or even if they still existed.

The album took seven weeks to complete, a mercifully far cry from the six months they'd spent on *Midnight To Midnight*. But it felt like an eternity regardless, one that was only drawn out even further when the album's release date was finally announced. June 1991 wasn't simply almost a year away. It was also at the height of one of the music industry's traditional dead

Andre Huckvale collection

Andre Huckvale collection

periods, the beginning of the summer holidays when buying records was the last thing on most peoples' minds. If the Psychedelic Furs needed any reminder of just how far down the list of industry priorities they had slipped, that was it.

Tim Butler: 'I think, partly because of our laziness, and our refusal to promote *Book Of Days* as it should have been promoted, people started to forget about us. So we decided, "Hey, we're going to make a great album," which we did with *World Outside*, and we were gung-ho for doing the whole interview, touring, video thing. It was almost like coming again from the first album to *Forever Now*. If you say *Book Of Days* is the first album again, then *World Outside* is like a *Forever Now*, so from then on, we could've been on a healthy course. But we'd lost our grip on our audience and, when it came out and was lukewarmly received, even though it got great reviews, I think we saw it as a slap in the face, the audience saying we don't want you anymore.'

The group's predicament, however, was not all their own doing. In September 1991, as the Psychedelic Furs hit the road in support of the album, Nirvana landed the one-two punch of 'Smells Like Teen Spirit' and the *Nevermind* album. And, though it now sounds absurdly melodramatic to say so, the established music scene would never be the same again.

Nirvana's impact was as immediate as it was profound, and the Psychedelic Furs were by no means the first, or the only, casualties. Robyn Hitchcock's latest album, *Perspex Island*, was top of the American alternative chart when *Nevermind* was issued; indeed, it was the Seattle band that knocked it off the #1 spot and, though Hitchcock is referring to his own role within the market, his observation is equally applicable to the Psychedelic Furs. 'Some of the people who came through at the same time as us had all moved up a notch to different planes...' – the Cure, Depeche Mode, REM, the Replacements, U2 of course – 'But everyone else was just there to be scattered, and that included us. We were still there as an alternative act, but it had altered, it all became "rock" again, people were allowed to have long hair and punch the air again, buy pretzels and shout "way to go." It had changed, and there wasn't really a place for what we did any more. Our stuff was far too musicianly and middle-aged.'

World Outside became the Psychedelic Furs' first album ever to miss the American chart; in Britain, it charted for just one week, at a lowly #68. Live audiences were more accommodating. Warming up in Washington DC on 3rd September 1991, with a predictably packed visit to the 9.30 Club, the Psychedelic Furs then headed straight for Britain and a concise series of gigs topped off with what should have been a triumphant Town & Country Club show. Unfortunately, the lethargy that appeared to afflict the album had now infiltrated the live act as well. Performing a distinctly crowd-pleasing set, the band never seemed to get out of first gear, with 'Sleep Comes Down' – scarcely the most animated song at the best of times – simply droning the wallflowers into submission.

'I wanted to smash my guitar, amongst other things...' Ashton says today, reflecting on his loss of interest during the tour and preceding sessions. 'I just could not be bothered anymore.'

Things improved somewhat once they crossed the ocean: a handful more club shows raised the band's confidence, a string of well-attended theatre gigs pushed morale up a few notches, too. Although there were a few nights when the empty seats yawned black and accusing, there were others that sold out almost as soon as tickets went on sale: the 9.30 in Washington DC, the Whisky a Go Go in Hollywood, St Louis' Mississippi Nights, Chicago's Metro, Cleveland's Empire. In Royal Oak, MI, more than 1,500 fans filled the Music Theatre; back in DC, almost 2,000 packed the Citadel.

Such brightspots aside, it appeared that the album and the tour were not going to make the desired impact. Things were grinding to an end for the band.

'I had flown in from London to spend thanksgiving with my girlfriend,' says Les Mills. 'I knew that it was all over. Columbia had already gone cold on the band and we were touring a dead album. The situation in the rest of the world was even worse.

'East/West had effectively given up and admitted that they would not be renewing their option. So I flew down to Washington and travelled back to New York on the tour bus with the band to break the news. I commandeered the lounge and spoke to everyone, one by one. First I had to explain to the hired musicians that there would be no retainers once the tour ended. Then the hardest part: explaining to Richard, Tim and John that we could continue touring into the new year – which would ensure that they would earn enough money to tide them over for a while. Everyone took it pretty well, particularly Richard who I think was more relieved than anything else. Only Tim seemed unable to comprehend what I was telling him. The hardest thing was explaining to Tim that he no longer was a successful rock star. Tim, you don't understand, it's over. We can carry on touring and make a bit more money, but it's over... Tim was really the baby of the band – when he joined the band, he was very young and he had never had a job in his life. He really thought the Furs were going to be the biggest band in the world. He lived life as a rock star.

'The fact that he would have to downsize his rock'n'roll lifestyle and move out of his expensive apartment on St. Mark's Place. I think he took it harder because the rest of us had at least lived in the real world but all he had ever really known was The Psychedelic Furs.'

Though Tim points out that he did hold down two jobs away from home before The Furs, Les stands by his general point.

Richard insists none of Les's revelations came as a surprise: 'Les assumes we weren't aware of our situation. We were fully aware of where we were and what was happening. It's not as if Les came in breaking tragic news about our unexpected decline.

'When we went in to make *Book of Days* I was so disenchanted by the mistakes we'd made on *Midnight to Midnight* and I wanted to make a statement in the opposite direction. I had made myself ill agonizing over what a mistake *Midnight to Midnight* was. I wanted to say to anyone listening that the record was not what I was about and that it was not what the Psychedelic Furs were about. I was teetering on the verge of quitting the band and said I'd do another Furs record only if it could be completely different from the previous one.

'I told everyone I didn't want to make a commercial record and I didn't want a single on it. We all knew the possible ramifications of this, so it was no surprise that the album was not a hit. It was a statement that was more honest and true to the spirit of me and the spirit of the Psychedelic Furs and to hell with commercial success.'

Richard knew *World Outside* was unlikely to restore the band to their previous commercial heights. Still, if having their reduced status spelled out to them must have been disheartening, the band kept this from the outside world.

Breaking for Christmas, the group pressed on in the New Year. They appeared on American TV's top-rated *David Letterman* Show and, stopping off in Seattle in mid-February, in spite of Mills' revelations, Tim Butler told the press, 'it's been a very long tour, but we're enjoying it immensely. When it started, we thought that, with the recession, people would not be so willing to put out for concert tickets. But it's been great.' Furthermore, he continued, 'we work like a band again, instead of being three people swimming in a sea of session men. It's more driving, more energetic. Dare I say it – this show really rocks!'[24]

Unfortunately – or, perhaps, not – it was soon to be rocking its last.

The final date of the tour was at the Academy in New York City, on 14th March 1992, and tour manager Martin Cole – now into his ninth year of nursemaiding the Psychedelic Furs – was determined that it should be a special event, for the band as well as the fans. John Ashton remembers, 'Martin secretly got Mars [Williams] and Gary [Windo] to come down and play, without us knowing. At that point we weren't using saxophones, just Joe [McGinty's] keyboards, it was pretty sad – and, all of a sudden, there they are. That for me was the highlight of that whole time. What a brilliant end!'

And he was right. It was the end.

'After telling the band the position before Christmas I had gone back to London and downsized my own office,' says Les Mills. 'Reluctantly letting Tony Linkin go. I had continued to manage the band up until the end of the tour. I saw it through and sorted it to the end, settling the final accounts. However it was apparent that things were going nowhere and after six weeks of silence from New York I realised Richard wasn't committed to another record. I wrote to Richard, Tim and John on April 25th 1992 tendering my resignation. It was a sad end to an exciting 13 years together.'

There had been portents. Earlier in the tour, Butler had prompted his band-mates to consider maybe taking a break from one another, 'to do a few other things to get away from being in each other's back pockets for 13 years or whatever,' as Tim Butler put it. Now, with the band off the road, it was time to take that course for himself.

Tim Butler: 'I think Richard, more than John or I, just thought it was time to go out now, rather than wind up playing to 200 people at small clubs. Go out on top, as opposed to right at the bottom again. I think, towards the end of that tour, there was a feeling going around that this was it. There was never actually a date where we came together and said, "After this we're going to quit." We just needed a break.'

In the meantime, Richard recruited new management in the shape of Richard Bishop, manager of hardcover punk poet Henry Rollins, to replace Les Mills, who remained on good terms with his ex-charges.

Richard's immediate plan was to cut a solo album. John Ashton: 'I had a con-versation with Richard a few weeks before the end of the tour, and asked, "Do you want to do another album?" And he said, "Oh yeah, yeah, sure. Definitely, but I want to do my own solo album first".' Various people, himself included, had been floating the possibility of a Butler solo shot since the early 1980s. 'The first time a solo album was mentioned to me was around *Forever Now*, and I said, "No, no, I'm too involved doing this." Then, after we did *World Outside*, I thought, "If I want to do something different, now is really the time I should be thinking about doing it. If I don't do it now, I'll definitely be with the Psychedelic Furs." And I felt that I didn't want to do that.

'I just didn't feel excited by the prospect of beginning all over again with the Psychedelic Furs. Tim, John and I had been together for so long, we'd just worn out what we had between us. Maybe if we'd been with Duncan, Roger and Vince, it would have felt more like a gang, but it had kind of lost that feeling. I kind of knew what any other records in future would sound like. I wanted to work with somebody where it would be different, that I would be surprised by. It was just becoming bor-ing, and I'm sure that they felt exactly the same thing. I wanted to do something else.'

The problem, at least for anybody actually waiting for him to get up and do it, was that he had no firm ideas of what form this 'something else' might take, nor when it might emerge. 'Unless you're a singer-songwriter type, going out on your own with an acoustic guitar, James Taylor or Cat Stevens, it's very difficult to do a "solo album" as such, because you're always going to be working with other musi-cians, and whether you like it or not, that means it's a band.'

While he wrestled with that dilemma, his brother and Ashton got back to work. Retaining drummer Don Yallech, and adding vocalist Chris Robertson, Tim Butler promptly formed a new band, Feed, then invited Ashton to join them. The guitarist turned him down: 'I felt Tim needed to be doing something on his own.'

Feed was eventually completed by Keith Otten, a member of a local band whose demos Butler had helped out on, and the group was soon playing live shows around New York City.

Ashton, meanwhile, moved into session work – his guitar immeasurably enlivens 'Empty Promises', on Kristen Hall's 1991 album *Fact and Fiction*. But he remained convinced that the Psychedelic Furs would be reconvening somewhere down the road, which is why – with Butler's solo album still nothing but a dream – Ashton finally called Richard Bishop to suggest the Psychedelic Furs do a small tour to pay off some of their debts. To his horror and shock, he was told – or, at least, came away with the impression that he'd been told – 'Richard has no intention of ever doing anything with the Psychedelic Furs again.' Those words effectively hammered the last nails into the band's coffin, and Ashton and Butler would not speak again for several years.

'I don't want to call John a liar,' Richard insisted to *Goldmine* in 1997, 'but I would never do that, and I'm sure it didn't happen that way. I get a bit foggy about how it actually happened. It certainly wasn't anything to do with bad feelings between any of us, that wasn't the issue. It wasn't like I came off the tour and said, "My God, I can't stand those guys." It wasn't that at all. But, by the end of the tour, I already knew what I was going to do. I decided to call it a day, and I think I did that quite soon after we came off tour. It wasn't like an age went by. I'd wanted to do something different for a long time now.'

Despite such resolutions, there never was a formal announcement that the Psychedelic Furs were no more. In fact, when the news did leak out, it came from an altogether unexpected source. Richard Butler recalls, 'I'll tell you one of the most touching things I ever heard. Somebody told me that Pete Townshend had accepted an award in Toronto, and he said "I'm very glad to accept this award because it's been a very bad year for music, because two of the best English bands of the '80s have split up, The Beat and the Psychedelic Furs."

'So a couple of years ago, I actually bumped into him, and said, "You know I heard you'd said something very sweet at Toronto." "Yeah, I did say that." And I said, "Well, thank you very much, that was a very nice thing to say, I'm really flattered." I mean, Pete Townshend is one of the greatest English writers of the '60s.'

18

I DON'T WANT YOUR TALK TALK TALK

ALTHOUGH THEY HAD NO IDEA whatsoever where the songs would actually end up, the Butlers began writing fresh songs together almost from the moment the Psychedelic Furs came off tour. They lived across the road from one another, were constantly hanging out; it was only natural that music would continue to flow. And, slowly but surely, the stockpile grew: 'Superman', 'Half A Life', 'Am I Wrong', 'Please' and 'More': by mid-1993, they had accumulated more than the rudiments of a new album, no matter what form it might ultimately appear in.

Slowly, however, Richard began to streamline his thoughts. The Psychedelic Furs were out of the question; so, he'd finally decided, was an album under his own name – because, what could he possibly hope to accomplish beyond, 'the first solo album by the Psychedelic Furs' Richard Butler,' and a long line of journalists queuing up to ask when the band was going to be back? If he was truly intending to strike out alone, then he had to make sure that that particular ghost would not be accompanying him. And that meant just one thing. 'Eventually I decided that these were songs for a new band, and Tim was "Okay," and we carried on writing songs together.'

There was no initial certainty as to what shape this new band would take. Butler continues, 'I wanted lots of different directions for the songs, as opposed to everything having one sound and every song sounding very similar. After that, I started thinking about guitarists I wanted to work with, and I started writing with Knox Chandler.' They completed a few songs, including the anthemic 'Change In The Weather', but something was still gnawing at Butler. 'I thought to myself, "You know what, Richard, this really isn't the way to go. You're just going to end up with another Furs' album with the secondary members," which was kind of ridiculous to do. So, the only other guitarist that I could think of, who really struck me as good, and that I liked as a person, was Richard Fortus.'

Thirteen years Butler's junior, born 17th November 1966, Richard Fortus was the stylishly individual guitarist with the St Louis-based Pale Devine, and a man whose own debt to the Psychedelic Furs had been building ever since he saw them play on the *Forever Now* tour and was converted on the spot. Proudly wearing that influence on his sleeve, he formed his own band, the Eyes, in the mid-1980s and, over the next five years, the group toured the mid-western college circuit relentlessly.

In 1989, the Eyes self-released their debut album; the following year, with an Atlantic Records contract in their laps, they changed their name to Pale Devine, delivering the *Straight To Goodbye* album in late 1991. Months later, in February 1992 – ten years after Fortus first clapped eyes on the group – they were booked as the support band on the Psychedelic Furs' final tour.

Fortus and Richard Butler hit it off from the start and had kept in touch ever since. Butler: 'So I called him up and said, "I want to do another record, I don't know what it's going to be yet, but would you like to have a go at writing some songs?" He said "Yeah".'

For the first few weeks, Fortus commuted between St Louis and New York, flying up whenever he could, crashing on Richard Butler's couch, and working on songs with the siblings – one of their first joint efforts was 'Seventeen'. As things progressed, however, and Butler's own vision of this new project coalesced, Fortus himself moved up to New York and the singer finally formulated what would become Love Spit Love.

With Tim Butler naturally confirmed as the band's bassist, the group put together a list of every drummer they thought might be suitable, and started auditioning. It was Fortus who suggested Frank Ferrer. Richard Butler remembers, 'Frank was one of the last to come in and he just was a better player than everybody else, he's got a great vibe about him, you meet Frank and you like him, he's one of those guys. So he walked out of the room at the end, and I turned to Richard and said, "Well, if he wants to do it, that's the guy that's got the job".'

The new band's name came just as easily. Richard Butler: 'A friend of mine had this art happening in New York City – a gay male couple, a gay female couple and a heterosexual couple, all making out on an American flag, and that was called *Love Spit Love*. As soon as I heard that, I called him up and said, "I want to use this as a song title, maybe," and he said, "Yeah, go ahead." But the more I sat with it, the more I liked it.'

The group was complete by summer 1993. But it was January 1994 before everything else came together and they were able to embark upon the crash course in edgy pop that became Love Spit Love's debut album. Richard Butler: 'With the Furs, we could go in and make a record without all the material but, when you're talking about going to a new record company, they want to hear a whole album's worth of stuff. And then, it always takes longer than I want to.'

Manager Richard Bishop ultimately signed the band with Imago, a label he was already familiar with via Henry Rollins and home, also, to Aimee Mann, Basehead and the Captain Hollywood project. However, there was further delay as the group waited for Butler's first choice of producer, Dave Jerden, to become available. 'I love the way he made Jane's Addiction sound, and what he did with Alice In Chains. I like the sound of those records. Then when I met him and he was talking about how he'd worked with Eno... [Jerden engineered Eno and David Byrne's *My Life In The Bush Of Ghosts*]. I really liked his ideas, and it turned out that the way he envisioned [our] record sounding was exactly the same as I'd heard it. Plus, he makes guitars sound fucking great, and that really attracted me as well.[25]

'Recording can get really boring,' Richard continued, 'and the only reason it didn't this time was because of Dave sticking in his two cents' worth, so we were arguing with him all the time.'

Recorded at Eldorado Studios in Los Angeles, *Love Spit Love* finally appeared in August 1994, and immediately drew comparisons with the best of the Psychedelic Furs – accusations that Richard Butler readily acknowledged. 'It's very difficult to pin exactly what's different on the album,' he pondered at the time, 'because I was and still am the same person. I'm kind of a pop writer in some ways, but I'm not going to go out and make a Spice Girls record.

'I'm more pop in terms of the Rolling Stones, bands like them. Richard Fortus can sit down and say, "Hey, I've got these four ideas, what do you think?" Maybe one of those will immediately suggest a melody, and I'll just start singing along with it, and then start writing words. And that's exactly the way it was with the Psychedelic Furs. I would say the real different is Richard Fortus, more importantly than anything else.'

Reviews of *Love Spit Love* were generally complimentary, the critics appearing genuinely pleased that Butler had bounced back so strong. *Cover* magazine described Love Spit Love as 'both the best new band and the best debut album of 1994,' while the American *Alternative Press* bellowed with similar effusiveness. 'What ho! Midlife apocalyptic grunge-pop crisis… except it's not a crisis. It could, in fact, be the album which re-establishes Butler in the MTV-mind, at the same time as remaining a record he can live with.' It was also, a few keen ears noted, the roughest-sounding album he'd made since the Psychedelic Furs' *Talk Talk Talk*.

The coincidence was not, in fact, wholly coincidental, as Richard Butler readily admitted. '*Talk Talk Talk* still sounds pretty good. I think that's the only album by the Furs that I actually have. Richard [Fortus] had it while we were in LA recording, and he put it on one time while we were driving around and I thought, 'Yeah, that sounds pretty good.' The sonic imprimatur of that album was suspended, too, over the song 'Superman'. 'There's a line "I don't want your talk talk talk"… I thought about that when I came up with that line. I thought "that sounds like… yeah, that'll do. I'll leave it in there".'

Elsewhere, however, *Love Spit Love* veered off in totally fresh directions – another Psychedelic Furs hallmark, of course, but one that nevertheless remained capable of shock. 'Jigsaw', a song which drew in the ghosts of Christopher Isherwood's Berlin, a comb-and-toilet-paper orchestra and the creepier musical aspects of Alice Cooper's *Welcome To My Nightmare*, was a vivid potpourri which Butler himself found difficult to resist. 'I keep getting this vision of this German SS soldier staggering down a dark alleyway at 4 in the morning, with lipstick on, and a garter over his uniform leg.'

One thing that hadn't changed, of course, was his method of writing. 'I have a particular group of obsessions that come up... and that's all I'm concerned with, putting those across so, when I listen back to it, I feel all those feelings again. I'm not really thinking about "will someone else understand this?" You have to be brutally honest when you write songs and, if you don't feel it when you listen back, then it hasn't worked.'[26]

The new group's development was not, of course, uncomplicated. Having completed the album, the assumption that Tim Butler, the predominant co-writer on the project, would automatically be involved in its promotion was shattered when the bassist announced that he was leaving to pursue a career in studio engineering and production. His course work would consume all the time he might have once have dedicated to the group. He was replaced for the upcoming tour by Lonnie Hillyer, fresh from stints with Billy Joel, Billy Squier and Jeffrey Gaines. In September 1994, Love Spit Love launched their first American tour by selling out the ever-loyal 9.30 Club in Washington.

Several shows paired the band with Detroit alt.rockers Sponge – hitting it off with the musicians, Butler then joined the group in the studio, during the recording of their *Wax Ecstatic* album, contributing vocals to one song, 'I Am Anastasia'. Love Spit Love were then back on the road for another month in March 1995, this time opening for Live, the original Poor Man's REM. Despite such a sonic mismatch, Butler's enthusiasm remained high – quizzed about earlier pronouncements, he admitted that dreams of a solo album had long ago bitten the dust. 'I wanted a band. It's exciting to be in a new band, just trying to get heard. For me, the most exciting part of making a record is writing songs, sitting down with the band and working them out and thinking, "Fuck, that sounds great!"'

Indeed, so much sounded so great that *Love Spit Love* was still awaiting release when Richard began talking to Imago about releasing a second album before Christmas, comprising the songs which didn't make it onto the first. That crop was then added to with a handful of acoustic remakes cut at Rondor Studios in Los Angeles in July; however, aside from serving up a steady supply of possible B-sides, his suggestions fell on deaf ears.

'They say, "We can't do that, we'll still be working on this one". But I just want to keep putting stuff out, because the longer you leave between records, the more precious you become about them. And you shouldn't be precious, you should just get in and do it, and if it's not as good as it could have been, then it doesn't matter because you've got another one coming out and you should start working on that.'[27]

Unfortunately, the messy demise of Imago, midway through the Live tour, put an end to any such plans. *Love Spit Love* itself was completely lost in the ensuing chaos and, while another three years would pass before the album resurfaced, through the British label Burning Airlines, it was almost as long before the group itself resurfaced. As Butler himself later admitted, the whole experience had so put him off record companies that he was postponing finding a new one for as long as he possibly could.

Nevertheless, even in the depths of silence, he was adamant, 'I've always thought of Love Spit Love as being a long-term thing, it was never a side project. The Psychedelic Furs are long gone.'[28]

Acting on a suggestion from Dave Jerden, ex-Indian Chris Wilson was brought on board as a permanent bassist, while the group at least maintained its profile by contributing a superbly distinctive rendering of the Smiths' 'How Soon Is Now' to the soundtrack to the similarly superlative movie, *The Craft*. Retaining all the dynamic tension of the original, with Fortus fearlessly recapturing the eerie echoes of Johnny Marr's guitar, the only irony was, it took Love Spit Love to finally confirm something that Smiths' drummer Mike Joyce, following his first own audition with the group, enthusiastically informed a friend: 'They sound fantastic. I think they could be the next Psychedelic Furs.'[29]

The two Richards, Butler and Fortus, meanwhile, continued writing – Tim Butler weighed in on occasion – and, by early 1996, the group was actively seeking a new deal. Once again, it was a slow process, but finally Madonna's Maverick label pounced, having heard a three-song demo comprising 'Believe', 'Long Long Time' and 'Fall On Tears.' Work on the second Love Spit Love album got underway at the end of the year, produced this time by Ben Grosse, a Detroit-based remix engineer with whom manager Richard Bishop had worked in the past, and whose resume included work alongside Filter, the Red Hot Chilli Peppers and the Violent Femmes. *Trysome Eatone*, was finished in February 1997, and finally reached the stores in mid-September.

It emerged, again, with a sound that was not a million miles removed from past glories, at least in places. 'I wanted to make a record that had all great songs,' Butler said at the time. 'Not all singles necessarily, just great songs. I also wanted the record to be varied, with lots of different moods, but make it so it all hung together.' He continued, 'There are a few songs here that don't sound like anything I've done before.' But there were others… Even he admitted, 'The one track that made me sit back and think "God, this sounds like me around the early Psychedelic Furs" was 'Sweet Thing'. That sounds like me singing on *Talk Talk Talk*.'

Such similarities were only heightened when Love Spit Love took to the road that October/November, building their set around the two albums to date, but throwing in a couple of extra numbers from that same old LP, 'Mr Jones' and 'I Just Want To Sleep With You'. An unplugged 'Love My Way' and a 'Ghost In You'/'Heaven' medley also appeared from time to time, faithfully recognisable, but subtly reworked all the same, proof that Butler had finally put the Psychedelic Furs behind him, and was able to treat his songs as, indeed, *his* songs once more.

Response to the band's renewal was again encouraging. Traveling through September, Love Spit Love made personal appearances at some 30 different radio stations across the US; among the critics, *Alternative Press* lauded the album to the skies, albeit somewhat unconventionally: 'Looking back over Butler's entire output, this is simultaneously his most complete album since *Mirror Moves*, and his most gratuitously enjoyable since *Midnight To Midnight*. It is relentless, slashing changing moods with ceaseless movement, and unleashing choruses that make your head spin round. Stark production adds to the excitement; the album has a spiky, edgy air, cut through with a barely-disguised naked violence. The closest parallel,' the review continued, 'is an unrelenting wall of sound... just as the wrecker's ball hits it.' And you can just imagine the readers stroking their chins – 'as enjoyable as *Midnight To Midnight*, eh? Wow, it must be good.'

Despite such responses, *Trysome Eatone* was criminally under-promoted, completely under-sold, and the group lapsed back into silence. Though nobody knew it at the time, their final shows fell in the run-up to Christmas, billed alongside the Cure at a handful of American radio-sponsored festivals.

It was a state of quiescence that Butler confirmed would remain in force the following year, with the birth of his and wife Annie's first daughter. At home in Cold Spring, New York, Butler would spend the next three years almost exclusively as a parent and a songwriter. It was a lifestyle he adored, but an environment that, sometimes, he didn't understand. One of the first new lyrics he wrote in that tiny, upstate town was 'Wrong Train' – music by John and Tim – wondering whether people who lived quiet lives in the country ever found themselves asking how on earth they'd got there; why on earth they were spending their lives washed up in 'a suburban wife-swapping hell.' Had they, indeed, caught the wrong train? 'My wife doesn't like me, neither does her boyfriend.'

Butler made only a handful of public appearances during this period. In 1997, alongside electronica hero Brian 'BT' Transeau, he performed one song, 'Shineaway', for the soundtrack to *The Jackal*; three years later, he appeared as a guest on Jazz Passengers alto/tenor saxophonist Roy Nathanson's *Fire At Keaton's Bar And Grill*, a concept album set in a smokey (literally) nightclub and co-starring Debbie Harry, Elvis Costello and Nancy King.

Butler also appeared in a stage play version of *Fire At Keaton's Bar And Grill*, at some Chapel Theatre in New York. He also recorded an excellent track, 'After All', for the soundtrack of a movie called Gossip (which was briefly made available as a download from The Furs' Burned Down Days Website). He also made a brief appearance in the closing sequence of the Bowie (Warhol) movie *Basquiat*.

While Love Spit Love slumbered, and Tim Butler concentrated on his studio studies, John Ashton kept busy in sessions, for country rockers Western Vogue, Mercury Rev, Gowan, and Marianne Faithfull among others. He toured alongside 10,000 Maniacs' John Lombardo and Mary Ramsey and contributed to the *Invitation To...* tribute album to New York art minimalists Suicide. Resuming the interest in production work which set the Sisters of Mercy off on such a brilliant tangent, he also oversaw recordings with Los Angeles' Silence, English band Field of Dreams, expatriate singer Ally Rogers and the New York bands Ornamental and Red Betty, a crunchy pop band fronted by the irrepressible Yahz. Ashton produced and played on the band's first recording, the self-released *Sister Rubber Limbs*.

The Psychedelic Furs remained a constant in all three members' lives, however, with each of them reflecting sadly upon the group's ignominious close. 'If it *was* a close,' Tim Butler cautioned in 1997. '*If* it was, it was definitely a sputtering close. We could've done something like the Cure, "this is our last tour, come and see us," one last blaze of touring glory. But it did just sputter. *If* it was a close. But, who knows, if John and Richard get to a stage where they can actually talk to each other again, we might get some kind of action on the Psychedelic Furs' front.'

'Tim said *that?*' a shocked Richard Butler retorted when his brother's words were relayed to him. 'He must have been joking.'

No, he wasn't.

Butler paused for almost a minute. 'I don't know, nothing's impossible down the road. I would say it's very unlikely. I can't imagine it being so. But, you never know.'[30]

19

I FELT LIKE ONE IN A MILLION...

NOBODY HAS EVER DOUBTED THE IMPACT that the Psychedelic Furs had on the British and American music scenes of the 1980s, nor denied the legacy that the band left. Nobody, that is, aside from the band members themselves. John Ashton: 'I always have people coming up to me going, "Oh, I was really influenced by you, or listened to you a lot,' but I don't think we were the only band that… we were influenced by the Velvet Underground and the Stooges, but I don't think one band ever influences anybody.

'Us along with the Bunnymen, the Cure and U2 probably influenced the whole next generation, but I couldn't say one band in particular were influenced by the Psychedelic Furs. We were just part of a generation that influenced the next generation. We led the way, maybe, in the early days, we had a lot of success in the early MTV days, so we led the way in that. And we had instrumentation that was maybe a little bit more oblique than your regular guitar, bass and drums. But there were other bands in England at that time, that were very influential in what was to come after us.'

He undersells the group. The early Smiths were firm devotees, while U2, the Cure, Bauhaus and Echo and the Bunnymen were certainly pushed into broader horizons of sound by the Psychedelic Furs' own effortless advances. Later, the early-mid 1990s unveiled a clutch of bands who, whether they openly acknowledged it or not, undoubtedly drew the soul of their attack from the group. Listen closely, and elements of the Psychedelic Furs leak from Radiohead, Catherine Wheel, Blur, Suede….

Another superstar tribute shoots across the landscape. In 1992, preparing his *Black Tie, White Noise* album, David Bowie was moved to reunite with former Spiders From Mars guitarist Mick Ronson. 'Ronno' had been diagnosed with liver cancer and his life expectancy was now being measured in months.

Anxious to work one final time with the man who had fired his own career to its most expansive heights, Bowie assembled four songs for Ronson to choose their collaboration from: Bob Dylan's 'Like A Rolling Stone', Cream's 'I Feel Free', a new Bowie original titled 'Lucille' (an early version of 'Lucy Can't Dance') and, according to some reports, the Psychedelic Furs' 'Pretty In Pink'. In the event, only the Dylan and Cream were ever issued but, if the legend is true (some sources replace the Furs' song with Bowie's own 'Pretty Pink Rose'), the Thin White Duke's watchful awareness of the band he'd once championed remained strong.

The success, and the succession, of Psychedelic Furs compilations that emerged during the late 1990s, too, heightened awareness of both the band and its importance.

The earliest collections were workaday efforts, a bundle of album cuts that were just slung together. In 1995, however, Columbia compiled an ill-fitting, but nevertheless intriguing collection of, as its title insisted, *B-Sides & Lost Grooves*, resurrecting songs previously buried away on the back of singles, or occasional 12-inchers. A handful of genuine gems were included – 'Mac The Knife', the *Forever Now*-era 'Aeroplane' and 'I Don't Want To Be Your Shadow', the *Midnight To Midnight* offcut 'New Dream'. But it wasn't a project that the band members themselves necessarily cherished; Richard Butler later complained, 'Those songs weren't lost. They were thrown away. It was like they went through our garbage for it.'

Two years later, a more coherent archive trawl pulled the band's BBC radio sessions out of Auntie's vault, while Tim Butler reunited with the band's old Columbia ally Bruce Dickinson, now an independent A&R man, to compile the aptly titled *Should God Forget: The Psychedelic Furs Retrospective*, a generous 2CD compendium of expected album cuts and unexpected rarities. Live versions of 'Heartbeat' and 'All Of The Law', caught in Berkeley on the *Midnight To Midnight* tour, completely give the lie to the band's own sour memories of that period; while the first album's 'Blacks'/'Radio' medley finally made its American debut and didn't raise a single eyebrow. Not for the lyric, anyway. The sound, on the other hand… Summing up in the liner notes to *Should God Forget*, John Ashton mused, 'we had all come a long way, but… had not reached our final destination. Perhaps this collection will help fan the flames.'

Tim Butler was also involved in sorting through material for a proposed 1983-era live album; that project ultimately fell off the schedules, but the group's catalogue continued revolving and, while not every release especially merited celebration, each confirmed what its predecessor had announced: that the Psychedelic Furs were not only one of the previous decade's most important bands, they were also one that was gathering new fans all the time.

Other forces were at work, too. No sooner were the 1980s over, it seemed, than the first '80s-era revivals began to appear, a storm of nostalgia-tinted hair-gel so tumultuous that, sometimes, it seemed there wasn't a retro-stone left unrolled: Culture Club, the Human League, New Order, Echo and the Bunnymen, ABC, Adam Ant, the Mission, the Alarm… They weren't all revivals, they weren't even all retro – the albums that the Bunnymen have cut following their reformation are arguably as strong as most of what they'd turned out first time around.

But, of course, the music isn't the only criterion by which such things are judged. Perception, too, plays a part, which means that a band that was big in one decade, then sank from sight until midway through another, is automatically going to look like a revival, no matter what its own intentions may be. It's a dilemma

Richard Butler and John Ashton on stage at the 9.30 Club, Washington, DC, 2001.

André Huckvale

Richard Fortus and John Ashton at Opus 40, Saugerties, NY, 2000.

Anna Dorfman

that none had yet found a way around; it was one that the smartest, therefore, simply opted to ignore – or celebrate.

By early 2000, Richard Butler was beginning to feel restless again. He'd written a bunch of songs and was writing more with his brother. 'Then, one day, Tim said, "You've got a lot of songs, what are they for?" I was, "I dunno, I'm just writing them at the moment." I was writing for another album, whether it was going to be Love Spit Love or a solo record or whatever, and he said, "Well, there's enough to do whatever you want to do, and do a Furs album as well." And, because I hadn't really thought about the Psychedelic Furs, that wasn't a bad idea.'

'About two weeks after Tim suggested making a new Furs record, our agent called and said, "Hey guys, would you like to go out and do a tour? If you think about putting the Furs back together at all, Richard, give me a call. There's a lot of interest out there." And I called him back and said, "It's funny, but Tim just mentioned making an album at some point. So yeah, I guess we are interested".'

The idea took on further impetus after Howard Thompson, now A&R at the Almo Sounds label, took the Butlers, John Ashton and Vince Ely out to dinner in New York City one night, seemingly with the express purpose of trying to engineer a reunion. It didn't quite happen – Ely returned to his home in Spain shortly after. It was a shame for Vince; he loved The Furs and had been here before. He'd not that long ago spent time at John's house in Woodstock working on music with a view to reforming the Furs. 'In the end Richard didn't want to do it,' he explains, 'as he had solo demos in the pipeline.'

Undeterred, the Butlers and Ashton pressed on together.

Deliberately, the trio kept everything as casual as possible. No promises, no guarantees, just a handful of rehearsals and songwriting sessions, simply to see how things went. That changed when Butler's phone rang again. 'Our agent called back and said, "Look, I've got this tour going out. It's the B-52s and the Go-Gos. You would have the opening slot, which means you would play for about 40 minutes, so there would be no pressure and it would be a great way for you guys to find out if you like playing together again". So I said yeah.'[31] In fact, rehearsals had already answered that question.

Richard Fortus was drafted in as second guitarist, hijacked away from his own band, Honky Toast; drummer Earl Harvin was borrowed from Matt Johnson's The The and, on 5th July 2000, the Psychedelic Furs played their first live show in eight years, a warm-up at Toad's Place in New Haven, CT. (In fact Harvin had to miss this and the other first few shows due to a previous commitment, replaced by Frank Ferrer). Two nights later, the band were at Clarkston MI's DTE Energy Music Theatre, appearing in front of 15,000 '80s addicts.

'It was definitely an '80s revival tour, that one,' Butler laughed. But the word 'revival' did not fill him with fear. 'You can't avoid it. For a lot of people who grew up in the '80s, the Psychedelic Furs will always be a part of their lives then, as Bob

Tim Butler, New York City, 2004.

'Alive' in New York City, 2004.

Anna Dorfman (2)

Richard Butler at Spirit, New York City, 2004.

Anna Dorfman

Dylan was for me in the late '60s… Led Zeppelin in the late '60s, early '70s, and David Bowie in the '70s. You kind of associate people with certain decades and, although [Bowie] still brings out good records that I like, he will always have a real special part in my life from when I was growing up in the '70s. And for me to play that part in someone else's life, I find quite flattering.[32]

'So, you are in that strange revival place, playing things everybody wanted to hear. But that's what we wanted. Go out, play the songs which the audience knew, find out if they were interested in hearing us again – find out if *we* were interested in hearing us again!'

Both criteria were eminently satisfied and, off the road, the group began sorting through new material. There'd been room for only one new song, 'Alive,' on the summer tour but, as they prepared for another outing, six weeks around the United States, beginning in late March 2001, three more would make their way in among the oldies: 'Anodyne (Better Days)' – its subtitle re-deploying a lyric first aired on *World Outside*; 'Cigarette' – the music for which was written by John Ashton during the band's hiatus, but with the Furs in mind and the scornful 'Wrong Train'.

Hitting venues much the same size as they'd played during the *World Outside* outing, and frequently drawing similar crowds, this tour was the first opportunity the band had had to break in new material on the road since the Mediterranean tour of 1986, on the eve of *Midnight To Midnight* – an ill-starred event, to be sure, but a valuable experience all the same. Richard Butler: 'It's so easy to fall into the album-tour-album trap. We could never write on the road, so we would usually come back from a tour, go home and lick our wounds for a while and then write a whole new batch of tunes. It works better when we can play new songs on the road and see how they go down. By the end of the tour, you know what works and what doesn't.'[33]

Early plans to record a full album were placed on hold while the group tried to decide for itself the best outlet for such a project – Butler's own experiences with record companies over the past decade had certainly soured him towards conventional outlets, but he was still uncertain about the potential of the Internet. 'You want to see the record in the shops,' he laughs. 'You want people to be able to pick it up and look at it, take it home and play it.' Instead of rushing into a new studio set, then, the group opted for the safer alternative of a live album and an accompanying DVD, recorded over two nights (April 13/14) at the House Of Blues in Hollywood.

The set all but picked itself. 'Mr Jones', 'Heaven', 'The Ghost In You', 'Sister Europe', 'Pretty In Pink', 'Dumb Waiters'… even 'Heartbreak Beat', a song that Richard could quite happily have spent the rest of his days never hearing again, crept in. One day in rehearsal, his brother started playing it and, listening quietly for a moment, Butler was finally forced to concede, 'You know, it's not a bad song after all.'

However, when conversation turned towards the next tour, this one coinciding with the autumn release of the less-than-imaginatively subtitled *Beautiful Chaos: Greatest Hits Live*, 'We decided we're not gonna do "India", we're not gonna do "Into You Like A Train", we're not gonna do all the songs people might be expecting to hear. We stuck some non-hits in there, instead.'

'Run and Run', 'Imitation of Christ', 'All That Money Wants' and 'All of This And Nothing' all made surprise appearances; among the scheduled shocks, meanwhile, was a newly worked-up version of Roxy Music's debut hit, 'Virginia Plain'. Richard Butler caught Roxy on their own reunion tour, in New York City, and was horrified that the song was omitted from the repertoire. Mindful of the days when the Psychedelic Furs themselves were being compared to Roxy, who better to resurrect 'Virginia Plain' in their stead?

Opening in November 2001, the tour initially took on the appearance of yet another revival outing, as Echo & The Bunnymen, themselves now three albums into their second lifetime, were announced as co-headliners. Richard Butler: 'We were tossing around a bunch of names that might be interesting to tour with. Originally, we wanted to put together a big tour of three or four acts, but the Bunnymen came up, and we'd only ever played with them once, with Teardrop Explodes in their early days, so we mentioned it to them and they were "Yeah, we'd love to".' The two bands agreed to alternate the opening slot – the Furs took pole position at the first show, at Atlanta's House Of Blues on November 15; the Bunnymen headlined New York City's Beacon Theatre; and so on.

Once again, the Psychedelic Furs' line-up had shifted dramatically. While Frank Ferrer of Love Spit Love filled the drum stool, bandmate Richard Fortus was absent, heading off to tour, instead, with Latin star Enrique Iglesias. He was replaced by Gordon Raphael, now best known as producer of the Strokes' *Is This It* album but, prior to that, keyboard player with Sky Cries Mary, a Seattle-based band who single-handedly came close to completely reinventing psychedelic space rock for the 1990s. Ironically, Raphael had been seriously considering moving back to Seattle from New York, when he received the Psychedelic Furs' call.

Fortus' absence was not permanent. Four nights into the tour, at the Beacon Theatre, he joined the group onstage for the closing three songs, 'Heartbreak Beat,' 'Wrong Train' and 'Pretty In Pink'. By mid-November, he was back on board whenever that other commitment permitted. He still missed some shows, though, including San Juan Capistrano, the night that past and present were merged into one unforgettable moment.

For the Psychedelic Furs, however, it is the future that matters, a future that might have begun a quarter of a century ago, but which is still being pursued today. In July 2003, the band brought on Rob Dillman & Ron Baldwin of Cabal Management as its new manager, though they remain on good terms with Richard Bishop. The band continues to tour... having played before 40,000 fans at a festival in Chicago in August, and before nearly 60,000 fans at the KROQ Inland Invasion

3 on September 20, 2003... where the band appeared with the Cure, Duran Duran, and others.

'It's great to be back together – very exciting,' says Richard. 'We're playing better than at the end of the 80s. Personalitywise we're getting along better than ever too. I'm getting along better with John than ever and John's playing better than ever before. The old material sounds fresh and it was good to take a breather.'

Richard Butler's long awaited solo album is nearing completion. Richard has been discussing a possible solo record for years. The album was written and recorded with his old friend Jon Carin – a musician and composer Richard met, ironically, when Chris Kimsey brought him in for *Midnight to Midnight*. It will be released in Autumn 2004 and with a less rock, more atmospheric sound, it will mark a musical departure from The Furs.

'There are a lot of acoustic guitars and a lot of electronics,' says Richard. '[Jon and I have] written together over the years and started making a record a year and a half ago. Jon plays everything on it and we're both producing it.... It plays to both our strengths – he's very different as a composer from The Furs. We adjust what we do to accommodate each other's individual strengths.'

After the solo record, next up will be a new Psychedelic Furs studio album. For the Furs, as Richard says, 'the test will be the next record.' They have half a dozen songs already written and recording will begin in earnest in the fall...

Though the Psychedelic Furs are unlikely ever to approach the same heights that they once climbed to contemplate, their very existence proves they conquered far rockier peaks than those.

Which brings us back to that ancient fable, and the man who didn't quite march to the top of the mountain. He went back to his village, the fuss all died down, and soon the whole affair was forgotten. He built a new house, surrounded by his friends and, though it wasn't quite as grand or as high as he'd planned, he was as comfortable there as he'd ever dreamed he could be. Because he knew that he'd survived. A lot of other people might not have.

FOOTNOTES

1 Butler quoted in *Boston Phoenix*, November 10, 1997.

2 Quoted in *Zig Zag*, November, 1983.

3 Butler quoted in *Alternative Press*, December 1991.

4 *Zig Zag #95*, July, 1979.

5 Ibid.

6 Quoted in the liners to the compilation *Should God Forget*.

7 Kilburn quoted in *Zig Zag*, March, 1980

8 Butler quoted in *New Musical Express*, 15th November, 1980.

9 Butler quoted in *Zig Zag*, October, 1980.

10 Personal posting from the unofficial Burneddowndays.com Psychedelic Furs website.

11 Butler quoted in *Zig Zag*, October, 1980

12 Ely quoted in *New Musical Express*, 15th November, 1980.

13 Quoted in the BBC Radio 1 series *The Record Producers*, 1981.

14 Ashton quoted in *Musician*, May 1983.

15 Calvert quoted in *Nick Cave: The Birthday Party & Other Adventures* by Robert Brokenmouth, 1996.

16 Howard quoted in *Nick Cave: The Birthday Party & Other Adventures* by Robert Brokenmouth, 1996.

17 Ashton quoted in *Musician*, May 1983.

18 Pope quoted in *The Cure: Faith* by Dave Bowler and Bryan Dray, 1995.

19 Butler quoted in *Sounds*, January 24, 1987.

20 Ibid.

21 Ibid.

22 Street quoted in *The Encyclopaedia of Record Producers* by Eric Olsen, Paul Verna, Carlo Wolff, 1999.

23 *Goldmine*, April 10, 1997.

24 Interview with the author, *Seattle Times*, 7 February, 1992.

25 Interview with the author, *Alternative Press*, September, 1994.

26 Butler quoted in Love Spit Love EPK (electronic press kit) 1994.

27 Interview with the author, *Pandemonium*, July 1994.

28 Quoted in Maverick Records press biography, 1997.

29 Reported in *Morrissey & Marr: The Severed Alliance* by Johnny Rogan, 1992.

30 *Goldmine*, April 10, 1997.

31 Butler quoted in *Choker Magazine*, August 2, 2000.

32 Ibid.

33 Butler quoted on Newsday.com, March 22, 2001

BIBLIOGRAPHY

MAGAZINES AND PERIODICALS

Alternative Press (US)
December 1991: The Ghost In Them – Susan Rees
December 1997: A Handle For The Door – Robert Cherry

B-Side (US)
Oct/Nov 1991: Psychedelic Furs Chemistry – Sandra Garcia

Creem (US)
Anniversary Issue 1991: After Midnight… In Search Of Redemption – Wilf Strenger

Goldmine (US)
10 April 1997: The Psychedelic Furs – Jo-Ann Greene

Melody Maker
31 January 1981: Weird Scenes Inside The Goldmine – Ian Pye
30 May 1981: Psychedelic Subversives – Steve Sutherland
19 October 1982: Inside The Outsiders – Steve Sutherland
5 May 1984: Two Way Mirror – Steve Sutherland
15 March 1986: Castles In Spain – Adam Sweeting
21 June 1986: Atom Heart Brothers – Steve Sutherland
7 February 1987: Kissing The Pink – Ted Mico
18 June 1988: Sleep Comes Down – Steve Sutherland
6 August 1988: Highwire Daze – Ted Mico
11 November 1989: Exile On Main Street – Steve Sutherland
1 June 1991: Alone Again Or – Steve Sutherland

Musician (US)
May 1983: Sleep Gets Down – Bill Abelson with Khaaryn Goertzel

New Musical Express
22 Sept 1979: Grown Up Strange – Paul Du Noyer
15 November 1980: Fake Furs Strictly For Fun – Paul Du Noyer
11 July 1981: Gentlemen P Fur Blondes – Paul Du Noyer

6 August 1988: Furs & Last & Always – Steve Lamacq
18 November 1989: FurtySomething – David Quantick
18 May 1991: The Fur Hoarseman Of The Apocalypse – Andrew Collins

Q
July 1991: Come In, Sit Down... – Robert Sandall

Record Mirror
12 April 1980: Eric's Last Stand – Mike Nicholls
27 September 1986: Pop's Outside – Andy Strickland
31 January 1987: This Man Talks To His Reflection In The Mirror – Nancy Culp

Sounds
6 October 1979: Which One's Psycho Derek – Giovanni Dadomo
29 March 1980: Victims Of The Furry – Pete Makowski
18 July 1981: Psychedelicatessence – Tim Somner
21 June 1986: Inside The Fur Trade – Chris Roberts
24 January 1987: Rock's Guardian Angel – Richard Cook
20 September 1988: The Butler Did It! – Roy Wilkinson
18 November 1989: The Dukes Of Hazard – Sam King

ZigZag
July 1979: The Flowers Of Evil Are In Full Bloom – Kris Needs
March 1980
October 1980: The Psychedelic Furs – Alan Anger
October 1982: Furs Psychedelic – Kris Needs
November 1983: What The Butler Saw – Johnny Waller

REFERENCE BOOKS

Guinness Book of Hit Singles, Hit Albums (various editions)
Fredric Dannen: Hit Men (Helter Skelter Publishing reissue edition, 2003)
Martin C Strong: Great Alternative Discography (Canongate)
Joel Whitburn: Top Pop Singles, Top Pop Albums (various editions: Record Research)

DISCOGRAPHY

THE PSYCHEDELIC FURS

UK SINGLES

October 1979 (Epic EPC 8005) We Love You/Pulse
7-inch single with picture sleeve – three different coloured sleeves were issued, pink, yellow and green. A-side censored on promo pressings (8005DJ).

February 1980 (Epic EPC 8179DJ) Sister Europe/Sister Europe
7-inch single. Promo featuring A-side only, short (3.45)/long (4.13). Release withdrawn.

February 1980 (CBS 8179) Sister Europe/****
7-inch single with picture sleeve. Reissue with reassigned catalogue number. Promos (8179DJ) feature A-side only, short/long versions as above.

October 1980 (CBS 9059) Mr. Jones/Susan's Strange
7-inch single with picture sleeve.

April 1981 (CBS A1166) Dumb Waiters/Dash
7-inch single. Limited edition of 5,000 featured playable pic sleeve. With specially printed stickers placed over the original song titles, these sleeves were also utilized in the US for promos of Pretty In Pink/No Tears.

June 1981 (CBS A1327) Pretty In Pink/Mack The Knife
7-inch single with picture sleeve.

June 1981 (CBS WA1327) Pretty In Pink/Mack The Knife
7-inch picture disc.

June 1981 (CBS TA 1327) Pretty In Pink/Mack The Knife/Soap Commercial
12-inch single – no picture sleeve.

June 1981 (CBS A 13327) Pretty In Pink/Mack The Knife/Soap Commercial
12-inch single – no picture sleeve; shrinkwrapped with free T-shirt.

July 1982 (CBS A2549) Love My Way/Aeroplane
7-inch single. Limited edition of 5,000 with gatefold sleeve.

July 1982 (CBS TA 2549) Love My Way/Aeroplane (Dance Mix)
12-inch single.

October 1982 (CBS A2865) Danger (Remix)/I Don't Want To Be Your Shadow
7-inch single with picture sleeve.

October 1982 (CBS TA 2865) Danger (Remix)/I Don't Want To Be Your Shadow (Extended Version)/Goodbye (Dance Mix)
12-inch single.

November 1982 (CBS A402909) *Greatest Original Hits* EP
Sister Europe/Pretty In Pink/Dumb Waiters/Love My Way
Cassette EP.

March 1983 (CBS A2909) *Greatest Original Hits* EP
Sister Europe/Pretty In Pink/Dumb Waiters/Love My Way
7-inch EP with picture sleeve.

March 1984 (CBS A4300) Heaven/Heartbeat (New York Mix)
7-inch single with picture sleeve. Limited edition shrinkwrapped with free poster.

March 1984 (CBS TA 4300) Heaven (Full Length Version)/Heartbeat (New York Mix)
12-inch single. Limited edition with free poster.

May 1984 (CBS A4470) The Ghost In You/Another Edge
7-inch single with picture sleeve.

May 1984 (CBS WA4470) The Ghost In You/Another Edge
7-inch picture disc.

May 1984 (CBS TA 4470) The Ghost In You/Another Edge/President Gas (Live)
12-inch single.

October 1984 (CBS A4654) Heartbeat (Mendlesohn Mix)/My Time
7-inch single with picture sleeve.

October 1984 (CBS DA4654) Heartbeat (Mendlesohn Mix)/My Time/Heaven (US single mix)/Here Come Cowboys (US single mix)
7-inch doublepack with picture sleeve.

October 1984 (CBS TA 4654) Heartbeat (Mendlesohn Mix – Long Version)/My Time
12-inch single.

August 1986 (CBS A7242) Pretty In Pink (86)/Love My Way (US Mix)
7-inch single with picture sleeve.

August 1986 (CBS WA7242) Pretty In Pink (86)/Love My Way (US Mix)
7-inch picture disc.

August 1986 (CBS DA7242) Pretty In Pink (86)/Love My Way (US Mix)/Heaven/Heartbeat
7-inch doublepack with picture sleeve.

August 1986 (CBS TA 7242) Pretty In Pink (86) (Berlin Mix)/Pretty In Pink (Dub)/Love My Way
12-inch single.

September 1986 (CBS 4501304) *The Twelve Inch Tape*
Pretty In Pink (Berlin Mix)/Love My Way (US Mix)/Heaven (Full Length

Version)/Heartbeat (New York Mix)/The Ghost In You
Cassette EP.

October 1986 (CBS 650183) Heartbreak Beat/New Dream
7-inch single with picture sleeve.

October 1986 (CBS 6501830) Heartbreak Beat/New Dream/Sister Europe/Into You Like A Train/President Gas
7-inch shrinkwrapped with free three-song cassette single.

October 1986 (CBS 650183) Heartbreak Beat (New York Mix)/Heartbreak Beat (7-inch mix)/New Dream
12-inch single. Heartbreak Beat was also released in an alternate version, Heartbreak Dub, as a limited 12".

January 1987 (CBS FURS 3) Angels Don't Cry/No Release
7-inch single with picture sleeve.

January 1987 (CBS FURS C3) Angels Don't Cry/No Release/We Love You/Pretty In Pink/Love My Way
7-inch shrinkwrapped with free three song cassette single.

January 1987 (CBS FURS T3) Angels Don't Cry (New York Mix)/Angels Don't Cry (Single Mix)/No Release
12-inch single.

July 1988 (CBS FURS 4) All That Money Wants/Birdland
7-inch single with picture sleeve.

July 1988 (CBS FURSEP 4) All That Money Wants/Birdland/No Easy Street (live)/Heaven (live)
7-inch doublepack with picture sleeve.

July 1988 (CBS FURS T4) All That Money Wants/Birdland/No Easy Street (Live)
12-inch single.

July 1988 (CBS CDFURS 4) All That Money Wants/Birdland/No Tears/No Easy Street (Live)
CD single.

January 1990 (CBS FURS 5) House/Watchtower

7-inch single with picture sleeve.

January 1990 (CBS FURS QT 5) House/House (flashback mix)/Badman/Torch (Electric)
10-inch single with picture sleeve.

January 1990 (CBS FURS T5) House (Flashback Mix)/House (extended)/ Watchtower
12-inch single.

January 1990 (CBS CDFURS 5) House/Watchtower/Badman/Torch (Electric)
CD single.

June 1991 (East West 78355) Until She Comes/Make It Mine
7-inch single with picture sleeve.

June 1991 (East West 74604) Until She Comes/Make It Mine/Sometimes/Until She Comes (Remix)
12-inch single.

July 1991 (East West 74055) Until She Comes/ Make It Mine/Sometimes/Until She Comes (Remix)
CD single.

September 1991 (East West –) Don't Be A Girl/Get A Room (acoustic)
7-inch single with picture sleeve.

September 1991 (East West –) Don't Be A Girl/Don't Be A Girl (remix)/Get A Room (acoustic)
12-inch single.

September 1991 (East West –) Don't Be A Girl/Don't Be A Girl (12" Mix)/Don't Be A Girl (Dancehall On Fire)/Get A Room (Acoustic)
CD single.

January 1992 (CBS 657750) Pretty In Pink/[Only Ones – Another Girl Another Planet/Lovers Of Today]
CD single.

US SINGLES

1980 (Columbia –) We Love You/Sister Europe
12-inch promo single.

June 1981 (Columbia –) Pretty In Pink/No Tears
7-inch promo single. Limited edition featured playable pic sleeve with specially printed stickers placed over the original UK song titles: Dumb Waiters/Dash.

September 1983 (Columbia 03197) Love My Way/Goodbye (Dance Mix)/ Aeroplane (Dance Mix)
12-inch single.

October 1983 (Columbia 03340) Love My Way/I Don't Want To Be Your Shadow
7-inch single with picture sleeve.

May 1983 (Columbia 03930) Run And Run/President Gas (live)
7-inch single with picture sleeve.

May 1983 (Columbia 1640) Run And Run/[Scandal – Love's Got A Line On You]
12-inch promo single.

April 1984 (Columbia 04416) The Ghost In You/ Heartbeat (7-inch remix version)
7-inch single with picture sleeve.

May 1984 (Columbia 04984) The Ghost In You (Full Length Version)/Heartbeat (New York Remix)
12-inch single.

July 1984 (Columbia 04577) Here Come Cowboys/Another Edge
7-inch single with picture sleeve.

July 1984 (Columbia AS 1908) Here Come Cowboys (Album Version)/Here Come Cowboys (12-inch Remix Edit)
12-inch promo single.

September 1984 (Columbia 04627) Heaven (US single mix)/Alice's House
7-inch single with picture sleeve.

April 1986 (Columbia 2826) Pretty In Pink/Pretty In Punk (dub version)
7-inch single with picture sleeve.

January 1987 (Columbia 06420) Heartbreak Beat/New Dream
7-inch single with picture sleeve.

January 1987 (Columbia 05969) Heartbreak Beat (Extended Mix)/Heartbreak Beat (Dub)/New Dream
12-inch single.

June 1987 (Columbia 07224) Shock/President Gas (live)
7-inch single with picture sleeve.

June 1987 (Columbia 06892) Shock (The Shep Pettibone Mix)/Shock (Instrumental – The Shep Pettibone Mix)/Shock (Single Mix)
12-inch single.

September 1987 (Columbia –) Angels Don't Cry (7-inch remix version)/Mac The Knife
7-inch single with picture sleeve.

June 1988 (Columbia CAS 1310) *Interchords*
12-inch promo interview disc featuring edited conversation between Richard Butler and WBCN program director Oedipus. The full-length version of the conversation was released the previous year. Also included Birdland/No Easy Street (live)

July 1988 (Columbia 07974) All That Money Wants/Birdland
7-inch single with picture sleeve.

August 1988 (Columbia 07862) All That Money Wants/Birdland/No Easy Street (live)
12-inch single.

August 1988 (Columbia 07862) All That Money Wants/Birdland/No Easy Street (live)
Cassette single.

November 1988 (Columbia 08499) Heaven/India
7-inch single with picture sleeve.

October 1989 (Columbia) Should God Forget/ Badman
12-inch promo single.

[Summer 1990] (Evatone 106532) Torch (Electric)/[cuts by Died Pretty, the Mekons].
7-inch flexidisc free with issue 39 of The Bob *magazine.*

July 1991 (Columbia 74055) Until She Comes/ Sometimes
7-inch single with picture sleeve.

November 1991 (Columbia) Don't Be a Girl/Don't Be a Girl (7" remix edit)/Don't Be a Girl (12" extended)/Don't Be a Girl (Dancehall on Fire mix)
CD promo single.

October 2001 (Sony/Legacy) Alive (single edit)/Pretty In Pink (live)/Pretty In Pink (acoustic)
CD promo single.

UK ORIGINAL ALBUMS

December 1979 (white label acetate – unissued) *The Psychedelic Furs*
India/Sister Europe/Imitation Of Christ (Lillywhite mix)/Fall (Lillywhite mix)/Girl's Song/Wedding Song/Blacks – Radio (Lillywhite mix)/Flowers (Lillywhite version)
The original completed LP, as cut to acetate in mid-December, 1979. Bootleg cassette copies were briefly available early in the new year.

March 1980 (CBS 84084) *The Psychedelic Furs*
India/Sister Europe/Imitation Of Christ (remix)/Fall (remix)/Pulse/We Love You/ Wedding Song/Blacks – Radio (remix)/Flowers (Thompson/Taylor version)
LP released with three limited edition (15,000 copies) different coloured sleeves – pink, green and yellow.

May 1981 (CBS 84892) *Talk Talk Talk*
Dumb Waiters/Pretty In Pink/I Wanna Sleep With You/No Tears/Mr Jones/Into You Like A Train/It Goes On/So Run Down/All Of This And Nothing/She Is Mine
Initial copies issued with limited edition folding poster.

September 1982 (CBS 85909) *Forever Now*
Forever Now/Love My Way/Goodbye/Only You And I/Sleep Comes Down/President Gas/Run And Run/Danger/No Easy Street/Merry Go Round
Free poster with initial pressings.

May 1984 (CBS 25950) *Mirror Moves*
The Ghost In You/Here Come Cowboys/Heaven/ Heartbeat/My Time/Like A Stranger/Alice's House/Only A Game/Highwire Days

Initial copies issued with limited edition folding poster.
February 1987 (CBS 450256) *Midnight To Midnight*
Heartbreak Beat/Shock/Shadow In My Heart/ Angels Don't Cry/Midnight To Midnight/One More Word/All Of The Law/Torture/Pretty In Pink (86 – remix) + No Release as CD bonus track.

November 1989 (CBS 465982) *Book Of Days*
Shine/Entertain Me/Book Of Days/Should God Forget/Torch/Parade/Mother-Son/House/Wedding/I Don't Mine

July 1991 (East West WX 422) *World Outside*
Valentine/In My Head/Until She Comes/Don't Be A Girl/Sometimes/Tearing Down/There's A World/Get A Room/Better Days/All About You

November 2001 (–) *Beautiful Chaos: Greatest Hits Live*
India/Mr Jones/Heaven/The Ghost In You/Alive (For Once In My Lifetime)/Love My Way/Heartbreak Beat/Sister Europe/President Gas/Into You Like A Train/Pretty In Pink/Dumb Waiters (all live, 2001)/ Alive (For Once In My Lifetime) (studio version)

US ORIGINAL ALBUMS

November 1980 (Columbia 36791) *The Psychedelic Furs*
India/Sister Europe/Susan's Strange/Fall/We Love You/Soap Commercial/Imitation Of Christ/Pulse/ Wedding Song/Flowers
Alternate sleeve.

May 1981 (Columbia CK 37339) *Talk Talk Talk*
Pretty In Pink/Mr Jones/No Tears/Dumb Waiters/She Is Mine/Into You Like A Train/It Goes On/So Run Down/I Wanna Sleep With You/All Of This And Nothing
Revised sleeve design.

September 1982 (Columbia CK 38261) *Forever Now*
Forever Now/Love My Way/Goodbye/Only You And I/Sleep Comes Down/ President Gas/Run And Run/Danger/No Easy Street/Yes I Do (alternate version of Merry Go Round)

May 1984 (Columbia CK 39278) *Mirror Moves*
Tracks and cover as UK edition.

February 1987 (Columbia CK 40466) *Midnight To Midnight*

Heartbreak Beat/Shock/Shadow In My Heart/ Angels Don't Cry/Midnight To Midnight/One More Word/All Of The Law/Torture/No Release
1987 (Columbia CAS 2719) *Interchords*
Promo interview LP featuring full conversation between Richard Butler and WBCN program director Oedipus. An edited version of the conversation was released as a 12-inch single the following year. Includes: Pretty In Pink/Love My Way/Ghost In You/Heartbreak Beat/Angels Don't Cry/Shock/Midnight To Midnight/Shadow In My Heart

November 1989 (Columbia CK 45412) *Book Of Days*
Tracks and cover as UK edition.

June 1991 (Columbia CK 47303) *World Outside*
Tracks and cover as UK edition.

November 2001 (Columbia/Legacy CK 86191 – US) *Beautiful Chaos: Greatest Hits Live*
Tracks and cover as UK edition.

SIGNIFICANT CD REISSUES

1996 (Columbia Rewind 493343 – UK) *Psychedelic Furs*
UK reissue as above + Susan's Strange, Soap Commercial

March 2002 (Sony/Legacy 85916 – US) *Forever Now*
US reissue as above + Alice's House (early version)/Aeroplane (non-LP B-side)/I Don't Want To Be Your Shadow (non-LP B-side)/Mary Go Round (previously unreleased version of Yes I Do)/President Gas (live; non-LP B-side)/No Easy Street (live)

March 2002 (Sony/Legacy 85917 – US) *Talk Talk Talk*
US reissue of original UK as above + Mr Jones (single version)/So Run Down (early version)/All Of This And Nothing (demo)/LP preview from "Dumb Waiters" picture sleeve (hidden track)

March 2002 (Sony/Legacy 85918 – US) *Psychedelic Furs*
US reissue of original UK as above + Susan's Strange/Soap Commercial/Mac The Knife (non LP B-side)/Flowers (demo)

COMPILATIONS AND RETROSPECTIVES

1987 (Music & Media MM 1257 – UK) *Psychedelic Furs*
12-inch interview picture disc featuring Tim Butler.

August 1988 (CBS 461101 – UK/Columbia 44377 – US) *All Of This And Nothing*
President Gas/All That Money Wants/Imitation of Christ/Sister Europe/Love My
Way/No Easy Street/ Highwire Days/She is Mine/Dumb Waiters/Pretty in
Pink/The Ghost in You/Heaven/Heartbreak Beat/All of This and Nothing

1989 (Relativity 1023 – US) *Crucial Music: The… Collection*
Sleep Comes Down/Pulse/She is Mine/Heartbreak Beat/My Time/Heaven/Here
Come Cowboys/Fall/India/Goodbye

October 1991 (Castle CCSCD 308 – UK) *The Collection*
Sister Europe/India/We Love You/Flowers/Dumb Waiters/Sleep Comes Down/Mr.
Jones/Love My Way/Forever Now/Danger/I Don't Want to Be Your Shadow/Pretty
in Pink/ Mac the Knife/Heaven/ Heartbreak Beat/No Release/Angels Don't Cry

May 1995 (Columbia 480363 – UK/57889 – US) *Here Came The Psychedelic Furs:*
B-Sides And Lost Grooves
Aeroplane (Dance Mix)/Another Edge/Badman/Birdland/Goodbye (Dance Mix)/I
Don't Want To Be Your Shadow/Heartbeat (7-inch remix version)/Mac The
Knife/New Dream/Here Come Cowboys (12-inch remix edit version)/Heartbreak
Beat (extended mix)/Angels Don't Cry (7-inch remix version)/Shock (Shep
Pettibone Mix)/President Gas (live)/No Easy Street (live)

1996 (Sony 26876 – US) *In The Pink*
Shadow in My Heart/Torture/Mr. Jones/It Goes On/India/Pulse/Fall/Here Come
Cowboys/Love My Way/My Time

February 1997 (Strange Fruit SFRSCD 003 – UK) *Radio One Sessions*
Imitation Of Christ/Fall/Sister Europe/We Love You (Peel: recorded 25/7/79,
broadcast 30/7/79); Soap Commercial/Susan's Strange/Mac The Knife (Peel:
recorded 18/2/80, broadcast 28/2/80); Into You Like A Train/On And Again/All
Of This And Nothing (Peel: recorded 2/2/81, broadcast 10/2/81); She Is
Mine/Dumb Waiters (Skinner: recorded 9/4/81, broadcast 21/4/81)/Entertain
Me/Book Of Days/Torch/Pretty In Pink (Campbell: recorded 7/2/90, broadcast
19/2/90)
This release rounds up all but two of the Psychedelic Furs' BBC session recordings.
Absent, to avoid title duplication, are two further cuts from the 9/4/81 Richard Skinner
set: 'All Of This And Nothing' and 'Pretty In Pink.'

1997 (Sony/Legacy C2K 65152 – US) *Should God Forget: A Retrospective*
India/Sister Europe/Pulse/Mac The Knife (18/2/80 BBC session)/Blacks – Radio
/We Love You/Imitation Of Christ/Soap Commercial (18/2/80 BBC
session)/Pretty In Pink/Mr Jones/Into You Like A Train/I Wanna Sleep With
You/Merry Go Round/ President Gas/Love My Way/Sleep Comes Down/I Don't
Wanna Be Your Shadow/Alice's House (Todd Rundgren version)/The Ghost In
You/Here Come Cowboys/Heaven/ Highwire Days/Heartbeat (live 1987)/All Of
The Law (live 1987)/Heartbreak Beat/All That Money Wants/Entertain
Me/Should God Forget/Torch/Get A Room (live 1991)/Until She Comes/All
About You/There's A World/Dumb Waiters (9/4/81 BBC session – hidden track)

2001 (Sony/Legacy CK 61481 – US) *Greatest Hits*
Sister Europe/Mr Jones (single version)/Dumb Waiters/Pretty In Pink/Love My
Way/ President Gas/Here Come Cowboys/Heaven/Heartbeat/The Ghost In
You/Heartbreak Beat/Angels Don't Cry/All That Money Wants/Sometimes/Until
She Comes/There's A World Outside/Only You And I (live 1987)

SIGNIFICANT BOOTLEGS, BROADCASTS AND DOWNLOADS

NOTE: dates refer to original broadcast/recording date only.

30 June 1981 – Into You Like A Train/Soap Commercial/She Is Mine/Mr Jones/
Dumb Waiters/ Pretty In Pink/So Run Down/It Goes On/Sister Europe/
Imitation Of Christ*/All Of This And Nothing*/India*/Pulse/Fall/Flowers*/
We Love You* (live: Metro, Boston). Tracks marked * available on bootleg (Good
Shape Records 109) *We Won't Hear Them Like This Anymore.*

November 1981 – Into You Like A Train*/President Gas*/Dumb Waiters*/Pretty
In Pink*/It Goes On/ Soap Commercial*/All Of This And Nothing/Sister
Europe/So Run Down/Pulse/India/Fall/We Love You (live: *Rockpalast*, German
TV). Tracks marked * available on bootleg (Good Shape Records 109) *We Won't
Hear Them Like This Anymore.*

10 October 1982 – Merry Go Round/Run And Run/ Love My Way/No Easy
Street/Only You And I [introduced as Angels]/Danger/Goodbye/Pretty In Pink/
She Is Mine/Sister Europe/Into You Like A Train (live: Hammersmith Odeon,
London, BBC broadcast)

3 January 1983 – President Gas/Pretty In Pink/Run And Run/Sister Europe/
Dumb Waiters (live: Ritz, New York City, King Biscuit Flour Hour broadcast).
Available on bootleg (PSYFUNYC 1383) *File Under Psychedelic Furs.*

1983 – President Gas/Run And Run/No Easy Street/Mr Jones/Love My Way/Sister Europe/Imitation Of Christ (source uncertain). Available on bootleg (Five Dolar Records FDR 132) *Molly Ringwald Blues*.

28 May 1984 – Here Come Cowboys/My Time/ President Gas/Sleep Comes Down/The Ghost In You/Heaven/Like A Stranger/Alice's House/ Heartbeat/ Forever Now (live: Hammersmith Odeon, London, King Biscuit Flour Hour broadcast). Available on bootleg (Baby Jones – no cat #) *Live Hammersmith Odeon 1984*.

5 June 1984 – Here Come Cowboys/My Time/ President Gas/Sleep Comes Down/The Ghost In You/Heaven/Only You And I [introduced as 'Angels…I think']/Sister Europe/Alice's House/ Heartbeat/Forever Now (live: Rolling Stone, Milan). Available on bootleg (Wind Records MB 5332) *Live In Milan At The Rolling Stone*.

10 September 1991 – Heaven/President Gas/Sleep Comes Down/Get A Room/The Ghost In You/Pretty In Pink/Love My Way/All That Money Wants (live: Town & Country Club, London). Available on bootleg (Kiss The Stone KTS 033) *Room At The Top*; reissued (Five Dolar Records FDR 132) *Molly Ringwald Blues*.

13/14 April 2001 – *Live From The House Of Blues* – one hour performance culled from VHS/DVD release of the same title – see below. (Hob webcast June 2001; DirecTV October, 2001)

15 November 2001 – Only You and I/Run and Run/Ghost in You/Wrong Train/Imitation of Christ/Alive/Maybe Someday/Broken Aeroplane/Sometimes/Love My Way/Heartbreak Beat/Virginia Plain/Pretty in Pink/All That Money Wants/Sister Europe/All of This and Nothing (live, House Of Blues, Atlanta, GA). Earthlink webcast.

2001 (XRT Radio broadcast) Love My Way/Wrong Train/Pretty In Pink (live, Chicago, IL). Acoustic performance.

ORIGINAL MATERIAL ON SOUNDTRACKS AND COMPILATIONS

1986 (A&M 75021-3293-2) *Pretty In Pink: Original Soundtrack*
Includes Pretty In Pink (86).

MISCELLANEOUS COMPILATION APPEARANCES (BY SONG TITLE)

Hardly an exhaustive list… but probably exhaus*ting*.

Heartbreak Beat on *Rock Of The 80s Volume 8* (1994)
Heartbreak Beat on *Sedated In The 80s Volume 2* (1994)
Heartbreak Beat on *Modern Rock: 1987* (1996)
Heartbreak Beat on *On The Edge* (2000)
Heaven on *Flashback Café Volume One* (1994)
Heaven on *Pop & Wave Volume 5* (1994)
Heaven on *Relax: The Ultimate 80s Mix Volume 2* (1999)
House (long version) on *Theodore: An Alternative Music Sampler* (1988)
Love My Way on *Sedated In The 80s Volume 1* (1993)
Love My Way on *Absolution* (1993)
Love My Way on *Rock Of The 80s Volume 5* (1993)
Love My Way on *Just Can't Get Enough Volume 9* (1994)
Love My Way on *Valley Girl: Original Soundtrack* (1994)
Love My Way on *Read The Hits: Best Of The 80s Volume 4* (1994)
Love My Way on *Greatest Hits of the 80s Vol 1* (1995)
Love My Way on *MTV Class of 83* (1995)
Love My Way on *Flashback Café Volume 2* (1995)
Love My Way on *Chart-Toppers: Modern Rock Hits Of The 80s* (1998)
Love My Way on *Newer Wave Volume 2* (1998)
Love My Way on *The Wedding Singer: Original Soundtrack* (1998)
Love My Way on *Let It Rock 1983* (2000)
Love My Way on *Alternative Evolution* (2000)
Love My Way on *Grand Theft Auto: Vice City, Vol. 2 Soundtrack* (2002)
Pretty In Pink on *Teenage Kicks* (1995)
Pretty In Pink (86) on *Modern Rock 1986: Hang The DJ* (1996)
Pretty In Pink on *Lost Property* (1996)
Pretty In Pink on *Once In A Lifetime* (1997)
Pretty In Pink (86) on *Flashback Flix* (1998)
Pretty In Pink on *CMJ: The Year In Alternative Music 1981* (1998)
Pretty In Pink (86) on *VH1: The Big 80s/The Big Movies* (1998)
Pretty In Pink (86) on *Relax: The Ultimate 80s Mix* (1998)
Pretty In Pink (86) on *Greatest Hits Of The 80s Volume 7* (1999)
Pretty In Pink (86) on *Greatest Hits Of The 80s Platinum Disc* (1999)
Pretty In Pink (86) on *Pop & Wave Volume 8* (1999)
Pretty In Pink (86) on *Train Kept A-Rollin'* (1999)
Pretty In Pink on *Guitar Club Classics* (2000)
Sister Europe on *Breaking The Rules* (1980)
The Ghost In You on *Richard Blade's Flashback Classics Volume 5* (1994)

The Ghost In You on *Rock Of The 80s Volume 13* (1994)
The Ghost In You on *Gag Me With A Spoon* (1995)
The Ghost In You on *New Wave Goes To Hell* (1998)
The Ghost In You on *Hits Of 1984* (1999)

MISCELLANEOUS COVER VERSIONS (BY SONG TITLE)

Includes unreleased/live versions. Released title noted where applicable.

All Of This And Nothing – Subway Riders
Dumb Waiters – The Rapture (B-side, 2000)
Heaven – Annie Lennox (*A Whiter Shade of Pale* EP, 1995)
Heaven – Buffalo Tom (CD *Birdbrain*, 1990)
Heaven – Face To Face (CD *Standards & Practices*, 2001)
Heaven – Love Spit Love (live)
House – Gameface (*Cupcakes* EP, 1997)
Into You Like A Train – Jawbreaker (CD *Dear You* 1995)
I Wanna Sleep With You – Love Spit Love (live)
In My Head – Echoing Green (CD *Hope Springs Eternal* 1997)
Love My Way – William Orbit (CD *Best Of Strange Cargoes* 1996)
A spacious, symphonic instrumental, the basic melody washed beneath a wall of grand electronics.
Love My Way – Assemblage 23 (CD *Newer Wave*, 1998)
Love My Way – Live
Love My Way – Mineral (B-side, 1998)
Love My Way – Powderfinger (B-side, 2001)
Love My Way – Love Spit Love (live)
Mr Jones – Love Spit Love (live)
Pretty In Pink – Elvis Costello
An in-concert rarity, a sparse cover is delivered all but a cappella, the ghost of an acoustic guitar barely audible.
Pretty In Pink – David Bowie
If it exists…
Pretty In Pink – The Grown-Ups (CD *In Their Eyes: 90s Teen Bands Vs. 80s Teen Movies* 1998)
Pretty In Pink – Schleprock (CD *Propellor*, 1994)
Pretty In Pink – Automatic 7 (CD *Before You Were Punk* 1997)
Sister Europe – Gary Windo (LP *Deep Water*, 1985)
Session sax player on Forever Now. Windo's solo album also features cellist Ann Sheldon.
Sister Europe – Iva Davis & Icehouse (CD *The Berlin Tapes*, 1996)
Bowie's 'Pretty In Pink' remains tantalisingly unconfirmed but, if you've ever wondered what he'd do to 'Sister Europe,' this remarkable classically-themed cover is a dead-ringer,

with the Mike Garson-styled piano only emphasising the comparisons.
The Ghost In You – Counting Crows (CD *Clueless: Original Soundtrack,* 1995)
The Ghost In You – Love Spit Love (live)
The Ghost In You – Robyn Hitchcock
An occasional live favourite, performed solo and acoustic.
The Ghost In You – Mark McGrath (CD *50 First Dates: Original Soundtrack,* 2004)

VIDEOS

1980 Sister Europe (dir. Don Letts, Mick Calvert)
1980 We Love You (dir. Bill Davis)
1981 Pretty In Pink (dir. Terry Bedford)
1981 Dumb Waiters (dir. Terry Bedford)
1982 Love My Way (dir. Tim Pope)
1982 Run And Run (dir. Bill Davis)
1982 Sleep Comes Down (dir. Bill Davis)
1984 Heaven (dir. Tim Pope)
1984 The Ghost In You (dir. Tim Pope)
1984 Here Come Cowboys (dir. Tim Pope)
1986 Pretty In Pink (dir. Wayne Isham)
1987 Heartbreak Beat (dir. John Shea)
1987 Angels Don't Cry (dir. Tim Pope)
1987 Shock
1988 All That Money Wants (dir. Walter Pitt)
1989 House (dir. Peter Scammell)
1991 Until She Comes (dir. Meiert Avis)

VIDEO COLLECTIONS

August 1988 (CBS Video 15V 49004 – UK/Sony Video 6962 – US) *All Of This And Nothing*
Sister Europe/Pretty In Pink/Dumb Waiters/Love My Way/Sleep Comes Down/
Heaven/Heartbreak Beat/All That Money Wants
VHS release.

October 2001 (Pioneer Artists PA 11611) *Live From The House Of Blues*
India/Mr Jones/Heaven/No Easy Street/The Ghost In You/Alive/Love My Way/
Wrong Train/ Heartbreak Beat/Sister Europe/Anodyne (Better Days)/Only You
And I/Into You Like A Train/Pretty In Pink/Dumb Waiters (live: House Of Blues,
Hollywood, 13-14 April, 2001)
VHS release.

October 2001 (Pioneer Artists PA 11611) *Live From The House Of Blues*
India/Mr Jones/Heaven/No Easy Street/The Ghost In You/Alive/Love My Way/
Wrong Train/ Heartbreak Beat/Sister Europe/Anodyne (Better Days)/Only You
And I/Into You Like A Train/Pretty In Pink/Dumb Waiters (live: House Of Blues,
Hollywood, 13-14 April, 2001)/Love My Way/Wrong Train/ Cigarette (acoustic)
+ documentary, commentary.
DVD and DVD (DTS Stereo) release.

DISCOGRAPHY

LOVE SPIT LOVE

UK SINGLES

October 1994 (Imago 25073) Am I Wrong/Codeine (acoustic)
CD single.

1994 (Imago –) *B-Sides*
Codeine (Acoustic)/More Than Money (alternate)/All She Wants/Song
*Cassette promo single. All four tracks subsequently released on UK Love Spit Love
enhanced edition – see below.*

1995 (Imago 25090) Change In The Weather/ Wake Up/Song
CD single.

1995 (Imago –) Wake Up (edit)/Wake Up (live)
CD promo single.

1996 (Columbia –) How Soon Is Now (edit: 3.45)/How Soon Is Now (full version: 4.25)
CD promo single.

1997 (Maverick –) Long Long Time/Well Well Well
Cassette single. One track CD promos were issued for Long Long Time and Fall On Tears.

UK ALBUMS

October 1994 (Imago 21055) *Love Spit Love*
Seventeen/Superman/Half A Life/Jigsaw/Change In The Weather/Wake Up/Am I
Wrong/Green/ Please/Codeine/St Mary's Gate/More/All She Wants

September 1997 (Maverick) *Trysome Eatone*
Long Long Time/Believe/Well Well Well/Friends/ Fall On Tears/Little Fist/It Hurts When I Laugh/7 Years/Sweet Thing/All God's Children/ More Than Money/ November 5

UK REISSUE

1998 (Burning Airlines PILOT 41) *Love Spit Love*
Enhanced 2CD package features *Love Spit Love* album (above) + Codeine (acoustic version)/More Than Money (alternate)/Song (acoustic)/Wake Up (acoustic)/ Wake Up (live)/Am I Wrong (video)/Change In The Weather (video)

US ALBUMS

October 1994 (Imago 72787 21030) *Love Spit Love*
Seventeen/Superman/Half A Life/Jigsaw/Change In The Weather/Wake Up/Am I Wrong/Green/ Please/Codeine/St Mary's Gate/More

September 1997 (Maverick 46560) *Trysome Eatone*
Tracks and cover as UK edition.

BROADCASTS/DOWNLOADS

1994 – Concert broadcast from Coach House, San Juan Capistrano. Source of the promo-only live 'Wake Up" (see above). Westwood One broadcast.

September 1997 – US radio sessions/interviews
Love Spit Love's promotional tour included appearances on the following radio stations (date in parentheses): (15) Denver/Boulder – KTCL; (18) Chicago – Q101, WXRT, JBTV; (19) Boston – WBCN, WFNX, WBOS, WXRV; (20) Providence – WDGE, WBRU; (21) Atlanta – 99X; (22) Washington DC – WHFS, Philadelphia – WPLY; (25) Detroit – CIDR, WHYT, Minneapolis – KEGE; (26) Dallas – KDGE, KKZN, Houston – KTBZ, KRBE; (27) San Francisco – Live 105, KOME, KLLC, KFOG; (28) Seattle – KNDD, KMTT, Los Angeles – KROQ; (29) Los Angeles – KROQ, Y 107, KYSR.

21 October 1997 – More Than Money/Mr Jones/Little Fist/Friends/Fall On Tears/7 Years/Believe/ Superman/It Hurts When I Laugh/Codeine/Long Long Time/Seventeen/I Wanna Sleep With You/A Change In The Weather/Love My Way/Am I Wrong (live; Galaxy Club, New York City). Webcast.

ORIGINAL MATERIAL ON SOUNDTRACKS AND COMPILATIONS

1994 (Volume 9222) *Volume 12*
Includes Wake Up (acoustic version).

1994 (–) *Live X II*
Includes Am I Wrong – exclusive live version recorded for 99X radio of Atlanta, GA. All profits were donated to Grady Health Systems Children With AIDS program.

1996 (Columbia CK 67626) *The Craft: Music From The Motion Picture*
Includes How Soon Is Now.

2003 (Private Music –) *Charmed: The Soundtrack*
Includes How Soon Is Now.

UNRELEASED MATERIAL IN CIRCULATION

Dusk
I Wanna Sleep With You (live)
Indecision
Love My Way (live)
Mr Jones (live)
Never Be Wrong
New Green
The Ghost In You/Heaven (medley) (live)

MISCELLANEOUS COMPILATION APPEARANCES (BY SONG TITLE)

Am I Wrong on *Angus: Original Soundtrack* (1995)
Am I Wrong on *Zima – Uncut* (1995)
Wake Up (acoustic version) on *Sharks Patrol These Waters* (1995)

VIDEOS

Am I Wrong (dir. Jake Scott)
Change In The Weather (dir. Michael Halsband)
Long Long Time (Paul Andresen)

SOLO/EXTRA-CURRICULAR RELEASES

JOHN ASHTON

March 1994 (Munster 40 – US) *An Invitation To Suicide: A Tribute To Suicide*
An expansive Suicide tribute also featuring contributions from Mudhoney, Luna, Flaming Lips, Ben Vaughn and more.

SISTERS OF MERCY

November 1982 (Merciful Release 015) Alice/Floorshow
7-inch single. Producer.

April 1983 (Merciful Release) Alice/Floorshow/1969 [+ Phantom]
12-inch single. Producer.

A fourth song, 'Good Things,' was recorded but remains unreleased. All represented a dramatic improvement on the band's murk-encrusted earlier releases; all, as the Sisters chronicle *Heartland* later enthused, 'were enhanced by [Ashton]'s more experienced production techniques. He taught Eldritch how to combine a crisp production which makes the song more listenable, whilst losing none of its original power or feeling.' Eldritch would ultimately remove Ashton's name from the single's production credits, but his influence, at least, was indelible.

KRISTEN HALL

1991 (Daemon 5053 – US) *Fact And Fiction*
Guitar on 'Empty Promises', the opening track on Atlanta-based country singer Hall's second album.

GOWAN

1993 (Anthem/Columbia – Canada) *But You Can Call Me Larry*
Guitar. Gowan was Larry Gowan, a founder member of Rheingold in the early 1980s. He quit to go solo; Larry was his fifth album and also features contributions from Robert Fripp, Tony Levin, Jerry Marotta and John Sebastian.

MERCURY REV

1993 (Columbia 53217 – US) *Boces*
Guitar on 'Meth Of A Rockette's Kick'. Boces was the Buffalo-based avant-garde-y Rev's second album.

RED BETTY

1998 (Radio Room – US) *Sister Rubber Limbs*
Guitar and production. Self-released debut by the New York band featuring singer Yahz, Michael DiLalla (guitar), WhyNot Janfeld (bass) and Chad LaRue (drums) This original line-up broke up soon after the release; Yahz leads a new Red Betty today.

RICHARD BUTLER

1985 (A&M 5104 – US) *Lost In The Stars: The Music Of Kurt Weill*
Includes 'Alabama Song' (with Ralph Schuckett etc).

October 1997 (MCA 11688 – US) *The Jackal*
Includes 'Shineaway' (with Brian Transeau of BT).

SPONGE

July 1996 (Columbia 67578 – US) *Wax Ecstatic*
Includes I Am Anastasia – vocals by Richard Butler. Detroit based hard rock band Sponge gigged with Love Spit Loves during autumn, 1994.

ROY NATHANSON

March 2000 (Six Degrees 1024 – US) *Fire at Keaton's Bar And Grill*
Concept album features Richard Butler as one of the performing characters.

TIM BUTLER

LEFTOVER SALMON

September 1999 (Hollywood 162142 – US) *The Nashville Sessions*
Assistant engineer. Leftover Salmon are, they say, a 'polyethnic cajun slamgrass' band, formed in Colorado in the early 1990s from the wreckage of two bands, the Left Hand String Band and the Salmonheads. The line-up features: Vince Herman (vocals/guitar/washboard), Mark Vann (banjo), Drew Emmit (mandolin, guitar), Tye North (bass) and Michael Wooten (drums). This was their fifth album.

TERROR SQUAD

1999 (Atlantic 83232 – US) *Terror Squad*
Mixing assistant. *Terror Squad* was the debut album by the Latin rap act featuring Fat Joe, Big Punisher, Cuban Link, Armageddon, Triple Seis, and Prospect.

THE BASTARD SONS OF JOHNNY CASH

2000 (Ultimatum 766672 – US) *Walk Alone*
Bass. Alt. country band formed in 1995 and self-released two CDs before cutting their major label debut.

CHANGING FACES

October 2000 (Atlantic 83401 – US) *Visit Me*
Assistant engineer. New York urban soul duo comprising Cassandra Lucas and Charisse Rose. *Visit Me* was their third album since 1995.

VINCE ELY

ROBYN HITCHCOCK

1981 (Armageddon 4 – UK) *Black Snake Diamond Role*
Drums on Brenda's Iron Sledge, Do Policemen Sing?, The Lizard, I Watch The Cars.

1986 (Glass Fish 2 – UK) *Invisible Hitchcock*
Out-takes collection.

1986 (Midnight Music DONG 2 – UK) *Eaten By Her Own Dinner* EP
Out-takes collection.

1997 (Rhino 72847 – US) *Uncorrected Personality Traits*
Compilation.

Robyn Hitchcock: '*Black Snake Diamond Role* was the first time I'd ever got to make a record by myself, it was the first time I'd got to pick who I was going to have on individual songs.' Aside from Ely, guests at the sessions included long-time collaborator Morris Windsor, Alaska studio owner and producer Pat Collier, guitarist Knox (Collier's old sidekick from Punk heroes the Vibrators), saxophonist and future Soft Cell collaborator Gary Barnacle and a then-unknown Thomas Dolby.

Some twenty songs were completed, including 'I Watch The Cars' – laid down while Hitchcock and co still recovered from the breaking news that John Lennon was dead. *The Perfumed Corpse* was an early, distinctly Edward Gorey-esque, working title, while Hitchcock also toyed with *Zinc Pear* for a while. Indeed, test pressings of *Zinc Pear* do exist; largely identical to what would finally be remixed as *Black Snake Diamond Role*, *Zinc Pear* is most notable for the inclusion of the old Soft Boys favourite, 'Give Me A Spanner, Ralph,' in place of the eventual 'Brenda's Iron

Sledge.' 'Ralph' later turned up on the *Invisible Hitchcock* compilation of odds and ends, alongside three more session refugees: 'All I Wanna Do Is Fall In Love,' the bizarrely titled 'A Skull, A Suitcase And A Long Red Bottle Of Wine,' and 'My Favourite Buildings,' a song which would be re-recorded during the *I Often Dream Of Trains* sessions.

Another out-take, 'Dancing On God's Thumb,' would appear as the B-side to Hitchcock's next single, 'The Man Who Invented Himself'; while 'It's A Mystic Trip' and 'Grooving On An Inner Plane' would be included on a flexi-disc issued free with that single. Finally, 'It Was The Night' would be demoed again for Hitchcock's next album before the original version, alongside an unreleased version of 'I Watch The Cars,' and the *Zinc Pear* mix of 'The Man Who Invented Himself,' were appended to Rhino's 1995 reissue of *Black Snake Diamond Role*.

MINISTRY

1983 (Arista 8016) *With Sympathy* (aka *Work For Love*)
Producer, percussion.
Dove-tailing perfectly with the prevalent new romantic synth sound of the day, Ministry's major label debut emerged a fascinating document of the young Al Jourgensen's period predelictions. Slick and eminently singable, it was a far cry indeed from the rampaging monster of future renown, and chart success and heavy club rotation for the attendant singles 'Revenge,' 'I Wanted To Tell Her' and 'Work For Love,' would not lessen Jourgensen's future disdain for the project. 'It's the same old story,' he complained. 'They sign you because you're unique, then they try to make you sound like someone else.'

SPECIMEN

1983 (demo) Syria included on CD compilation *Gothic Rock* (Cleopatra CLEO 0109, 1993)
Producer.

SHRAPNEL

1984 (Elektra 9602811) *Shrapnel*
Producer. Shrapnel were a New York band featuring Dave Wyndorf (vocals), Daniel Rey – aka Dan Rabinowitz (guitar), Phil Caivano (bass), Dave Vogt (guitar) and Dan Clayton (drums). Formed in 1979, the band cut two self-released singles before signing to Elektra in 1984. This five track EP includes a cover of Gary Glitter's 'I Didn't Know I Loved You (Til I Saw You Rock'n'Roll),' alongside four originals.

THE CURE

October 1984. Robert Smith: 'We arrived on the West Coast with a three week tour ahead of us, without a drummer and in a bit of a panic. We were in this bar deciding whether to cancel the tour… or we should carry on as a four piece when Phil [Thornally] phoned up a mate of his, Vince Ely… who was now living in this beach house with someone from the Go-Gos, mellowing out as a West Coast producer. Vince hadn't drummed in a band for about two years, but he was up for it so, he did a day-and-a-half's rehearsal with us and played 11 concerts, 40 minute sets, learning the songs in soundcheck. Unfortunately, he was doing advertising work, producing jingles or something, so we knew he'd have to leave the tour somewhere around Texas.'[i]

JANE WIEDLIN

1985 (IRS 5638) *Jane Wiedlin*
The first solo album by Go-Gos guitarist Wiedlin. Ely was producer of five tracks: Goodbye Cruel World, East Meets West, Forever, Modern Romance, I Will Wait For You.

LIMITED WARRANTY

1986 (Atco 90513 – US) *Limited Warranty*
Producer. Band featuring Greg Sotebeer (vocals, bass), Dale Goulette (guitar), Erik Newman (guitar), Paul Hartwig (keyboards) and Jerry Brunskill (drums).

JETBOY

September 1999 (Cleopatra 718 – US) *Lost And Found*
Producer. Los Angeles glam rockers formed by former Hanoi Rocks bassist Sam Yaffa with Mickey Finn (vocals), Fernie Rod (guitar), Billy Rowe (guitar) and Ron Tostenson (drums). Having cut two albums during their 1989/90 prime, the band disappeared for a decade but returned in 1999 with, among other releases, this collection of out-takes and rarities.

i Robert Smith quoted in *The Cure: 10 Imaginary Years* by Barbarian, Steve Sutherland, Robert Smith (1988)

ABOUT THE AUTHOR

DAVE THOMPSON is the author of 75 books, including biographies of Kurt Cobain, David Bowie, the Cure and Depeche Mode, encyclopaedias of Alternative Rock, Reggae & Caribbean Music, Industrial and Glam Rock, and the 2002 ARSC Awards nominated *Essential Listening Guide to Funk*. He is also a regular contributor to *Mojo*, *Alternative Press*, *Goldmine* and the All Music Guide. Born in Devon, he now lives in Seattle, USA.

PHOTOGRAPHS BY LES MILLS

A LARGE PROPORTION OF THE PHOTOGRAPHS in this book are from the private collection of Les Mills.

Between 1979 and 1983 Les Mills combined his twin passions of music and photography. Whilst managing The Psychedelic Furs he took the opportunities afforded by his unrestricted access to the band to take the extraordinarily candid behind the scenes pictures reproduced in this book. However, by 1984, the rapid worldwide success of the band meant he had to set the camera aside to concentrate on on business. By 1992, increasingly disillusioned by the music industry, he turned his attention back to photography full-time.

Initially based in New York City, in 1993 Les moved upstate to the Catskill Mountains where he explored the twin disciplines of studio work (making and photographing sculptured forms) and landscape photography. Since moving back to London in 1996 he has continued to focus on photography, digital multimedia and video.

Using a combination of analog photographic processes and digital imaging Les produces unique images for both a gallery and online audience. He is currently writing a book on art photography in the digital domain.

Examples of his work, including colour images of the black and white reproductions in this book, can be found at www.lesmills.co.uk

www.helterskelterbooks.com

All Helter Skelter, Firefly and SAF titles are available by mail order from
www.helterskelterbooks.com
Or from our office:
Helter Skelter Publishing Limited
South Bank House
Black Prince Road
London SE1 7SJ

Telephone: +44 (0) 20 7463 2204 or Fax: +44 (0)20 7463 2295
Mail order office hours: Mon-Fri 10:00am - 1:30pm,
By post, enclose a cheque [must be drawn on a British bank],
International Money Order, or credit card number and expiry date.

Postage prices per book worldwide are as follows:

UK & Channel Islands	£1.50
Europe & Eire (air)	£2.95
USA, Canada (air)	£7.50
Australasia, Far East (air)	£9.00

Email: info@helterskelterbooks.com